Office 2000

by Jennifer Fulton

QUE®

A Division of Macmillan Computer Publishing
201 W. 103rd Street, Indianapolis, Indiana 46290 USA

International Standard Book Number: 0-7897-1847-2

Library of Congress Catalog Card Number: 98-86862

Printed in the United States of America

00 99 98 4 3 2 1

Trademarks

All terms mentioned in this book that are known to be trademarks or service marks have been appropriately capitalized. Que cannot attest to the accuracy of this information. Use of a term in this book should not be regarded as affecting the validity of any trademark or service mark.

Warning and Disclaimer

Every effort has been made to make this book as complete and as accurate as possible, but no warranty or fitness is implied. The information provided is on an "as is" basis. The authors and the publisher shall have neither liability nor responsibility to any person or entity with respect to any loss or damages arising from the information contained in this book.

Publisher *John Pierce*

Acquisitions Editor *Jamie Milazzo*

Development Editor *Laura Bulcher*

Managing Editor *Thomas F. Hayes*

Project Editor *Karen S. Shields*

Copy Editor *Margo Catts*

Book Designer *Anne Jones*

Indexer *Bruce Clingaman*

Technical Editor *Glenda Friesen*

Proofreader *Tricia Sterling*

Production *Steve Geiselman*

Contents at a Glance

Contents

Part 1 The Basics

Part 2 Word 2000

Part 3 Excel 2000

Part 4 PowerPoint 2000

Part 5 Outlook 2000

Introduction

Whenever someone asks me what book they should buy to learn about some new program they've just acquired, I of course say, "Something I've written."

OK, what I really say is, "Buy a good used book." My reasoning is that, with a used book, chances are the person who read it first has already marked up all the important parts, and maybe even added some practical notes in the margin. That way, all you've got to do is skim the parts that the first person has already determined are important.

This book is kinda like that, except that you get a book without any chewed-up pages. But like a well-worn treasure, in this book, all the important information is already highlighted for you. And yes, I've added some important notes in the margins, so you can feel free to just skim.

Why You Need This Book

This book, unlike many others you might choose, cuts right through the technical stuff. Here, you'll learn only what you need to know, not what somebody else wants you to know. This book minimizes the time you take to learn a new program, because it's got the features that get you up and going in a hurry:

- The chapters in this book are short, which makes learning what you need to know easy and less time-consuming.
- In each chapter, the stuff you must know for basic survival is covered first. Later on, after you're feeling more confident, you can read the stuff at the end of each chapter, under a section called "Beyond Survival."
- Stuff you need to remember is already highlighted for you.
- The most important points are repeated in the margin notes, where you can find them fast.

How This Book is Organized

This book is divided into five parts:

Part 1, The Basics, covers the absolutely-need-to-know stuff about using your Office 2000 applications. Here you'll learn how to start and exit a program, how to create a new document or open an existing one, how to spell check your work, how to save it and print it, and how to get help.

Part 2, Word 2000, covers all the things you need to know if you want to create letters, reports, fax covers, memos, and the like. You'll learn the basics of using a word processor: how to enter and edit text, how to format text, how to create numbered and bulleted lists, and how to add a header or footer, among other things.

Part 3, Excel 2000, shows you how to use this spreadsheet program to enter and analyze all sorts of numeric data. Here you'll learn how to enter and edit your worksheet data, how to format data, how to work with multiple worksheets, and tricks that will make your worksheets look professional. You'll even learn how to enter formulas and create charts!

Part 4, PowerPoint 2000, details the process of creating a dynamite presentation. Here, you'll learn the many ways in which PowerPoint can help you create a presentation with style. In addition, you'll learn how to add and delete slides, how to rearrange them to your liking, and how to add clip art. Finally, you'll learn how to review your presentation slide by slide.

Part 5, Outlook 2000, shows you how to keep track of the things you do by managing your electronic mail, calendar, tasks, and contacts. Here you'll learn how to send and receive electronic mail as well as schedule appointments, meetings, and events on your calendar. You'll also learn how to add contacts to your contact list and create a distribution list.

About the Author

Jennifer Fulton is a computer trainer, consultant, and best-selling author of more than 50 books covering many areas of computing, including DOS, Windows, and Microsoft Office. Jennifer is a self-taught veteran of computing, which means that if something can happen to a computer user, it has happened to her at one time or another. As a computer veteran, Jennifer brings what's left of her sense of humor to her many books, including *Big Basics Book of Windows 95*, *Netscape Navigator 6 in 1*, *10 Minute Guide to Excel 97*, *Big Basics Book of Office 97*, *Easy Outlook*, and *Big Basics Book of PCs.* Jennifer began her writing career as a staff writer for Alpha Books, a former division of Macmillan Computer Publishing, before escaping to the life of a freelance author. Jennifer lives in Indianapolis with her husband, Scott, who is also a computer book author. They live together in a small home filled with many books, some of which they have not written.

Dedication

To my husband Scott, whom I love with all my heart, and to my daughter Katerina, whom I love more than life.

Acknowledgments

I'd like to thank Jamie Milazzo for giving me a chance to update this book. And thanks to Laura Bulcher and Glenda Friesen, my editors, who helped turn this book into something sensible. Thanks also to everyone else at MCP who helped make this book a great one.

Tell Us What You Think!

As the reader of this book, you are our most important critic and commentator. We value your opinion and want to know what we're doing right, what we could do better, what areas you'd like to see us publish in, and any other words of wisdom you're willing to pass our way.

As a Publisher for Que, I welcome your comments. You can fax, email, or write me directly to let me know what you did or didn't like about this book—as well as what we can do to make our books stronger.

Please note that I cannot help you with technical problems related to the topic of this book, and that due to the high volume of mail I receive, I might not be able to reply to every message.

When you write, please be sure to include this book's title and author as well as your name and phone or fax number. I will carefully review your comments and share them with the author and editors who worked on the book.

Fax: 317.581.4666

Email: `office_que@mcp.com`

Mail: John Pierce, Publisher
Que
201 West 103rd Street
Indianapolis, IN 46290 USA

PART 1

The Basics

Before you learned how to drive a car, you probably already had some idea of which pedal did what. If you've used any Windows programs at all, then you already found the pedals for Office 2000. Even so, there are still some things you must learn before you can put any of Office 2000's applications into "drive."

In this part, you'll learn about the following topics:

- Starting an Office 2000 Application
- Creating a New Document
- Opening an Existing Document
- Saving a Document
- Checking Your Spelling
- Changing Margins and Other Page Options
- Printing an Office Document
- Exiting an Office 2000 Application
- Getting Help

Cheat Sheet

Starting an Application

1. Click the Start button.
2. Select Programs.
3. Select the Office 2000 program you want to start.

Starting an Application from the Office Shortcut Bar

Click the button on the Shortcut bar that corresponds to the application you want to start, such as Microsoft Word.

Starting an Application Automatically When You Start Windows 98

1. Click the Start button.
2. Select Settings, the taskbar, and then Start Menu.
3. Click the Start Menu Programs tab.
4. Click Add.
5. Click Browse, and then select the program you want to start automatically. Click Open.
6. Click Next>.
7. Select the StartUp folder and click Next>.
8. Type a name for your shortcut and click Finish.
9. Click OK.

1

Starting an Office 2000 Application

Before you can use any of your Office 2000 applications (such as Microsoft Word), you must first start it. You can use many methods to start an Office application, as you'll learn in this chapter.

After an application has been started, it's said to be *running*. After an application is running, it appears as a button on the Windows taskbar, located at the bottom of your screen. To switch to a running program, just click on this button. When you're finished with a running program, you *exit* it. Exiting a program turns it off and removes the program window from the screen.

Basic Survival

Starting an Application

When you install Office 2000, it places commands on your Windows Start menu that you can use to start any of its programs, such as Excel 2000. Follow these steps:

1. Click the Start button.
2. Select Programs.
3. The Office 2000 applications are listed toward the bottom of this menu. Select the one you want to start.
4. If this is your first time starting an Office application, you will see a dialog box asking you to enter your name and initials. Do so, and click OK. The program you selected appears in its own window, and on the Windows taskbar.

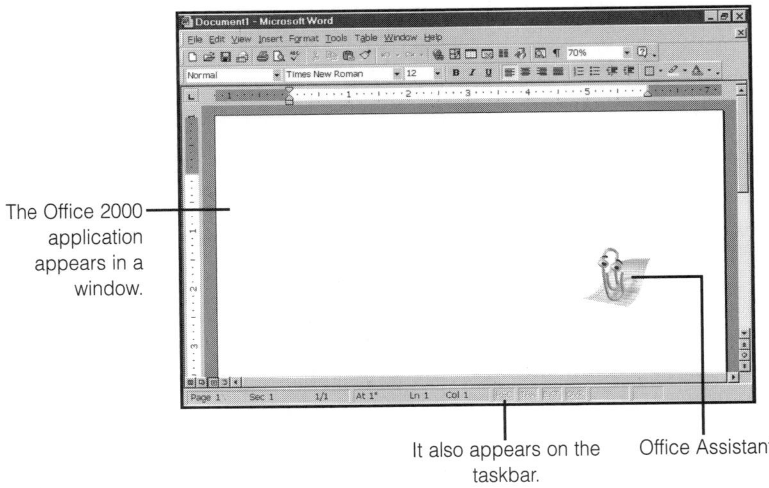

Need help? Ask the Office Assistant!

When you start any Office application for the first time, the Office Assistant appears. He's there to offer help. Click Start using *X* (where *X* represents the Office application you have launched) to begin using the program. If you need help with the Assistant, see Chapter 9.

Starting an Application from the Office Shortcut Bar

If you installed the Office Shortcut bar when you installed Office 2000, it should appear on your desktop when you start Windows. If so, you can use it to start your Office 2000 application. Just click the appropriate button: For example, to start Word, Excel, or PowerPoint with a new document, click the New Office Document button, as shown. (If the Shortcut bar is not visible, choose Start, Programs, Microsoft, Microsoft Office Tools, Microsoft Office Shortcut bar.)

If you use Outlook 2000, you must start it by clicking the Outlook button on the Shortcut bar. Within Outlook, begin a particular task by clicking the corresponding button, such as New Message (to send an email message), New Appointment, New Task, New Contact, New Note, or New Journal Entry.

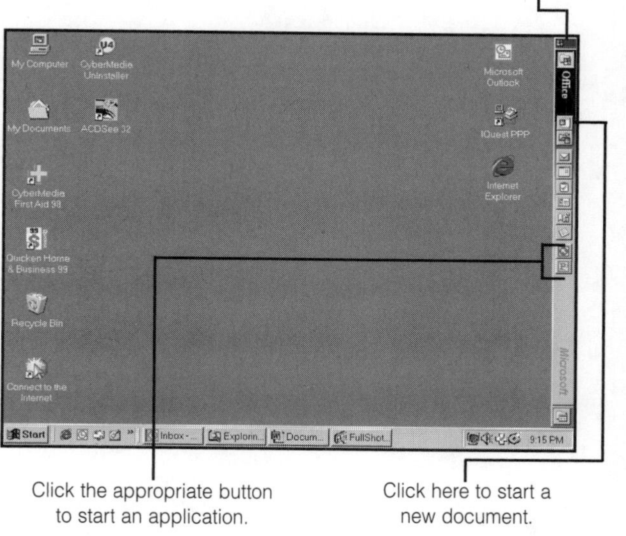
Office 2000 Shortcut bar
Click the appropriate button to start an application.
Click here to start a new document.

Beyond Survival

Starting an Application Automatically When You Start Windows 98

You can do this in Windows 95, too!

If you use Excel or some other Office 2000 program every day, why not have Windows start the program for you automatically when you turn on your PC? It's simple to do:

1. Click the Start button.
2. Select Settings and then Taskbar & Start Menu.
3. Click the Start Menu Programs tab.
4. Click Add.
5. Click Browse, and then select the program you want to start automatically. (Your Office 2000 programs are in the `Program Files\Microsoft Office\Office` directory on your hard disk.) Click Open.
6. You're returned to the Create Shortcut dialog box, and the filename you selected appears in the Command Line text box. Click Next>.
7. Select the StartUp folder and click Next>.

8. Type a name for your shortcut, such as Excel 2000, then click Finish.

9. You're returned to the Taskbar Properties dialog box. Click OK. The program you selected now appears on the `Start/Programs/StartUp` menu, and from now on, it will be started for you automatically whenever you start Windows 98.

Cheat Sheet

Starting a New, Blank Document

To start a new document, click the New button on the Standard toolbar.

Starting a New Document from a Template or Wizard

1. Open the File menu.
2. Select New. The New dialog box opens.
3. Click the tab that contains the template or wizard you want to use. For example in Word, click Letters & Faxes.
4. Click the template or wizard you want, then click OK.

Using a Template Wizard

- To move to the next screen, click the Next> button.
- To go back to a previous screen so you can change a selection, click <Back.
- After making all your selections, click Finish.
- If you want to bail out of the wizard at any time (and not create a new document), click Cancel.

Starting a New Document When You Start an Office Application

1. Click the Start button.
2. Select New Office Document. The New Office Document dialog box appears.
3. Click the tab that contains the template you want to use. For example, click Spreadsheet Solutions.
4. Click the template you want.
5. Click OK. The appropriate Office application is started, and a new document is created using the template you chose.

2

Creating a New Document

When you start Word or Excel, it automatically opens a new, blank document for you. (When you start PowerPoint, it gives you the option up-front of starting a new presentation or opening an old one.) At that point, all you need to do to create your document is type. If you complete your first document and want to start a new one, you can do so, without having to restart the application.

New documents: from scratch or a template

When you decide that you want to start a new document, you're presented with a few choices. You can start a new document from scratch, or you can get some help in the form of a template. A template is a preformatted document, such as a letter or a memo, that you use as a guide for creating your own document.

Basic Survival

Starting a New, Blank Document

One way to create a new document is to start from scratch with a blank page, worksheet, or PowerPoint slide. To do that, click the New button on the Standard toolbar, and a new, blank, document is created.

Click the New button on the Standard toolbar to create a blank document.

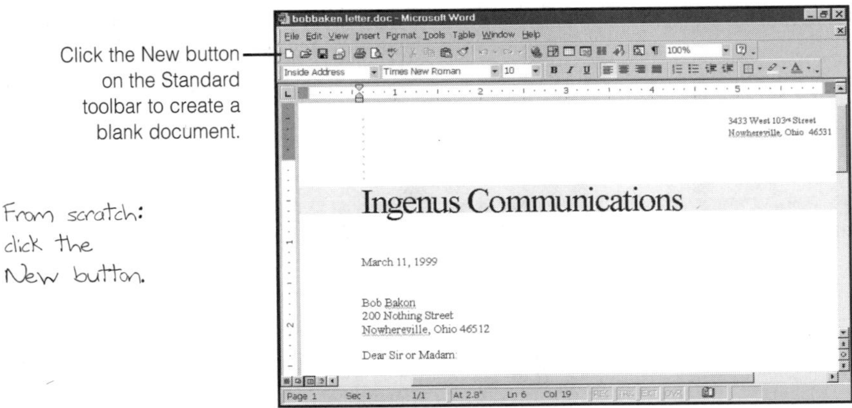

From scratch: click the New button.

Starting a New Document from a Template

One advantage of using Office is that it comes with multiple templates that enable you to create a variety of standard documents. These include letters, memos, and fax transmittals (using Word), purchase orders, invoices, and expense account statements (using Excel), or slide presentations for a company meeting or an organizational overview (using PowerPoint). Using one of the Office templates to create your document saves you the trouble of designing a professional-looking document or presentation from scratch. You can even use a template to create a document for publishing on the Web.

Templates do the work for you!

The Word and Excel templates typically provide some sample text, graphics, formulas, and so forth that you can quickly modify to create your finished document. PowerPoint templates also provide some of this help, depending on which one you choose: You can choose a *presentation design* (which provides the background for your slides), a *presentation template* (which also supplies an outline and sample slide), or an *AutoContent template* (which supplies all of these and a lot of hand-holding, too).

Create from template: use File/New.

1. Open the File menu.
2. Select New. The New dialog box opens.
3. Click the tab that contains the template you want to use. For example in Word, click Letters & Faxes.

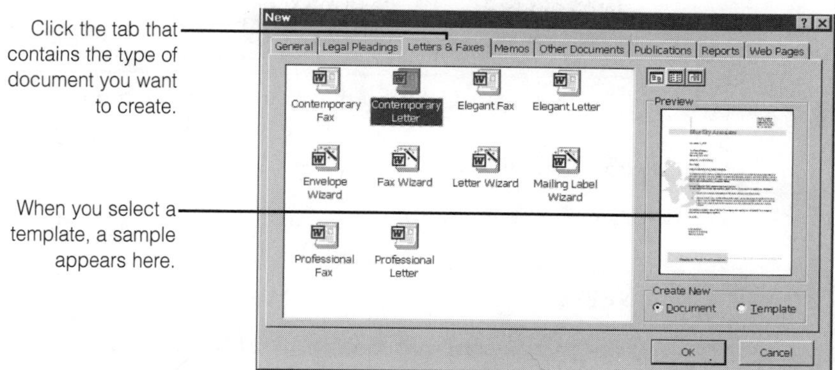

4. Click the template you want, then click OK. Some templates are not yet installed; if prompted, insert the Office CD-Rom and click OK to continue.

Using a Template Wizard

Wizards step you through a complex process.

Some of the Office templates (such as the AutoContent template in PowerPoint) are *wizards*. A wizard is a series of dialog boxes that step you through the process of customizing the template to fit your exact needs. If a wizard appears when you select a template, keep these things in mind:

- To move to the next screen, click the Next> button.
- To go back to a previous screen so you can change a selection, click <Back.

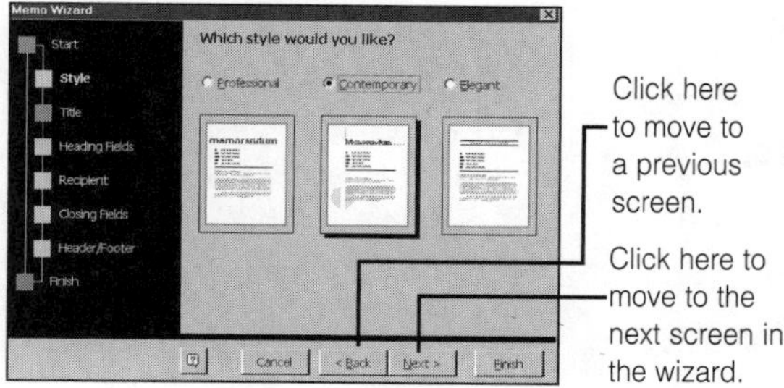

- After making all your selections, click Finish.
- If you want to bail out of the wizard at any time (and not create a new document), then click Cancel.

Beyond Survival

Starting a New Document When You Start an Office Application

Rather than start your Office application and then choose a template for your new document, why not perform both tasks at one time? Follow these steps:

1. Click the Start button.
2. Select New Office Document. The New Office Document dialog box appears.
3. Click the tab that contains the template you want to use. For example, click Spreadsheet Solutions.

Create new doc + start Word/Excel/PP!

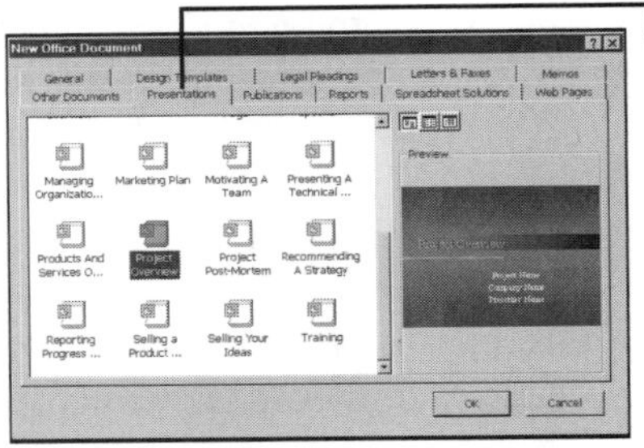

4. Click the template you want.
5. Click OK. The appropriate Office application is started, and a new document is created using the template you chose.

Switching from Document to Document in the Same Application

After creating your new document, you can close it if you want (which gives you the option to save it to the hard disk before closing, as explained in Chapter 8). You can also start another document or open an existing document, and move between any of your open documents as needed.

To switch from one document to another:

1. First, save your current document (as explained in Chapter 4), then start a new document or open an existing document (see Opening a Document in Chapter 3). The document you open or start fills the screen, replacing the document on which you were working.

Docs are open until you close them.

2. To switch back to the original document, click its button on the Windows taskbar.

Taskbar button: switch between docs.

You can use this same process to switch between any Office documents—not just those in the same program. If you are switching between documents within the same program (such as two Excel workbooks), try this: Open the Window menu and select the document you wish to view from those listed.

If you're working with several documents within the same program, you can view more than one document at a time by arranging them onscreen:

1. Open the Window menu and select Arrange or Arrange All. (If Arrange does not appear on the menu, point to the double arrows to view these menu options.)
2. If prompted, select how you want the windows arranged. For example, in Excel, you can have your worksheets arranged in a tiled, cascaded, horizontal, or vertical pattern.
3. To view only one document again, click on that document's Maximize button.

Click this Maximize button to view only this document.

The screen is split between open documents.

Cheat Sheet

Opening a Document

1. Click the Open button on the Standard toolbar from within the program.
2. Click the drop-down arrow next to Look in: and select the drive and directory that contain the document you want to open.
3. Select the document you want to open from the file list.
4. If you want to preview the contents of the file before you open it, click the drop-down next to the Views button and click Preview.
5. Click Open.

Starting an Office Application with an Existing Document

1. Click the Start button.
2. Select Open Office Document. The Open dialog box appears.
3. Click the drop-down arrow next to Look in: and select the drive and directory that contain the document you want to open.
4. Select the document you want to open from the file list.
5. Click Open.

Opening a Recent Document

1. Open the program such as Word, Excel, or PowerPoint.
2. Open the File menu.
3. The four most recently used documents appear at the bottom of the File menu. Select the document you want to open from this list.

3

Opening an Existing Document

After starting your Office 2000 application, you can begin a new document, or you can open a previously saved document and make changes to it. When you open a document, its contents are displayed onscreen so that you can make changes to it. After making your changes, save the document, and this new version will automatically replace the old one on your hard disk.

Open: already saved docs.

To open a document, you must tell the Office application the specific drive and directory in which the file is kept. You must also identify the document by its filename. For this reason, you should use careful thought in deciding on the document's filename when you save it for the first time. (Saving a document is explained in detail in Chapter 4.)

Name docs carefully!

Basic Survival

Opening a Document

To work on a document you have previously created and saved, you must open it:

1. Click the Open button on the Standard toolbar. The Open dialog box is displayed.

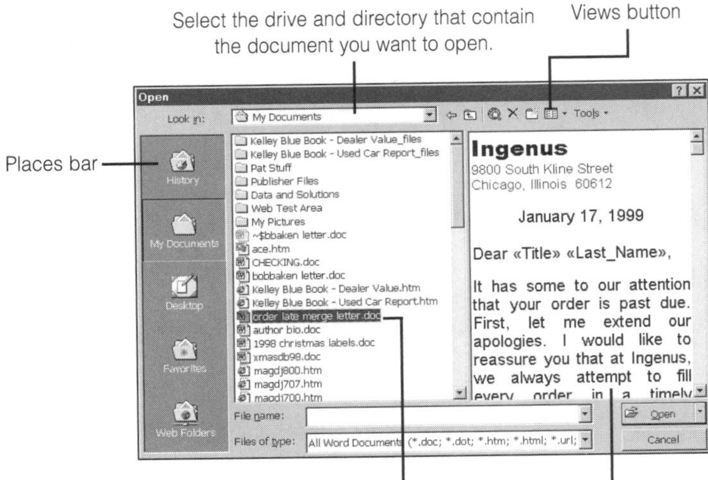
Select the drive and directory that contain the document you want to open.
Views button
Places bar
Select a file from those listed.
Preview window

You can preview documents before you open them.

2. Select the drive and directory that contain the document you want to open from the Look in: drop-down list. You can quickly change to certain folders by clicking their icon in the Places bar. Most Office documents are saved to the My Documents folder, although you can save them to the Favorites folder as well. The History folder contains a list of documents and folders you've used recently. The Desktop folder contains a list of any icon you've placed on the desktop, and the Web Folders folder contains links to folders on the Web that you have access to.

3. Select the document you want to open from the file list. If you want to open multiple documents, press Ctrl and click each one. However, in PowerPoint, you can open only one presentation at a time.

4. If you want to preview the contents of the file before you open it, click the drop-down arrow next to the Views button and select Preview. The contents of the file appear in the Preview window.

5. Click Open.

Beyond Survival

Starting an Office Application with an Existing Document

Start Word/Excel/PowerPoint and open a document!

Sometimes when you start an Office 2000 application, it's because you want to work on something you've already created and saved. So rather than start your program and then open the document you want to change; why not accomplish both tasks in a few simple steps? (If you want to create a new document when starting your Office 2000 application, see Chapter 2 for help.)

Follow these steps:

1. Click the Start button.
2. Select Open Office Document. The Open dialog box appears.
3. Select the drive and directory that contain the document you want to open from the Look in: drop-down list.
4. Select the document you want to open from the file list.
5. Click Open. The application associated with the document you selected is started for you, and the document is opened onscreen.

Opening a Recent Document

Recently used docs on File menu

If you want to make changes to a document that you have worked on lately, there's a simple shortcut you can use (rather than clicking the Open button):

1. Open the File menu.
2. The four most recently used documents appear at the bottom of the File menu. Select the document you want to open from this list.

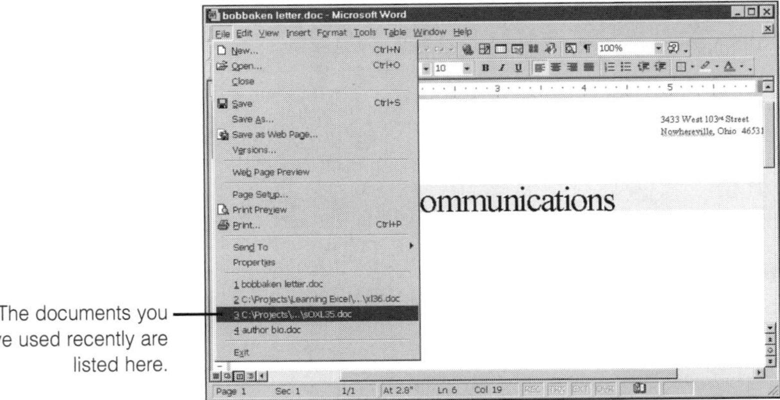

The documents you have used recently are listed here.

Change number of documents listed on File menu.

To change the number of recently used documents that are displayed on the File menu, open the Tools menu and select Options. If needed, click the General tab. Then change the number displayed in the Recently Used File list box. Click OK.

If you haven't started your Office program yet, you can still open a recently used document. Just click Start, select Documents, then select the document you want from the list that's displayed.

Cheat Sheet

Saving a Document for the First Time

1. Click the Save button on the Standard toolbar.
2. Type a name for the document in the File name text box.
3. If you want to save your document in some other folder (directory), change to that directory using the Save in drop-down list box.
4. Click Save.

Saving a Document Again

- Click the Save button on the Standard toolbar, or
- Press Ctrl+S, or
- Open the File menu and select Save.

Saving a Document with a New Name

1. Open the document upon which you want to base your new document.
2. Open the File menu and select Save As.
3. Type a name that's different than the original document's filename in the File name text box.
4. Click Save.

4

Saving a Document

As you create your new document, it is stored only temporarily in the memory of your computer. The contents of the document exist only as long as the computer is on and the application that you used to create it is still running. To avoid losing all your hard work, you should save your document to disk. In fact, you should save the document even before it is actually finished to reduce any chance that you might lose something important.

Save a document before it's done.

If you continue to make changes to a document after you've saved it, you should resave the document. That way the file on your hard disk will contain all of your current changes and revisions. In fact, it's recommended that you save your document frequently as you work. Doing so will save you the headaches (and possible loss of data) that come with power outages, computer freezes, and so forth.

Save documents often!

Basic Survival

Saving a Document for the First Time

The first time you save a document, you must give it a name. This name can contain letters, numbers, and even spaces, up to 256 characters. Consider carefully the name you give your document; the name should be descriptive enough of the document's contents so that you can easily identify the document again should you have a need. The name should also be unique; if you pick the same name as that of another document, you could end up replacing that document with your new one.

Filename = 256 char, letters, numbers, spaces.

After you save your document, the Office 2000 application gives it a file extension, such as .doc, .xls, or .ppt. The file extension helps Windows to identify the program that created the document.

Sample filenames include:

Budget Proposal.doc

Qtr 2 Sales Figures.xls

Employee Orientation.ppt

Follow these steps to save your document the first time:

1. Click the Save button on the Standard toolbar. The Save As dialog box appears.

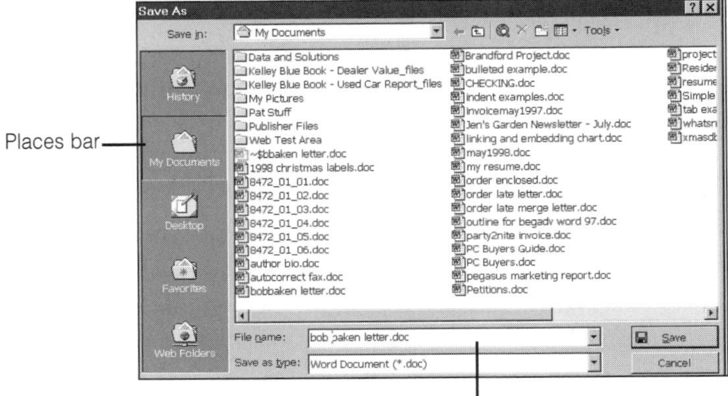

2. Type a name for the document in the File name text box. Remember that Windows 98 allows you to use up to 256 characters, including letters, numbers, and spaces, which is much better than the eight characters you were allowed under Windows 3.1. You don't have to type the file extension; the application adds it for you automatically.

3. By default, Office 2000 saves all your documents in a folder called My Documents. If you want to save your document in some other folder (directory), change to that directory using the Save in drop-down list box or by clicking the appropriate icon in the Places bar. You can save documents to your hard disk, the floppy drive, a network (if you are connected to a network at the office, for example), or to any other drive hooked to your computer (such as a second hard drive or an Iomega Zip drive). You can also save documents to a folder on the Web by using the Web Folders button.

Docs are saved in My Documents folder.

4. Click Save. The document is saved to disk. If you make any changes to the document, be sure to save it again. When you're through with a document, you must close it to remove it from the screen. See Chapter 8 for help.

Saving a Document Again

Office saves docs every 10 min.

As you continue to work on a document, Word and PowerPoint will automatically resave it at periodic intervals, usually every 10 minutes. This prevents you from losing any of the changes you might make to a document after saving it for the first time. You can change the intervals for this automatic save by selecting the Tools menu and choosing Options. From there, simply choose the Save tab and change the Save AutoRecover info every *XX* setting.

Excel's AutoSave feature is an optional Add-in. To add this select Tools, Add-Ins and check the box next to AutoSave Add-In. Click OK then follow the prompts to add the AutoSave feature. Once the add-in is installed, select Tools, AutoSave and change the automatic save time intervals.

If you make an important or complex change to a document, you may want to resave it yourself, rather than wait for the Office 2000 application to do it for you. Use any of these methods:

- Click the Save button on the Standard toolbar.
- Press Ctrl+S.
- Open the File menu and select Save.

Beyond Survival

Saving a Document with a New Name

Why start from scratch? Reuse!

If you need to create a document that's similar to one you've already saved, there's an easy way to do it:

1. Open the document on which you want to base your new document.
2. Open the File menu and select Save As. The Save As dialog box appears.
3. Type a name that's different than the original document's filename in the File name text box.

4. Click Save. The original document is closed, and a new document is created. This new document starts out with the same contents as the original document; simply make the changes you want and save them, and you'll end up with two documents: the original and a new one that is similar but includes your changes.

Cheat Sheet

Checking the Spelling in a Document

1. Click the Spelling button (or in Word, the Spelling and Grammar button) on the Standard toolbar.
2. When an error is found, it's highlighted. To correct the error, perform one of the following:
   - Select one of the suggested spellings and click Change to change the highlighted word to the suggested spelling. Click Change All to change all occurrences of the misspelled word to the word you selected.
   - If there are no suggestions listed, or if a correct suggestion is not listed, make the correction manually.
   - If the word is actually spelled correctly, then click Ignore. Click Ignore All to ignore any further occurrences of the "misspelled" word.
   - To add the word to the dictionary so it is no longer listed as misspelled, click Add.
   - To add the word to the AutoCorrect list (so that the word will be automatically corrected for you in the future), click AutoCorrect.

5

Checking Your Spelling

Prior to printing your document, you should proofread it for errors. Checking a document for errors is the single most important step you can take if you desire professional-looking results.

Check all documents before printing!

The first thing most people do when proofing a document is check for spelling errors. This is why your Office 2000 programs contain a spelling checker. In addition, Word 2000 contains a grammar checker that you can use to check for grammatical errors in your Word documents.

Basic Survival

Checking the Spelling in a Document

When you use the spelling checker, it verifies the spelling of each word of your document against the words in the spelling dictionary. If a word is suspected of being misspelled (because it cannot be found in the dictionary), it's flagged for your review. At that point, you can choose to correct the error (with a suggested substitute or with your own typed correction) or you can simply ignore the error. In Word, your spelling and grammar are checked at the same time (unless you turn the grammar feature off, in which case only your spelling is checked).

Checks grammar, too!

To start the spelling checker, follow these steps:

1. Click the Spelling button (or in Word, the Spelling and Grammar button) on the Standard toolbar.
2. When an error is found, it's highlighted. To correct the error, perform one of the following:

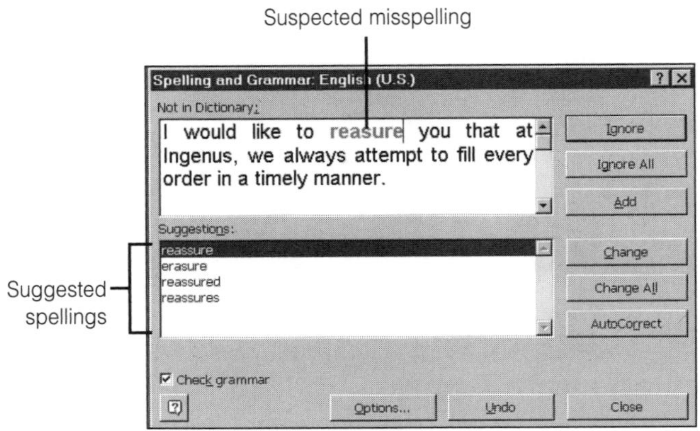

- Select one of the suggested spellings and click Change to change the highlighted word. You can also click Change All to change all occurrences of the misspelled word to the word you selected.
- If no suggestions are listed, or if a correct suggestion is not listed, make the correction manually by editing the text in the top box.
- If the word is actually spelled correctly, then click Ignore. Click Ignore All if you want to ignore any further occurrences of the "misspelled" word.
- To add the word to the dictionary so it is no longer listed as misspelled, click Add.
- To add the word to the AutoCorrect list (so that the word will be automatically corrected for you in the future) click AutoCorrect.
- To turn off grammar checking (this time only), click the check box next to Check Grammar to remove the check mark.

Red = spelling error
Green = grammar error

Besides checking your spelling whenever you start the spelling checker, Word can also check your spelling and grammar as you type. When this option is turned on (by default) and a misspelled word is typed, it's underlined with a red wavy line. Grammatical errors are underlined with a green wavy line. To check an error when it occurs, right-click on the underlined word. A shortcut menu appears, listing several options for correcting the suspected error. This shortcut menu also gives you the option to ignore the suspected error.

Beyond Survival

Using AutoCorrect

AutoCorrect fixes errors as you type.

Your Office 2000 applications come with a feature called AutoCorrect, which corrects certain spelling errors as you type them. For example, if you were to type "teh," it would automatically be changed to "the." You don't have to do anything to use AutoCorrect; it's turned on for you by default. When a misspelling occurs that is in the AutoCorrect list, it is automatically fixed for you.

If you often mistype a particular word, such as "donaton" instead of "donation," you can add that misspelling to the AutoCorrect list:

1. Open the Tools menu and select AutoCorrect. The AutoCorrect dialog box appears.

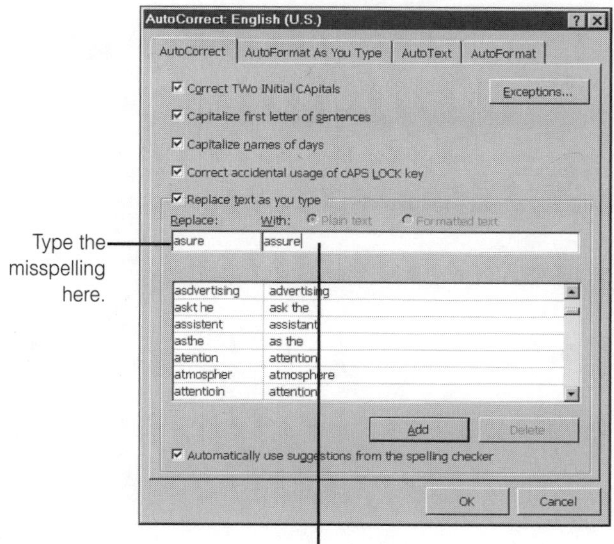

2. Type the misspelling in the Replace text box.
3. Type the correction in the With text box.
4. Click Add.
5. Repeat steps 2 to 4 to add more misspelled words. Click OK when you're finished.

If you mistype a word after adding it to the AutoCorrect list, it will automatically be corrected for you. You can also add words to the AutoCorrect list when checking your document for spelling errors; see the earlier section, "Checking the Spelling in a Document," for help.

Cheat Sheet

Setting Margins

To change the margins in Word or Excel:

1. Open the File menu and select Page Setup.
2. If needed, click the Margins tab. Specify the amount you want for the top, bottom, left, and right margins.
3. Set the gutter margin if applicable. Set the Mirror margins option as well. Click OK.

Changing Margins While in Page Preview

1. Click the Print Preview button on the Standard toolbar.
2. In Word, click the View Ruler button. In Excel, click the Margins button instead.
3. Drag a margin guide to change the corresponding margin.
4. To return to normal view, click the Close button.

Centering a Page

To center a page in Word:

1. Open the File menu and select Page Setup.
2. Click the Layout tab.
3. Select Center from the Vertical Alignment drop-down list. Click OK.

To center a page in Excel:

1. Open the File menu and select Page Setup. The Page Setup dialog box appears.
2. Click the Margins tab.
3. Under Center on page, select either the Horizontally or Vertically option, or both. Click OK.

6

Changing Margins and Other Page Options

Prior to printing your document, you may want to preview it to see whether it looks the way you want. For example, is there enough whitespace (margin area) on either side of the page? Would the document look better if you printed it using landscape (lengthwise) orientation rather than portrait (widthwise) orientation? What would the document look like if it was centered on the page both vertically and horizontally? You'll learn how to change each of these options in this chapter.

Basic Survival

Setting Margins

Each page of your document is printed within four margins: top, bottom, left, and right. A margin is whitespace that lies between the edge of the paper and the page contents. Margins give the eye a visual resting spot.

Normally, in Word, the left and right margins are set at 1 1/4 inches (in Excel, they are set at 3/4 inch), and the top and bottom margins are set at 1 inch. This is usually fine for most documents, but if you plan to print on company letterhead, you may need a larger top margin. If you need to conserve paper, you can print more on each page by reducing the size of the left and right margins.

To change the margins in Word or Excel, follow these steps (You can't, by the way, change the margins in PowerPoint):

1. Open the File menu and select Page Setup. The Page Setup dialog box appears. (The dialog box shown here is the Word Page Setup dialog box. The Page Setup dialog box in Excel is slightly different.)

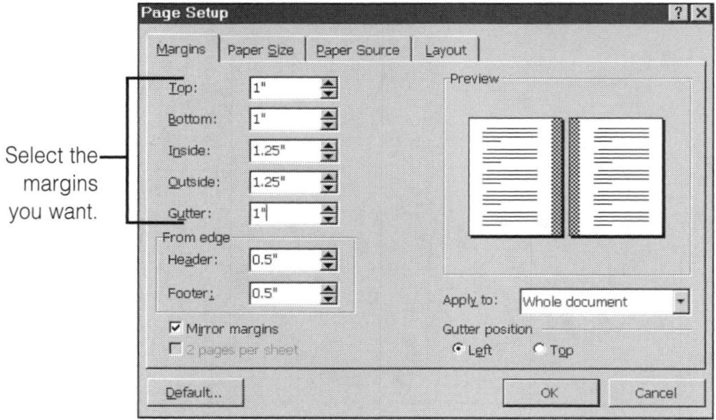

2. If needed, click the Margins tab. Specify the size—in inches—you want for the top, bottom, left, and right margins. Space is automatically allotted for a header or footer, but you can increase the margin between them and the page contents if you wish.

3. Word has an additional margin you can set, called the *gutter*. The gutter is the center margin of a book or similarly bound document. It allows space for the binding. If you plan to present your document in the manner of a book, magazine, or similar material, then you should choose a gutter margin. You should also choose the option Mirror margins.

4. Click OK.

Beyond Survival

Changing Margins While in Page Preview

Because you typically preview your document prior to printing it, it's a simple matter to make changes to your margins and then:

1. Click the Print Preview button on the Standard toolbar.

2. In Word, click the View Ruler button. In Excel, click the Margins button instead.

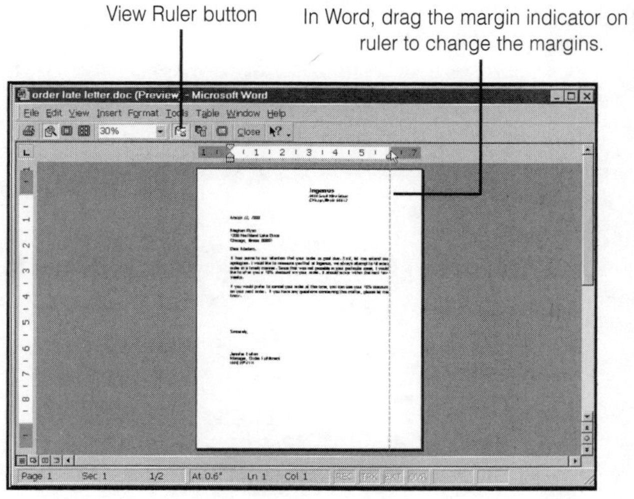

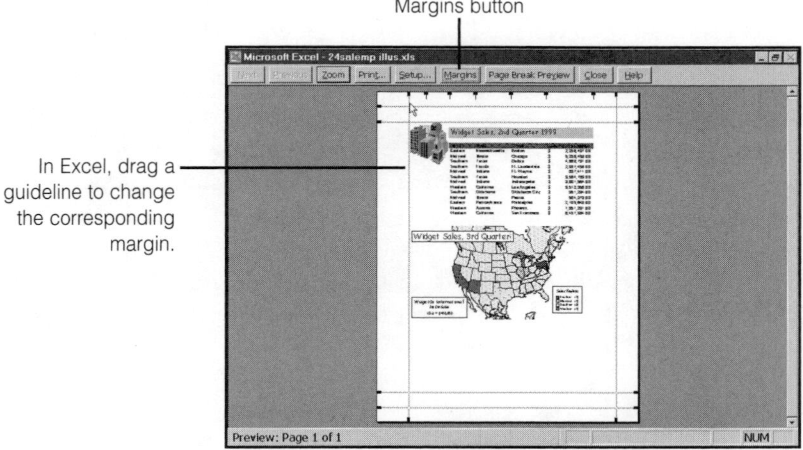

3. Drag a margin guide to change the corresponding margin.

4. To return to normal view, click the Close button.

Centering a Page

A page can be centered *vertically* (its contents placed equally between the top and bottom margins) or *horizontally* (its contents placed equally between the left and right margins). You might want to center a short letter or a spreadsheet that does not contain a lot of data.

To center a page in Word:

1. Open the File menu and select Page Setup. The Page Setup dialog box appears.
2. Click the Layout tab.

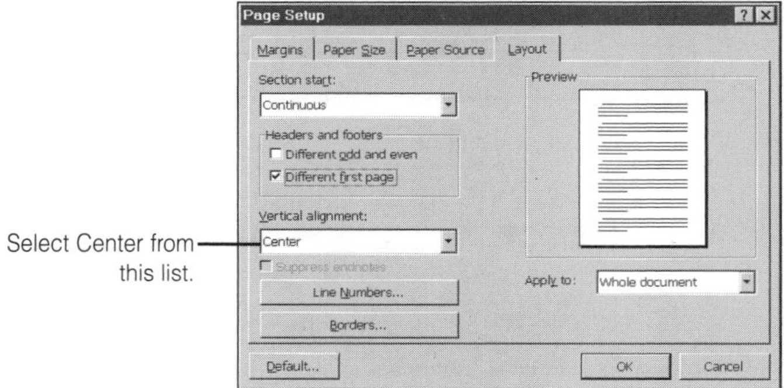

3. Select Center from the Vertical alignment drop-down list. (To center text horizontally between the left and right margins, simply select it and click the Center button on the Formatting toolbar.)
4. Click OK.

To center a page in Excel:

1. Open the File menu and select Page Setup. The Page Setup dialog box appears.

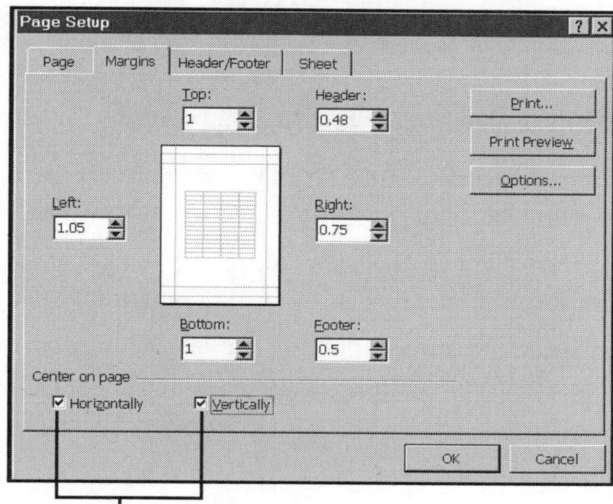

You can center your page vertically, horizontally, or both.

2. Click the Margins tab.
3. Under Center on page, select either the Horizontally or Vertically option, or both.
4. Click OK.

Changing Page Orientation

When a page is printed, its text is typically oriented so that its text is read across the smallest dimension of the paper. So, if you use 8 1/2 by 11-inch paper, the text is typically printed across its 8 1/2-inch width. This type of orientation is called portrait orientation.

The opposite of portrait orientation is landscape orientation. Here, the text is printed across the largest dimension of the page. That would mean the text would be printed along the 11-inch width of an 8 1/2 by 11-inch sheet of paper.

To change the orientation of the page:

1. Open the File menu and select Page Setup. The Page Setup dialog box appears.
2. In Word, click the Paper Size tab. In Excel, click the Page tab.
3. Select the orientation you want and click OK. (PowerPoint allows you to set the orientation of your slides differently from the orientation of your notes, handouts, and outline.)

Cheat Sheet

Previewing a Document Before You Print It

To preview a Word or an Excel document prior to printing it, click the Print Preview button on the Standard toolbar. Then click any of the following buttons, as appropriate.

- Click the Print button to print the document.
- To zoom in on any part of the document, simply click on it. To zoom back out, click again.
- To edit the document while zoomed, click the Magnifier button (Word only).
- Click the Multiple Pages button to view more than one page at a time. Click the One Page button to view only a single page (Word only).
- Click the View Ruler button to display or hide the ruler (Word only). In Excel, click the Margins button to display or hide the margin guides.
- To shrink the size of the text so that it fits on a single page, click the Shrink to Fit button (Word only).
- To view the document full-screen so that no distractions are on the screen, click the Full Screen button (Word only).
- To display the Page Setup dialog box, click the Setup button (Excel only).
- To move from page to page in a document (Word only), click Next Page or Previous Page.
- To preview where the page breaks fall within your worksheet (Excel only), click the Page Break Preview button (more on this feature later in the chapter).

When you finish previewing your document, click Close.

Printing a Document

To print a document, click the Print button on the Standard toolbar. Or select File, Print to view the Print dialog box where print options can be selected.

7

Printing an Office Document

Typically, after spending hours writing, editing, and proofing a document, you print it so you can have a hard copy for your records or for others to review. Printing a document is a simple enough process: You open the document you want to print, tell the Office application to print it, and Office feeds the necessary information to Windows so that it can be printed.

Can keep working while printing.

The Windows printer can handle many documents at once, so feel free to load it up with anything you want to print. If Windows is sending several documents to print at the same time, it organizes them in a long list called a "queue," and then prints them one at a time until it has nothing left to print. Meanwhile, your Office program is freed from the burden of managing the printing process—this enables you to continue working while your document is printing, if you like.

A few additional printing options apply to Excel only; those options are covered in Chapter 36.

Basic Survival

Previewing a Document Before You Print It

Prior to actually printing your Word or Excel document, you should preview it to review its overall appearance. With Print Preview, you can tell whether or not the graphics look nice with your text, the margins are sized correctly, and the headers and footers are pleasing to the eye. To preview a document:

Preview first!

1. Click the Print Preview button on the Standard toolbar. The document is displayed as a full page.

In Print Preview, your document appears as it will when printed.

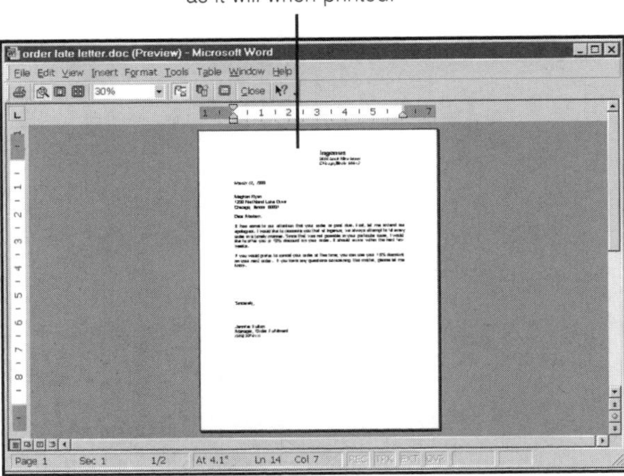

2. Click any of the following buttons (you cannot preview your presentation in PowerPoint):

   - Click the Print button to print the document.
   - To zoom in on any part of the document, click on the zoom button. To zoom back out, click again.
   - To edit the document while zoomed, click the Magnifier button (Word only).
   - Click the Multiple Pages button to view more than one page at a time. Click the One Page button to view only a single page (Word only).
   - Click the View Ruler button to display or hide the ruler (Word only). In Excel, click the Margins button to display or hide the margin guides.
   - To shrink the size of the text so that it fits on a single page, click the Shrink to Fit button (Word only).
   - To view the document full-screen so that there aren't any distractions onscreen, click the Full Screen button (Word only).
   - To display the Page Setup dialog box, click the Setup button (Excel only).

- To move from page to page in a document (Word only), click Next Page or Previous Page.
- To preview where the page breaks fall within your worksheet (Excel only), click the Page Break Preview button (see Chapter 36). If you've selected this option and want to return to regular view, select View, Normal.

3. When you finish previewing your document, click Close.

Printing a Document

After previewing your document, you're ready to print it. You can do so by clicking the Print button in the Print Preview window, or, if you're in the main document window, by using the Print command from the File menu.

1. Click the Print button on the Standard toolbar.
2. Your document starts to print. You can continue to work while your document is printing. You can even open another document and click Print to send it to the printer as well, even before your first document is done printing. (If you wish to print a range of pages rather than the entire document, or several copies of your document, see the "Beyond Survival" section for help.)

Beyond Survival

Printing a Range of Pages

If you don't want to print your entire document, you don't have to. You can print a single page or a series of pages in Word; a single worksheet or a range of cells in Excel; or a single slide, a series of slides, handouts, notes, or your outline in PowerPoint. Here's how:

Can print select pages, worksheets, or slides.

1. Open the File menu and select Print. The Print dialog box appears. (The dialog box shown here is from Word; Excel and PowerPoint's dialog boxes are slightly different.)

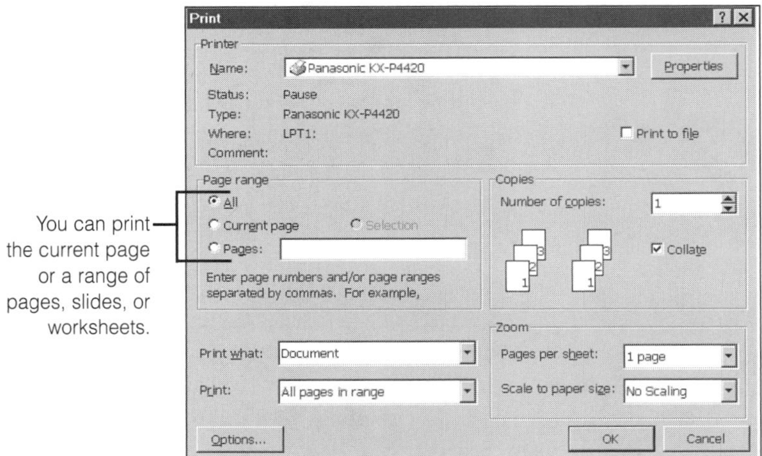

You can print the current page or a range of pages, slides, or worksheets.

2. To print the current page, worksheet, or slide, select that option in the Print range area.

   To print a range of pages or slides, enter that range in the Pages or Slides text box. For example, to print pages 2, 4, 5, and 6 in Word, enter **2, 4-6** in the text box. To print pages 2 to 6 in Excel, enter **2** in the From text box, and **6** in the To text box. To print slides 1, 2, 5, 7, 8, and 9 in PowerPoint, enter **1, 2, 5, 7-9** in the text box. To print just odd or only even pages in Word, select that option from the Print list.

3. In Excel, you can also print a selected range of cells or selected worksheets. To do that, select the cell range or the worksheets you want to print *first*, prior to using the File/Print command. (See Chapter 23 for help in selecting ranges. See Chapter 26 for help in selecting worksheets.)

4. In PowerPoint, you can print slides, notes, handouts or your outline by selecting the appropriate option from the Print what drop-down list box.

5. Click OK to begin printing.

Printing More Than One Copy

Don't use this unless the copier is broken!

If you need more than a single copy of your document for distribution, you can print several copies at one time. This process, however, is perhaps only marginally faster than standing in a long line at the copier; for long documents, it may actually be *slower*. However, if you want to try, follow these steps:

1. Open the File menu and select Print. The Print dialog box appears.

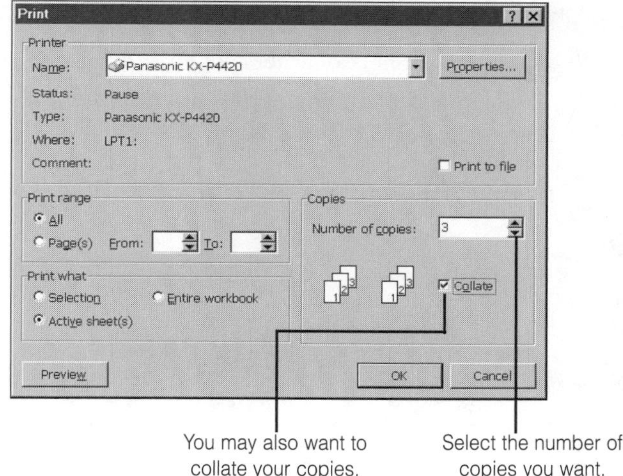

You may also want to collate your copies.

Select the number of copies you want.

2. Select the number of copies you want to print from the Number of copies list box.
3. To collate your pages, select the Collate option.
4. Click OK.

Cheat Sheet

Exiting an Application

1. Open the File menu and select Exit. (You can also click the application window's Close button.)
2. If for some reason you have not saved changes to a particular document, you'll see a warning telling you so. To save the document, click Yes. Then type a filename for the document and click Save.

Closing a Document and Continuing to Work

- To close a single document, open the File menu and select Close.
- To close all documents, press and hold the Shift key, then open the File menu. Select Close All.

8

Exiting an Office 2000 Application

When you finish working in an Office application, you should exit it. Doing so frees up resources within your computer, making the applications you are working with even faster.

Exit when done!

Prior to exiting any program, however, you should save all open documents. (See Chapter 4 for help.) If you don't save your documents, you will lose any changes you have made since you last saved the document.

If you're finished with a particular document, but you want to continue working in your Office application, you can. In this case, you do not exit the application (because you haven't finished using it). Instead, you close (put away) the document.

Basic Survival

Exiting an Application

When you are finished working within an Office application, exit it. However, before you do so, make sure you take a moment to save all your open documents. Then follow these steps:

Save documents first!

1. Open the File menu and select Exit. (You can also click the application window's Close button.)
2. If for some reason you have not saved changes to a particular document, you'll see a warning telling you so. To save the document, click Yes. Then type a filename for the document and click Save.

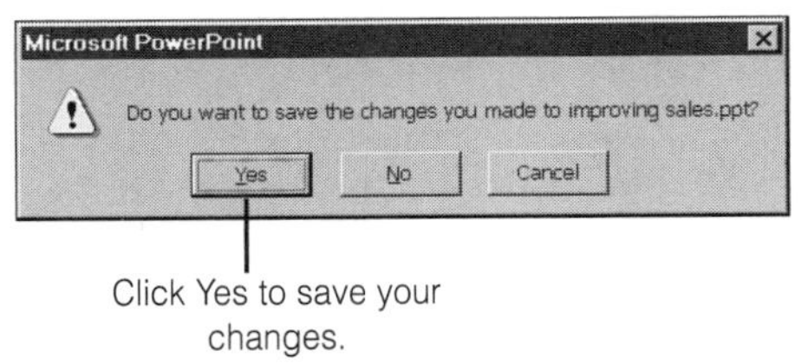

Click Yes to save your changes.

Beyond Survival

Closing a Document and Continuing to Work

When you're finished with a document, you should close it. Doing so frees up computer resources that can then be used for something else.

Closing a document removes it from your screen. To work on the document at some later time, open it again. (See Chapter 3 for help.)

To close a document:

Close documents when done!

1. Open the File menu and select Close.
2. If for some reason you have not saved your changes to the document, you'll see a warning telling you so. Click Yes, type a filename for the document, and click Save.

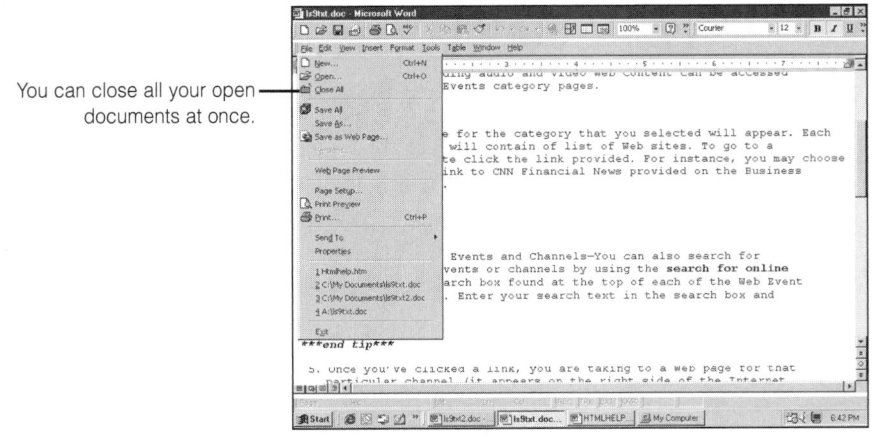

You can close all your open documents at once.

If you want to close all your open documents, press Shift when you open the File menu. The Close command changes to Close All. If you select Close All, you will close all open documents.

Cheat Sheet

Turning the Office Assistant On and Off

- To display the Office Assistant at any time, click the Office Assistant button [?] on the Standard toolbar.
- To remove the Office Assistant from the screen, simply right-click on it and choose Hide.
- To leave the Office Assistant running, so you can ask a future question more quickly, click in the document to hide the bubble.
- To redisplay the bubble so you can ask the Office Assistant a question, click the Office Assistant.

Asking the Office Assistant a Question

1. If the Office Assistant is not visible, click the Office Assistant button [?] on the Standard toolbar to display it.
2. Type your question or just a few keywords into the text box.
3. Click Search or press Enter.
4. Click the topic that best fits your question or problem.
5. After reviewing the contents in the Help window, click its Close button to remove it from the screen.
6. To remove the Office Assistant as well, click the Office Assistant Close button.

Selecting a Different Office Assistant

1. In the Office Assistant, select Choose Assistant.
2. Click Next> until you find an assistant you like and click OK.

9

Getting Help

The Office Assistant is new to Office 2000. Even so, you've probably seen the Office Assistant already—it's the paper-clip character that appeared when you started one of your Office applications for the very first time. (If you don't see an animated paper-clip, don't worry; it's possible that you or another user—if you are using Office in a work environment—has switched to another Office Assistant.) In addition, the Office Assistant has a knack for showing up automatically whenever it senses you're in trouble. (In fact, if the Office Assistant has a suggestion to make, a tiny light bulb appears on the Office Assistant button on the Standard toolbar.)

Despite its often comical appearance, the Office Assistant is pretty talented when it comes to providing help. In this chapter, you'll learn how to get the Office Assistant to deliver the exact help you need.

Basic Survival

Turning the Office Assistant On and Off

The Office Assistant automatically pops its head up the very first time you start an Office program. At that point, to get it out of the way, you can simply select the option Start using X (where "X" represents the name of the application). But how do you get the Assistant back when you need it? And how do you get it out of the way when you don't?

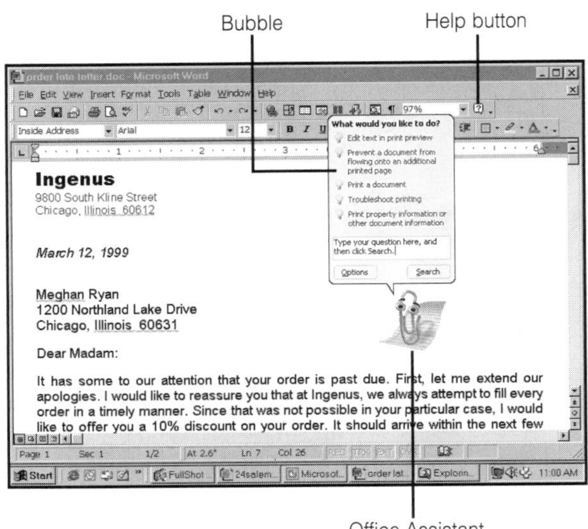

- To display the Office Assistant at any time, click the Office Assistant button [?] on the Standard toolbar. You can also press F1 to call on the Assistant.
- You can leave the Office Assistant onscreen as long as you like; it does not interfere with your documents. However, if you want to get it out of the way so you can see what you're working on, simply right-click on it and choose Hide.
- If you want to leave the Office Assistant running, but you want to remove its bubble from the screen, click in the document to hide the bubble.
- To redisplay the bubble so you can ask the Office Assistant a question, click the Office Assistant.
- Keep in mind that there is only one Office Assistant. So, if you close it while using Excel, and then switch to Word, it does not appear onscreen. You need to call the Office Assistant back up when you need to use it again.

Asking the Office Assistant a Question

If you need help with a problem or question while you are working in an Office application, just ask the Office Assistant. Here's how:

1. If the Office Assistant is not visible, click the Office Assistant button on the Standard toolbar or press F1 to display it.

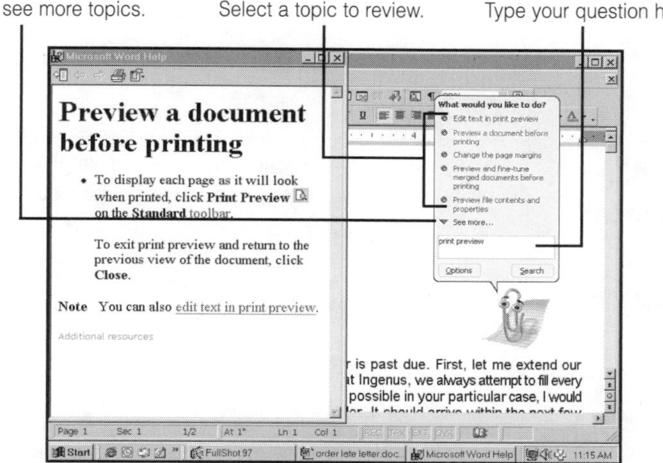

2. Type your question or just a few keywords into the text box.
3. Click Search or simply press Enter. The Office Assistant displays a list of suggested topics for you to review.
4. Click the topic that best fits your question or problem. The Help window appears, displaying help for the topic you selected. If you don't see a topic you like, click See more at the bottom of the bubble (if displayed). To return to the previous list, click See previous, which appears at the top of the list.
5. After reviewing the contents in the Help window, you can click the Print button to print the help topic for a handy reference, click the Back or Forward buttons to review previous help screens, click the Close button to remove the Help window, or click another topic in the Office Assistant bubble to display it.

6. The Office Assistant stands poised and ready for another question. If you're finished with it, you can remove the Office Assistant from the screen by right-clicking it and selecting Hide.

Light bulb on button = suggestion

If the Office Assistant has a suggestion to make, a light bulb appears above the Office Assistant, as well as on the Office Assistant toolbar button. To display the suggestion, display the Office Assistant [?] if needed, then click the light bulb.

Beyond Survival

Selecting a Different Office Assistant

When the Office Assistant first appears, it takes the form of a paper-clip. If you grow tired of it, you can change the appearance of the Office Assistant to any number of characters:

1. If needed, display the Office Assistant by clicking the Office Assistant button [?] on the Standard toolbar.

Check this out!

2. Right-click the Assistant and select Choose Assistant. The Office Assistant dialog box appears.

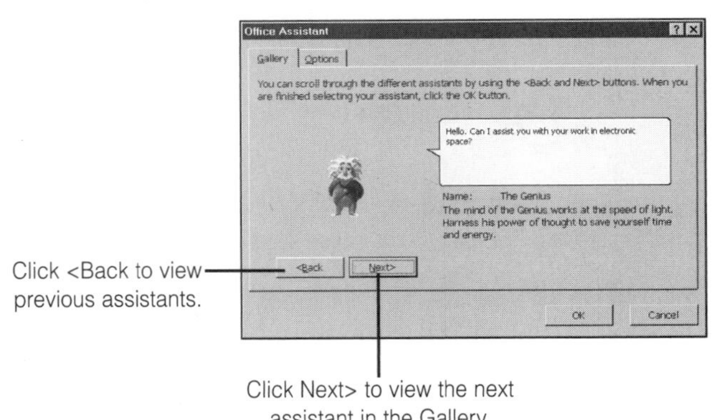

Click <Back to view previous assistants.

Click Next> to view the next assistant in the Gallery.

3. Click Next> until you find an assistant you like.
4. Click OK.

PART 2

Word 2000

Word 2000 is one of the world's most popular word processors. With it, you can create letters, memos, reports, fax covers, resumes, and even Web pages. Of course, before you can create any of these things, you should get to know Word a bit better.

In this part, you'll learn about the following topics:

- Taking a Look Around
- Entering and Editing Text
- Selecting Text
- Copying, Moving, and Deleting Text
- Viewing a Document
- Finding and Replacing Text
- Changing How Text Looks
- Changing How Paragraphs Look
- Setting Tabs
- Creating Numbered and Bulleted Lists
- Adding a Header or a Footer

Cheat Sheet

Understanding the Word 2000 Screen

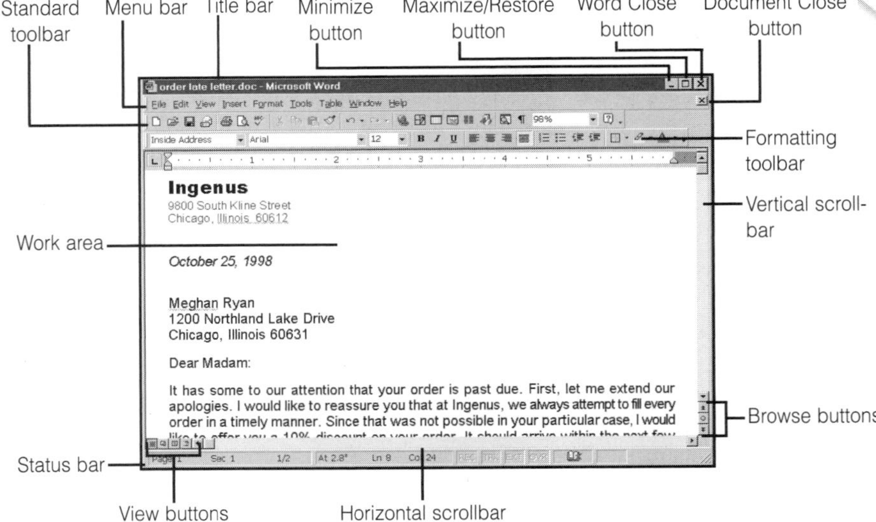

10

Taking a Look Around

When you start Word 2000, you're presented with a blank document into which you can begin typing your text. Word provides many tools you can use to fill this "blank canvas," as you will learn in this chapter.

The screen elements in Word provide access to the commands you need, such as the commands for cutting and pasting text. These elements also enable you to move through your document quickly, resize the window, and so on.

Basic Survival

Understanding the Word 2000 Screen

Before you begin using Word, you need to understand the purpose of each of its screen elements:

- **Title bar** Displays the name of your document.
- **Window controls** With the Minimize, Maximize/Restore, and Close buttons, you can control the size of the window in which you work. There are rows of buttons: the top row includes all three buttons and controls the Word window; while the other row contains only a Close button and controls the document window.
- **Menu bar** This bar contains the Word menus. To open a menu, click on it. For example, to open the File menu, click on the word File. A list of commands appears; to select one, click on it.

Click menu, click command.

- **Toolbars** Word has many specialized toolbars that you can use to accomplish specific tasks. Initially, only the Standard and Formatting toolbars are displayed—in a single row, just below the menu bar. But you can display other toolbars whenever you like. You'll learn how to do this in the next section, "Hiding, Displaying, and Moving Toolbars."

Vertical ruler doesn't show normally.

- **Ruler** Horizontal and vertical rulers are used to change a variety of format options, such as setting tabs, adjusting page margins, and changing paragraph indents. Depending on how you are viewing your document, the horizontal ruler may be the only ruler displayed. To display the vertical ruler, you must change the Print Layout view, by selecting Print Layout from the view menu. You might use the vertical ruler to change your top or bottom margins, header and footer margins, table row height, positioning of graphics, and so on. (Double-clicking on either ruler will quickly display the Page Setup menu.) To hide both rulers, open the View menu and select Ruler to remove the check mark.
- **Work area** This is the area into which you type your text. The cursor (the vertical blinking line) marks the spot at which text is inserted when you begin typing.
- **Scrollbars** Use these to scroll the onscreen contents to view data that is not currently being displayed.
- **Browse buttons** The browse buttons are located at the bottom of the vertical scrollbar. You can use them to quickly jump to a different location in the document. You'll learn more about the browse buttons in Chapter 11.

Use View buttons to change display.

- **View buttons** To the left of the horizontal scrollbar are the view buttons, which you can use to change your view of the document. You'll learn more about this feature in Chapter 14.
- **Status bar** This bar displays the status of your document. Here, you can see the number of the page on which you're currently working, the section number (you can use sections to divide your document and use different formatting in each area), and cursor location. Reminders are also displayed here, such as the letters OVR to remind you that the overtype feature is on.

Beyond Survival

Hiding, Displaying, and Moving Toolbars

Initially, only the Standard and Formatting toolbars are displayed. Other toolbars appear automatically when needed; however, if you want to display a specific toolbar, such as the Drawing toolbar, follow these steps:

1. Open the View menu.
2. Select Toolbars. A cascading menu appears.
3. Slide the mouse pointer to the right, onto the cascading menu, then click the name of the toolbar you want to display. Toolbars that are currently being displayed appear with a check mark in front of them.

To hide a toolbar, follow these same steps. When you click on a toolbar name that appears with a check mark, the check mark is removed, and the toolbar is hidden from view.

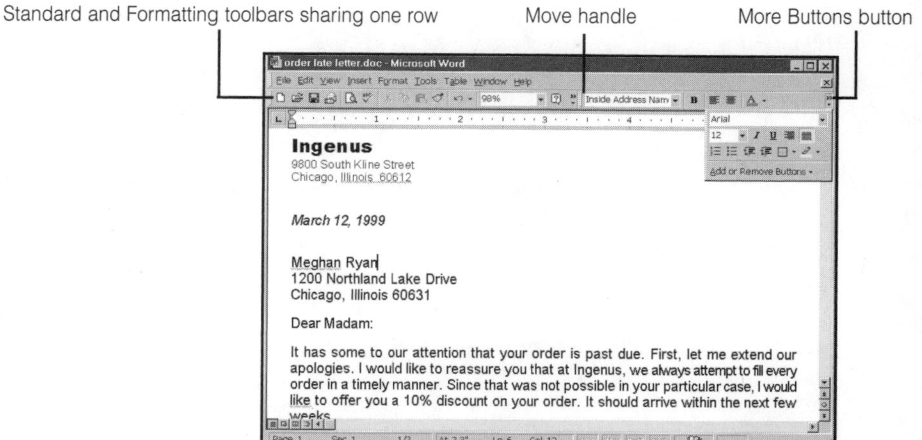

Once a toolbar is displayed, you can click any toolbar button to activate its command. If you don't know what a particular button does, just position the mouse pointer over the button, and a ScreenTip appears, displaying the button's name. If a button is not displayed (which will happen when two toolbars appear together on the same row), click the More Buttons button to display a list of buttons from which you can select.

As I mentioned before, initially, the Standard and Formatting toolbars share the same space, just below the menu bar. This prevents all of their buttons from being displayed, but it does provide a larger work area. However, if you want, you can move one toolbar below the other, in order to display all of their buttons. You can also "dock" a toolbar along the sides or bottom of the window. You can even drag them into the work area to make them more convenient:

1. Position the mouse pointer over the toolbar's move handle (the mouse pointer changes to a four-headed arrow.
2. Drag the toolbar to the top, bottom, left, or right side of the window until it attaches itself to one of the sides. Release the mouse to anchor the toolbar to its new position.

You can also drag a toolbar (using the move handle) into the work area so that it "floats" on your screen. This allows you to move the toolbar anywhere on the screen by dragging the colored title bar to a new position.

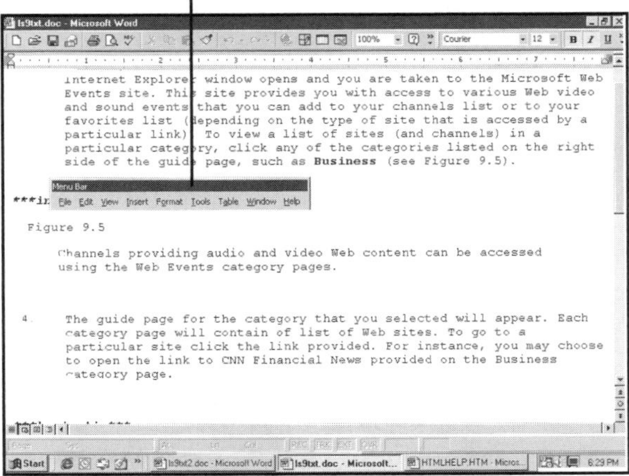

Cheat Sheet

Correcting Your Mistakes

To correct a simple typo:

- Press the Backspace key as needed to back the cursor up and erase characters to the left, or
- To erase a character to the right of the cursor, press Delete instead.
- Select the mistake and then type your correction.

Moving the Insertion Point with the Mouse

- Click in the spot at which you want to place the cursor, or
- Use the scrollbars to scroll to the spot you want, then click on it, or
- Use the Previous Page or the Next Page button on the vertical scroll-bar to jump to the spot you want, then click on it.

Moving the Insertion Point with the Keyboard

To move here	Press this
End of the line	End
Beginning of the line	Home
One character left, right, up, or down	Arrow keys
Beginning of the document	Ctrl+Home
End of the document	Ctrl+End
Next word	Ctrl+→
Previous word	Ctrl+←
Next paragraph	Ctrl+↓
Previous paragraph	Ctrl+↑
One screen	Page Up, Page Down
A specific page	Ctrl+G then type a page number and press Enter

11

Entering and Editing Text

Because Word is a word processing program, it makes sense that one of the tasks you will perform is entering text. Not surprisingly, Word makes it easy for you to enter text, make changes, and add new text.

Basic Survival

Entering Text

When you start Word, it presents you with a blank document. To enter text, start typing. A vertical line called the *insertion point* or *cursor* marks your place in the document. The cursor (or insertion point, if you prefer) moves as you type, keeping pace with you.

As you type, the text *wraps* between the margins; this means that unlike when you use a typewriter, you do not press Enter at the end of every line. Instead, keep typing, and text that won't fit on the current line is automatically wrapped down to the next line. If you delete some text later on, text following the deleted text is moved backwards to fill the gap.

When you want to begin a new paragraph or insert a blank line, press Enter to force the cursor to move down one line. Otherwise, type, and let word wrap place the words on the page for you. If you want to begin typing in the middle of a page, just click where you want to start; then begin typing.

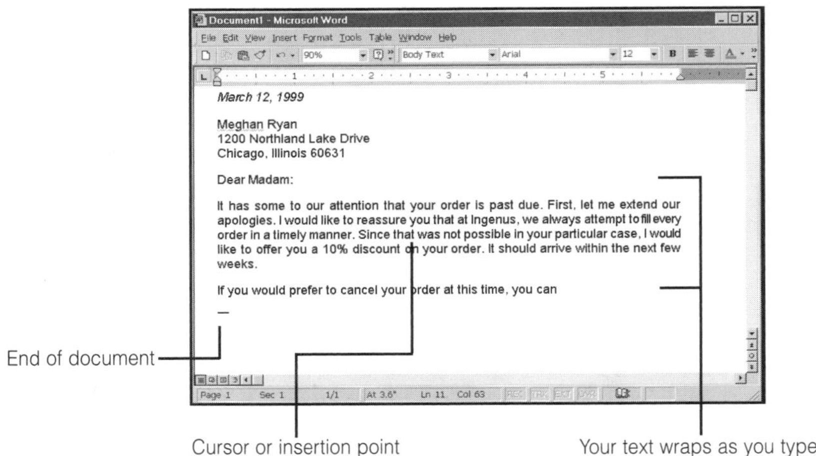

Another marker onscreen—a horizontal line—marks the end of your document. As you add text, this line also moves down so that it is always located at the end of the document's contents.

Correcting Your Mistakes

If you make a mistake as you are typing, Word usually corrects it for you automatically. Word knows many common misspellings, so it watches for them, and corrects them on the spot. If you type a common mistake, Word automatically fixes the typo for you. For example, if you type "teh," Word changes it to "the."

If you type a mistake that Word does not correct, use one of the following methods to correct the mistake:

- Press the Backspace key as needed to back the cursor up and erase characters to the left.
- To erase a character to the right of the cursor, press Delete instead.
- Select the mistake and then type your correction; the new text replaces the text you selected. To select text, drag over it. (To learn more about selecting text, see Chapter 12.)

Moving the Insertion Point

If you need to correct a mistake farther back in the text, you need to position the cursor, or *insertion point*. To do that, click in the spot at which you want to place the cursor. If you can't see the spot you need, use the scrollbars to back up: click a scroll arrow (located at either end of the scrollbar) or drag the scroll box. As you drag the scroll box, the page number you're scrolling through appears in a yellow box. You can also scroll through the document with the Previous Page or Next Page buttons, which are located at the bottom of the vertical scrollbar.

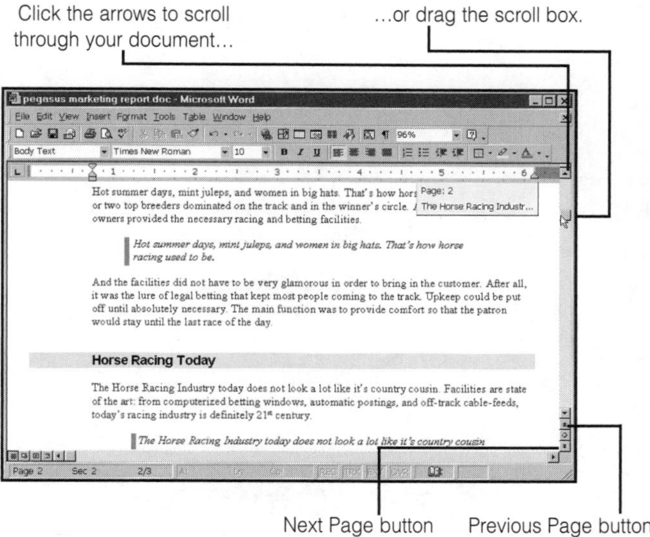

If you prefer the keyboard, you can use these shortcuts to move the cursor:

To move here	Press this
End of the line	End
Beginning of the line	Home
One character left, right, up, or down	Arrow keys
Beginning of the document	Ctrl+Home
End of the document	Ctrl+End

continues

continued

To move here	Press this
Next word	Ctrl+→
Previous word	Ctrl+←
Next paragraph	Ctrl+↓
Previous paragraph	Ctrl+↑
One screen	Page Up, Page Down
A specific page	Ctrl+G then type a page number and press Enter

Inserting Additional Text

If you type something and then want to add more text in the middle of it, it's easy to do:

1. Position the cursor at the point at which you want to add your text.
2. Begin typing, and the text is inserted—existing text is shifted to make room.

Beyond Survival

Typing Over Text

You can replace text you want to correct by typing over it, if you like. By default, when you type text, it's inserted at the cursor. This is called *insert mode.* However, at any time, you can switch from insert mode to *overtype mode,* and then, as you type, the characters replace existing text, as if you were typing over them. Follow these steps:

1. Position the cursor at the point where you want to type over existing text.
2. Press the Insert key on your keyboard once, or double-click on the word "OVR" on the right side of the status bar on your screen.

3. Begin typing. The characters you type replace existing characters, beginning at the cursor.
4. When you want to return to insert mode, press the Insert key again, or double-click on OVR on the status bar.

Cheat Sheet

Selecting Text with a Mouse

1. Click at the beginning of the text you want to select.
2. Hold the left mouse button down as you drag the mouse pointer over it.
3. Release the mouse button, and the text you selected is highlighted.
4. To deselect the text (remove the highlight), click anywhere within the document.

Selecting Text with the Keyboard

1. Position the cursor at the beginning of the text you want to select.
2. Press and hold the Shift key.
3. Press the arrow keys or any other keyboard movement key, such as Page Up or Page Down.

Selection Shortcuts to Use with the Mouse

If you like to use the mouse when selecting text, here are some shortcuts:

To select this	Do this
Word	Double-click on it.
Sentence	Press Ctrl and click on it.
Paragraph	Triple-click on it, or double-click in front of the paragraph, within the selection bar.
Line	Click once in front of the line, within the selection bar.
Document	Triple-click within the selection bar, or press Ctrl+A.

12

Selecting Text

If you want to do something to a bit of text, such as copying or moving it, you will need to select it first. By selecting text you want to copy or move, you tell Word exactly which characters you want it to work with. When you select text, it is highlighted, appearing onscreen in reverse video (white text on a black background).

Selected text is highlighted.

In addition, if you want to delete large amounts of text, you can select any amount of text you want, and then remove the entire section from your document in one step.

Selecting text also enables you to do other things with it, such as formatting your text. For example, to make a heading bold, you select the text first and then click the Bold button on the Formatting toolbar. All the text you've selected is changed to bold text. By the same token, selecting text already using the bold format and then clicking the Bold button returns the selection to plain text.

You can turn formatting ON and OFF.

While text is selected, you can apply or remove multiple formats, such as bold, italic, underline, or shadow effects. See Chapter 16 for more information.

Basic Survival

Selecting Text with a Mouse

Selecting text with the mouse is similar to using a highlighter. Just as you might drag a pen over text to highlight it, you drag your cursor over text to select it:

To select: click and drag pointer over text.

1. Click at the beginning of the text you want to select.
2. Hold the left mouse button down as you drag the mouse pointer over it. You can select as much or as little text as you desire.

3. Release the mouse button, and the text you selected is highlighted. It will remain selected until you click the mouse button anywhere within the document.

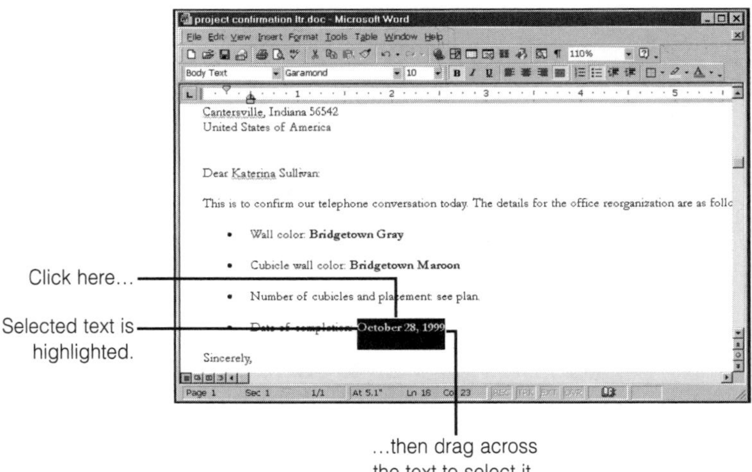

Selecting Text with the Keyboard

Select with keyboard, press Shift.

If you prefer, you can use the keyboard to select your text:

1. Position the cursor at the beginning of the text you want to select.
2. Press and hold the Shift key.
3. Use the arrow keys to select as much text as you like. You can also use any other keyboard movement key, such as Page Up or Page Down. See Chapter 11 for help.

Beyond Survival

Selecting Shortcuts to Use with the Mouse

word: double-click
paragraph: triple-click

If you like to use the mouse when selecting text, here are some shortcuts:

To select this	Do this
Word	Double-click on it.
Sentence	Press Ctrl and click on it.
Paragraph	Triple-click on it, or double-click in front of the paragraph, within the selection bar.
Line	Click once in front of the line, within the selection bar.
Document	Triple-click within the selection bar, or press Ctrl+A.

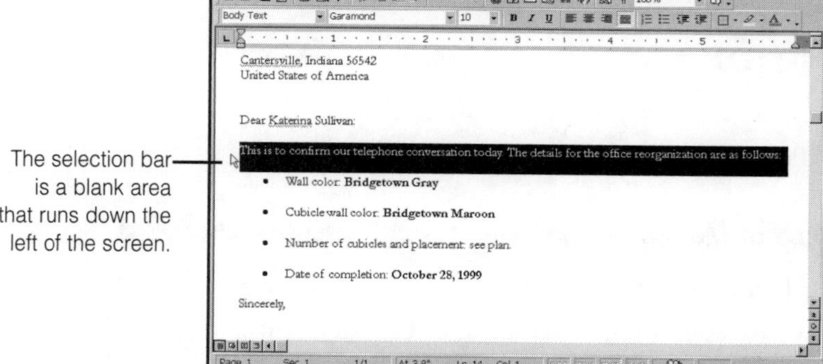

The selection bar is a blank area that runs down the left of the screen.

Cheat Sheet

Copying Text

To copy text, perform any of the following:

- Select the text and click Copy. Then click at the point where you want the text copied, and click Paste.
- Select the text and press Ctrl+C. Then move the cursor where you want the text copied, and press Ctrl+V.
- Select the text, press Ctrl, point to the highlighted text, and drag it to a new location.

Moving Text

To move text, perform any of the following:

- Select the text and click Cut. Then click at the point where you want the text moved, and click Paste.
- Select the text and press Ctrl+X. Then place the cursor where you want the text moved, and press Ctrl+V.
- Select the text and drag it.

Deleting Text

1. Select the text you want to delete.
2. Press Delete.

Copying or Moving Multiple Items with the Office Clipboard

- To copy a selected item, click the Copy button.
- To paste all the items on the Office Clipboard at the current cursor location, click Paste All.
- To paste a selected item from the Office Clipboard, click its icon.
- To remove everything from the Office Clipboard, click Clear Clipboard.

13

Copying, Moving, and Deleting Text

After you've learned how to select text, you are ready to copy, move, or delete it when needed. When you copy text, a "picture" of the selected text is made in memory, and this copy is placed where you indicate. Thus, you end up with two pieces of text that look exactly alike. When you move text, the text you select is deleted from the document and placed in memory, and then moved where you indicate. So, unlike copied text, text that has been moved exists only once within the document.

Can copy, move between docs

The area in memory in which text is stored when it is copied or moved is called the Clipboard, and it's a common area, shared by all your Windows programs. So if you like, you can use the techniques discussed here to copy or move text between documents, even documents created with other applications. In fact, text that you copy or move remains on the Clipboard until your next copy or move operation, so you can place that same text in several different spots if you like. If you're working within only Office documents, moving or copying data, you can use the Office Clipboard (described in the "Beyond Survival" section) to select lots of different items, and copy or move them in one step.

By the way, if you copy, move, or delete text, and you do not like the result, you can undo the change by clicking the Undo button on the Standard toolbar or by pressing Ctrl+Z.

Basic Survival

Copying Text

To copy text, you have to select it, use the Copy command (which places a copy of the text on the Clipboard), then *paste* that text to the spot where you want it. Follow these steps:

1. Select the text you want to copy.

2. Click the Copy button on the Standard toolbar or press Ctrl+C. The text is copied to the Clipboard.

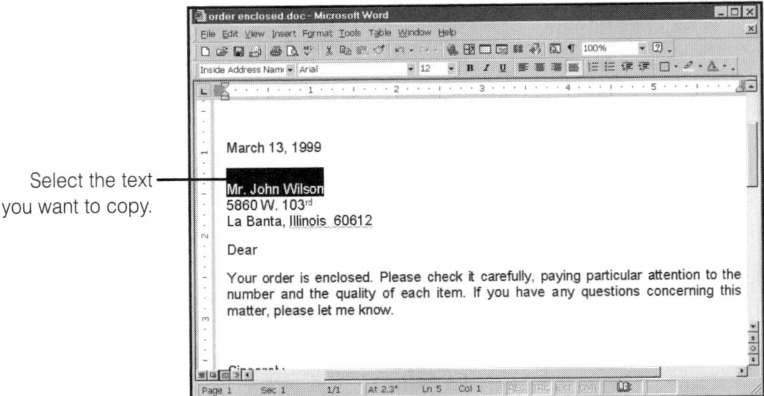

Select the text you want to copy.

3. Click at the point where you want a copy of the text placed. Remember you can open another document and copy the text there, if you like.

4. Click the Paste button on the Standard toolbar, or press Ctrl+V. The text is copied from the Clipboard to the spot you indicated. You can paste the same text in several spots by repeating just this step. (If you opened another document and need to switch back to your current document, open the Window menu and select a document from the bottom of the list.)

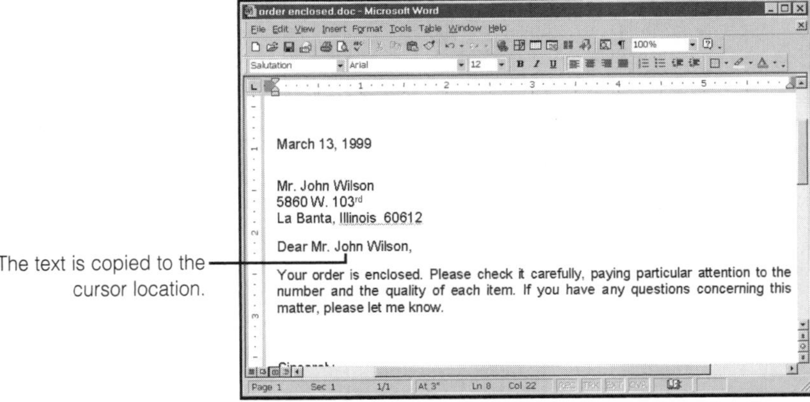

The text is copied to the cursor location.

Moving Text

To move text, you select it, then use the Cut command to remove the text from the document and place it on the Clipboard. You then *paste* that text from the Clipboard to the spot where you want it. Follow these steps:

1. Select the text you want to move.

Copy = copy,
Cut = move

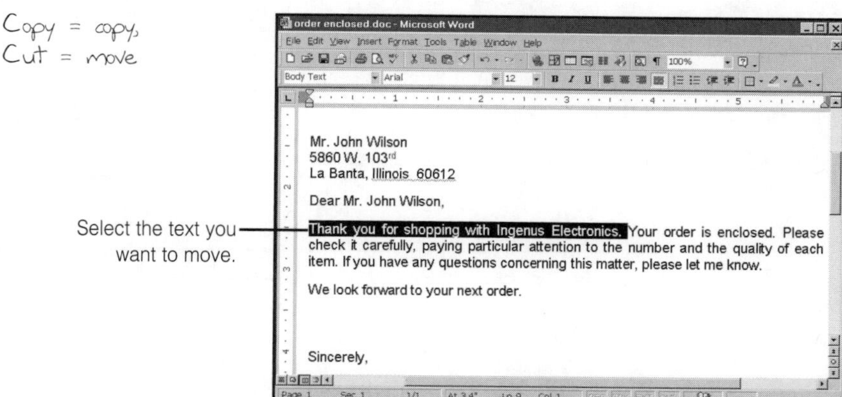

Select the text you want to move.

2. Click the Cut button on the Standard toolbar or press Ctrl+X. The text is removed and placed on the Clipboard.
3. Click at the point where you want the text moved. You can open another document and move the text there, if you want.
4. Click the Paste button on the Standard toolbar, or press Ctrl+V. The text is moved from the Clipboard to the spot you indicated; however, a copy of the text remains on the Clipboard itself. You can paste the same text in several spots by repeating just this step. (If you opened another document and need to switch back to your current document, open the Window menu and select a document from the bottom of the list.)

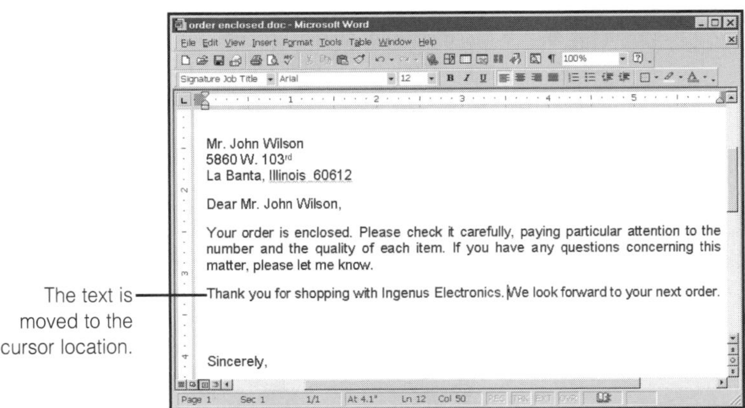

The text is moved to the cursor location.

Deleting Text

When you delete text, it's *removed* from the document, so you should be careful of the text you select when you perform these steps:

1. Select the text you want to delete.
2. Press the Delete key. If you've made a mistake, you can undo it with the Undo button.

Beyond Survival

Copying Text Using Drag and Drop

If you like using the mouse, there's a faster way to copy your text, called *drag and drop*. The only hitch: This process works best when you can simultaneously see both the text you want to copy and the spot to which you want to copy it onscreen. Although you can drag and drop to an area off-screen, the scrolling happens so fast that it's very hard to control. As a result, you'll probably like the old Copy/Paste or Cut/Paste operations better. Follow these steps to drag and drop:

Remember to use drag and drop!

1. Select the text you want to copy.
2. Press and hold the Ctrl key.
3. Point the mouse inside of the highlighted text and then click and hold the left mouse button, as you drag the text to the spot to which you want it copied. You'll notice that as you drag, the mouse pointer is displayed with a

tiny plus sign. This is to remind you that you're performing a copy process.

4. Release the mouse button, and the text is copied for you.

Moving Text Using Drag and Drop

Drag and drop also provides a quick method for moving text. However, once again, this process works best if you can see both the text you want to move and the place to which you want to move it. Follow these steps:

1. Select the text you want to move.
2. Point the mouse inside of the highlighted text then click and hold the left mouse button, as you drag the text to the spot to which you want it moved. You'll notice that as you drag, the mouse pointer is displayed with a plain square that does not contain the plus sign. This tells you that you're performing a move process.
3. Release the mouse button, and the text is moved for you.

Undoing a Change

Earlier, I mentioned that if you perform a copy, move, or delete process that you don't like, you can undo it by clicking the Undo button on the Standard toolbar. This button will soon become your favorite friend!

You can use Undo to undo several operations, not just the last action you have performed. To undo a previous action, click the down arrow on the Undo button, and select the point to which you want your document returned. The actions you've selected are undone, and your document is restored to its previous unchanged state.

After you perform an Undo, you can undo it. This process is called Redo. When you redo a change, it's restored, which returns the document to the point prior to the Undo. To redo a change, click the Redo button on the Standard toolbar. Like Undo, you can redo several previous actions; just click the down arrow on the Redo button, and select the actions you want to redo.

Can undo almost anything

Copying or Moving Multiple Items with the Office Clipboard

With the Office Clipboard, you can copy or move multiple items in one step—to any Office document. You don't have to perform any extra steps to activate the Office Clipboard—just select an item, and copy or cut it as usual. After you've selected all the items you want, use the Office Clipboard toolbar to paste them into a document.

If for some reason your Office Clipboard toolbar doesn't appear, select View, Toolbars, Clipboard. For more help with displaying and removing toolbars, see Chapter 10.

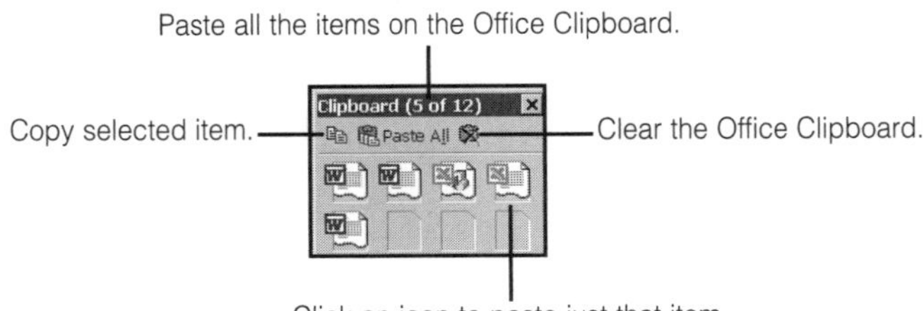
Paste all the items on the Office Clipboard.
Copy selected item.
Clipboard (5 of 12)
Paste All
Clear the Office Clipboard.
Click an icon to paste just that item.

Perform any of the following:

- To copy a selected item, you can click the Copy button on the Office Clipboard, or the Copy button on the Standard toolbar. They're the same.
- To paste all the items on the Office Clipboard at the current cursor location, click Paste All.
- To paste a selected item from the Office Clipboard, click its icon. If you're not sure which icon you want, move the mouse pointer over it, and a ScreenTip appears, displaying a description of the item's contents.
- To remove everything from the Office Clipboard, click Clear Clipboard. This also clears the Windows Clipboard, which contains the last item you cut or copied.
- To remove the Office Clipboard from the screen, click its Close button. The Office Clipboard will normally reappear when needed, but if you want to display it, choose View, Toolbars, Clipboard.

Cheat Sheet

The Different Views

• Normal View	The default view; good for most editing tasks.
• Web Layout View	Displays a Web document (HTML document) as it will appear on the Internet/intranet.
• Print Layout View	The best view for working with graphics, headers, footers, and general page layout.
• Outline View	This view displays your document headers in outline form, making it easy to rearrange large sections of a document.
• Full Screen View	Here, the menu bar, toolbars, and scrollbars are removed from the screen so that your document gets the maximum amount of onscreen space.

Changing Views

- Click the appropriate View button, located to the left of the horizontal scrollbar.
- To change to Full Screen view, open the View menu and select Full Screen.

Zooming a Document

1. Click the arrow on the Zoom button 100% .
2. Select the zoom you want from those listed.

Splitting the Screen

1. Click on the split box and drag the split bar.
2. To return to an unsplit window, double-click the split bar, or drag it back to its original position.

14

Viewing a Document

Word provides many views that you can use when editing your document. The view you choose does not affect your document's printed output, only its onscreen appearance. There are four views, including:

Four views are available

- **Normal View** The default view; good for most editing tasks.
- **Web Layout View** This view displays an HTML document as it will appear when viewed through a Web browser.
- **Print Layout View** The best view for working with graphics, headers, footers, and general page layout. This view was called Page Layout View in previous versions of Word.
- **Outline View** This view displays your document headers in outline form, making it easy to rearrange large sections of a document.

Basic Survival

Changing to Normal View

Normal view is the default view—the view in which your document is displayed when you start Word. It's the best view for general editing. In Normal view, you can see your text and all its formatting, and your text appears onscreen as it will when printed. However, certain elements are not displayed in this view, such as the page headers and footers, and multiple columns laid out on the page. You will probably find it easier to focus on your text and edit it if these elements are not displayed. Therefore, you will probably use Normal view more than any other view.

Normal: use for editing text

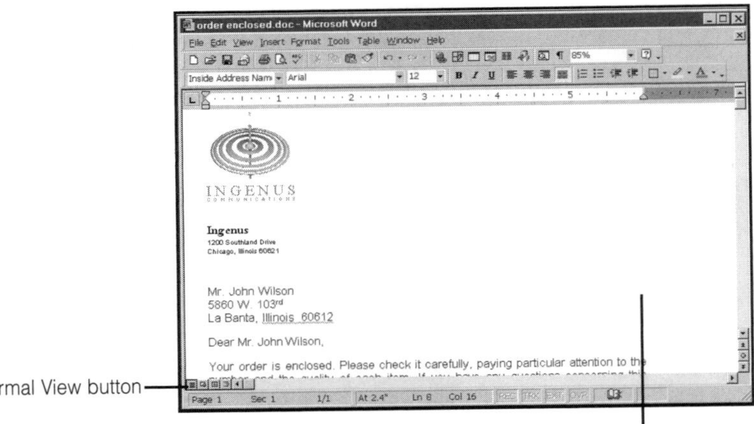

To change to Normal view, click the Normal View button.

Changing to Web Layout View

If you're working on an HTML document (a Web document), you need to be able to see more than just the text. In Web Layout view, you'll be able to see the text, graphics, backgrounds and other objects as they will appear when viewed in a Web browser. (Some objects, such as animated GIFs, will not appear properly, until you use Web Page Preview to actually view them in your Web browser.) In this view, if you resize the Word window, text is wrapped to fit its new dimensions—just like on the Web.

Web pub? Use Web Layout view.

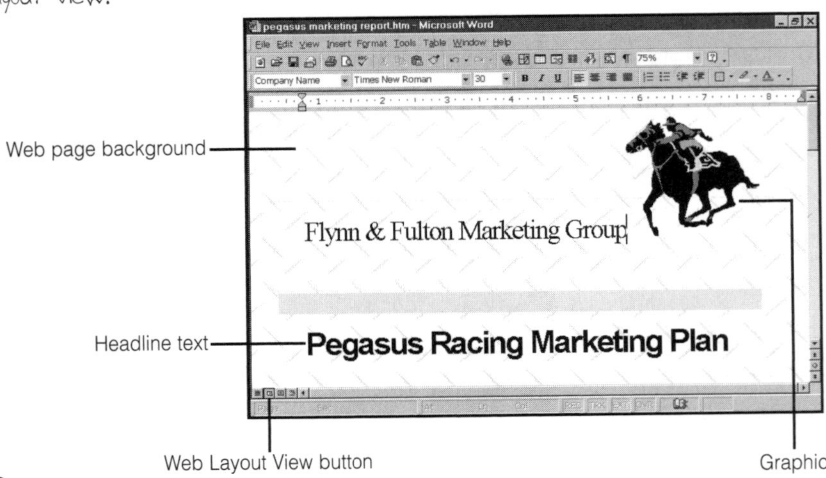

To change to Web Layout view, click the Web Layout View button.

Changing to Print Layout View

Headers/footers/graphics: use Print Layout

In Print Layout view, you see your document exactly as it will look when printed. In this view, headers and footers are displayed, along with page numbers, columns, and graphics. The vertical ruler displays only if the View/Ruler option is on and you are in this view—keep that in mind. Print Layout view is the best view to use when you are concentrating on the overall look of your document, such as editing headers and footers, resizing and positioning graphics, changing the size of columns, adjusting the look of tables, and so on. It is not the best view for working with text, since text is displayed slightly smaller than normal.

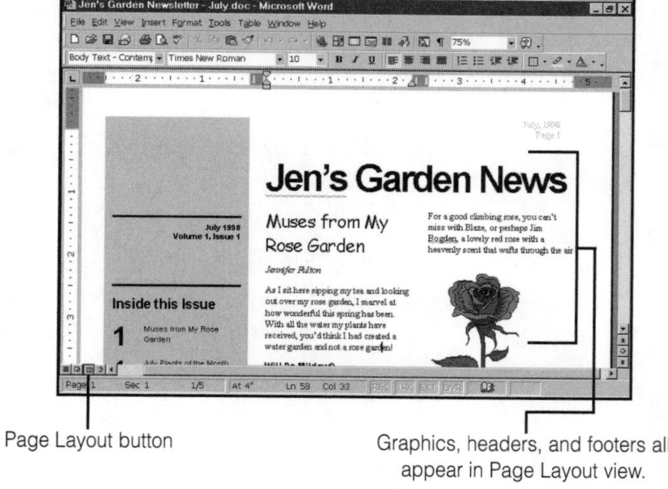

To change to Page Layout view, click the Page Layout View button.

Changing to Outline View

Must use heading styles for Outline view.

Outline view is the best view to use when you want to rearrange large sections of your document. In Outline view, you can display just your document headings (and hide the text), so that you can easily move parts of your document around. You can also use this view to create the general outline of your document before you begin adding text. To get the most out of this view, however, you must use the heading styles and apply them to the various headings in your document. To change to Outline view, click the Outline View button. You can ask your Office Assistant to teach you more about styles.

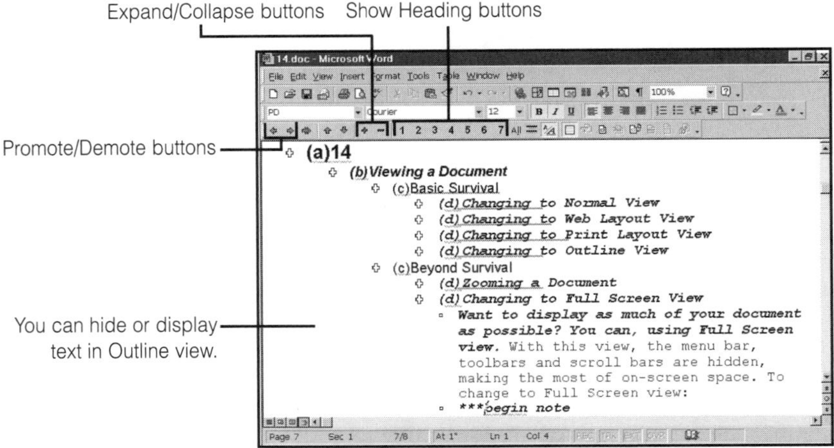

- To hide text and display only the headings up to a certain level within your outline, click on the appropriate Show Heading button.
- To expand the subheadings underneath a particular heading, select the heading and click the Expand button. To hide the subheadings, click the Collapse button.
- To promote a heading in the outline (and its coordinating text), click on the heading, then click the Promote button.
- To demote a heading, select it and click the Demote button.
- To demote a heading to regular body text, click the Demote to body text button.
- To move a section, collapse the heading so that its text is not displayed. Then drag the heading wherever you want and drop it within the outline.

Beyond Survival

Zooming a Document

Zoom in or out!

If you want to enlarge your text so you can view it better, or shrink it so you can see more text at one time, you can with a tool called Zoom. The current zoom percentage is displayed on the Zoom button 100% on the Standard toolbar.

Zoom button

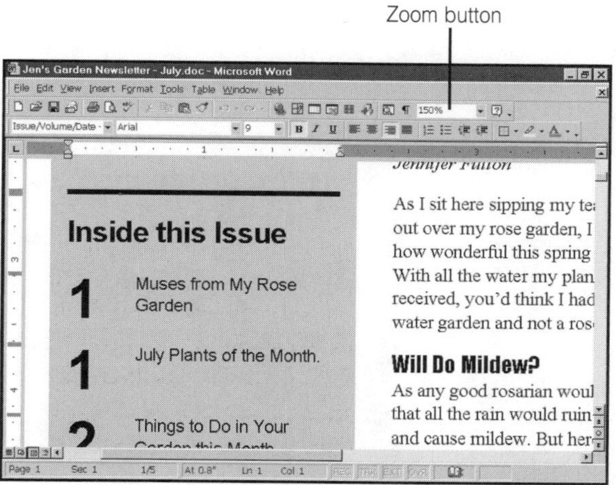
Jen's Garden Newsletter - July.doc - Microsoft Word
Inside this Issue
1 Muses from My Rose Garden
1 July Plants of the Month.
As I sit here sipping my te
out over my rose garden, I
how wonderful this spring
With all the water my plan
received, you'd think I had
water garden and not a ros
Will Do Mildew?
As any good rosarian woul
that all the rain would ruin
and cause mildew. But her

To select a zoom:

1. Click the arrow on the Zoom button 100%.
2. Select the zoom you want from those listed. Page Width zoom scales the document so that the entire page width is displayed. Text Width displays the page from margin to margin. Whole Page displays the entire page. Two Pages displays two pages at a time. (These last three options are available in Print Layout view only.)

Just type % in Zoom box.

To enter a custom percentage, just type it into the Zoom box and press Enter.

Changing to Full Screen View

Want to display as much of your document as possible? You can, using Full Screen view. With this view, the menu bar, toolbars rulers and scrollbars are hidden, making the most of onscreen space. To change to Full Screen view:

Hide everything with Full Screen view.

1. Open the View menu.
2. Select Full Screen.
3. To return to Normal view, click the Close Full Screen button that appears.

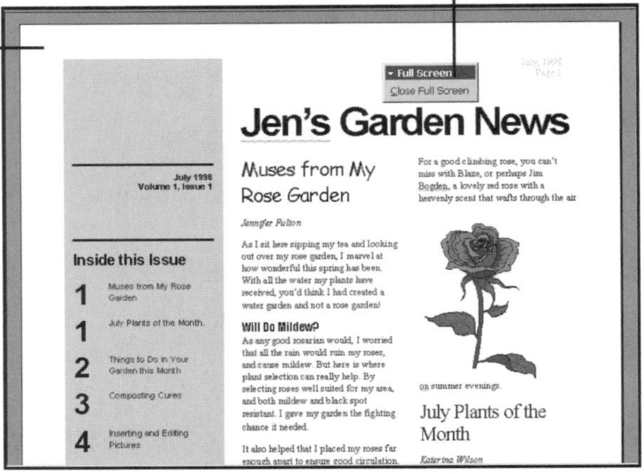

Click here to return to Normal view.

To display the menu bar, move the mouse pointer to the top of the screen.

Jen's Garden News

Muses from My Rose Garden

Jennifer Fulton

Inside this Issue

1 Muses from My Rose Garden

1 July Plants of the Month.

2 Things to Do in Your Garden this Month

3 Composting Cures

4 Inserting and Editing Pictures

As I sit here sipping my tea and looking out over my rose garden, I marvel at how wonderful this spring has been. With all the water my plants have received, you'd think I had created a water garden and not a rose garden!

Will Do Mildew?

As any good rosarian would, I worried that all the rain would ruin my roses, and cause mildew. But here is where plant selection can really help. By selecting roses well suited for my area, and both mildew and black spot resistant. I gave my garden the fighting chance it needed.

It also helped that I placed my roses far enough apart to ensure good circulation.

For a good climbing rose, you can't miss with Blaze, or perhaps Jim Bogden, a lovely red rose with a heavenly scent that wafts through the air on summer evenings.

July Plants of the Month

Katerina Wilson

If you need to use the menus while in Full Screen view, move the mouse pointer to the top of the window, and the menu will appear.

Splitting the Screen

If you need to work in two different parts of your document at one time (perhaps for copying or moving text), you can split the screen by following these steps:

Split screen: work on two parts of same document!

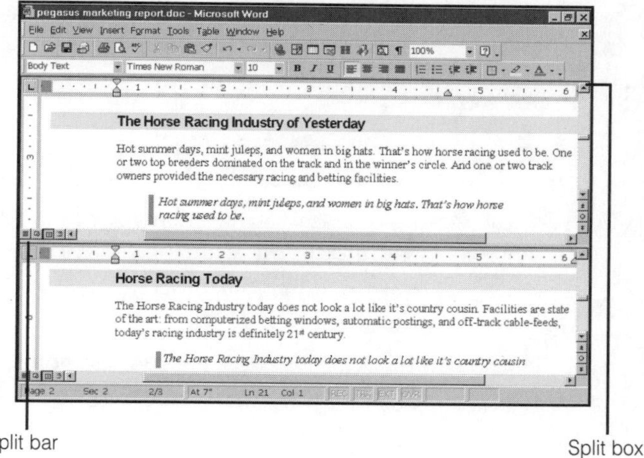

1. Click on the split box.
2. Drag the split bar to split the window.
3. The blinking cursor indicates which pane is currently active. Remember, if you start typing, text appears at the cursor. To switch to the other pane, click in it.
4. To return to an unsplit window, double-click the split bar, or drag it back to its original position.

Cheat Sheet

Finding and Replacing Text

1. Open the Edit menu and select Replace or Press Ctrl+F. (If you just want to find text, select Edit, Find instead.)
2. Type the word or phrase you're looking for in the Find what text box. (If you're only trying to find text, skip to step 4.)
3. Type the word or phrase you want to use as the replacement text in the Replace with text box.
4. Click the More button to select additional choices for your search, such as matching case and finding whole words.
5. Click Find Next to locate the first occurrence of the word or phrase.
6. If you're replacing text, perform one of the following:
    - To replace this occurrence only, click Replace.
    - To replace every occurrence without further confirmation, click Replace All.
    - To skip this occurrence and continue searching, click Find Next.
7. To find additional occurrences, continue to click on Find Next.
8. When finished searching, click Cancel to close the Find and Replace dialog box.

Creating an AutoText Entry

1. Select the phrase or graphic you want to save as an AutoText entry.
2. Open the Insert menu, select AutoText, and select New.
3. Type a name for your entry.
4. Press Enter to save your entry.

15

Finding and Replacing Text

If you are working with a fairly short document, such as a one-page letter, scanning that document for a particular word or phrase is pretty simple. However, if your document is larger than a few brief paragraphs, scanning the text for a word or phrase could be pretty tedious. Unless, of course, you used Word's Find and Replace feature.

With Find and Replace, you can search your document for text and quickly move the cursor to its location. If you like, you can even search for text and replace it with other text.

Basic Survival

Finding Text

When you use the Find command, Word searches the document for text that matches your criteria. When the text is found, it's highlighted—if, however, this first occurrence of the text is not the one you want, you can continue the search.

Put the cursor at the top of the document!

When you use the Find command, the entire document is searched, beginning at the cursor. If you want to search only part of the document, select the part you want to search *before* you use the Find command.

1. Open the Edit menu and select Find. The Find and Replace dialog box appears.

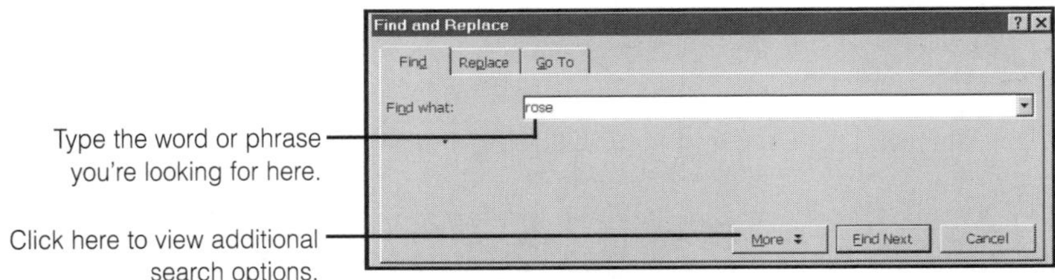

2. Type the word or phrase you're looking for in the Find what text box.
3. Click Find Next.
4. Word searches for a word or phrase that matches what you typed and highlights it. Based on the results of your Word search, you have several options:
    - If the text found is not the correct occurrence, click Find Next again to continue the search.
    - If the text found is the correct occurrence, press Esc to get rid of the dialog box and return to your document. The cursor is moved to the selection, and the word or phrase is highlighted for you.
    - If Word searches the entire document without finding another occurrence, you see a message asking if you want to continue the search. Click No to return to the Find and Replace screen, and click the Close box to end the search.

Use More to narrow search.

If you click the More button in the Find and Replace dialog box, it expands so that you can make additional selections, such as:

- Match case. This matches exact upper- and lowercase, so "Top" matches only "Top," and not "top" or "TOP."
- Find whole words only. This matches only the exact word you typed, and not words that might contain the letters you typed, so "top" matches only "top" and not "topological" or "stop."
- Use wildcards. Enables you to use wildcards in your search, such as ? for a single unknown character, as in

"t?p" and ?* for multiple unknown characters, as in "top*."

- Sounds like. Attempts to match words that sound similar to the one you typed. So "there" matches "their" and "they're."
- Find all word forms. Matches other forms of the word you typed, as in "teach," "taught," and "teaching."

You can even search for words with particular formatting (such as bold) by clicking the Format button and selecting the characteristics for which you want to search. In addition, you can search for special characters such as a column break by clicking Special and selecting it from the list.

Repeat search = Ctrl+F, Enter

After you use the Find command, it remembers the word or phrase for which you searched. So, if you want to repeat that search, you can select the Find command (or press Ctrl+F) and click Find Next.

Want to search for other phrases you looked for recently? Just click the down arrow next to the Find what text box, and select a recently searched-for item.

Replacing Text

As you search for text in a document, you can easily tell Word to replace that text with something else:

1. Open the Edit menu and select Replace.

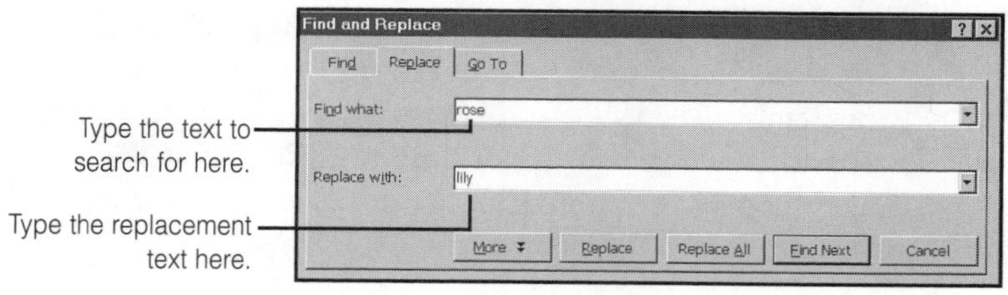

2. Type the word or phrase for which you want to search in the Find what text box.
3. Type the word or phrase you want to use as the replacement text in the Replace with text box. To replace the

search phrase with nothing (to delete it), leave the Replace with text box blank.

4. Click Find Next.
5. When Word finds a matching word or phrase, it is highlighted in your document. Now, choose one of the following options:
    - To replace this occurrence only, click Replace.
    - To replace every occurrence without further confirmation, click Replace All.
    - To skip this occurrence and continue searching, click Find Next.
    - If Word searches the entire document without finding your selection, you'll see a message telling you so. Click OK and press Escape to return to the document and end the search.

Can search and replace formatting.

If you want to search and replace formatted text, or if you require any of the special options described in the "Finding Text" section, click the More button to expand the Find and Replace dialog box and make your selections.

Beyond Survival

Using AutoText to Replace What You Type

One of the nicest features in Word is its capability to figure out what you're typing, and to insert the complete word or phrase for you. For example, you might start typing a date, such as September 19, 1999, and after typing only "Sept," a little box appears with the word "September" in it. When a "guess" such as this appears, you need only press Enter to accept it, and have Word finish the typing for you.

Create AT entry for closing paragraph.

In addition to these guesses, Word has stored a number of common phrases that you can quickly insert into a document, such as RE:, Sincerely, and so on. To insert one of Word's built-in phrases, follow these steps:

1. Open the Insert menu and select AutoText.

2. Select the category of the phrase you want to insert. For example, to insert "Sincerely," select Closing.
3. Select the phrase you want to insert from the list. The word or selection appears in your document.

If you are a fast typist, you may find it simpler to just type the phrase "Respectfully Yours," instead of using the AutoText feature to insert it. But, if you must repeatedly type the same long paragraphs in work documents, AutoText can be a real lifesaver. You can even save a graphic image—such as a company logo—for quick insertion.

To put AutoText to work for you, follow these steps:

1. Select the phrase or graphic you want to save as an AutoText entry.
2. Open the Insert menu, select AutoText, and select New.
3. Type a name for your entry. This name is what you will type to insert the entry later, so make it short and easy to remember.
4. Press Enter. The entry is saved.

To insert your entry at any time, type its name, then press F3. (In some cases, your entry appears in a yellow box above your text, and all you need to do is to press Enter to accept it.) You can also open the Insert menu, select AutoText, and select your entry from the menu.

Cheat Sheet

Changing the Text Font

1. To change the font of existing text, select it first.
2. Click the down arrow on the Font list Arial.
3. Select a font by clicking on it.

Changing the Size of Text

1. To change the size of existing text, select it first.
2. Click the down arrow on the Font Size list 14.
3. Click a new point size.

Making Text Bold, Italic, or Underlined

1. To change existing text, select it first.
2. Click one of the following buttons, located on the Formatting toolbar:

   Bold B

   Italic I

   Underline U

Copying Text Formatting

1. Select the text that has the characteristics you want to copy.
2. Click the Format Painter button. To copy formatting to several sections of text, *double-click* the Format Painter button instead.
3. Drag your "paintbrush" over the text to which you want to copy your formatting.
4. If you double-clicked on the Format Painter button in step 2, then repeat step 3 to format additional text. When you're through copying formatting, click the Format Painter button again, or press Esc.

16

Changing How Text Looks

To improve the overall effect of your words, you may want to experiment with various text styles, called fonts. Some fonts project a dynamic style, while others are more sedate. Some fonts are easier to read when printed in a small size, while others look better when used in large headlines.

In addition to changing a text's font and size, you can add bold, italic, or underlining. In this book, italic is used to emphasize a point or to highlight a new term. Bold is used to point out important information. You can add these effects to your text to emphasize your message as well.

If you're using a color printer, you can add color to your text. Because there are hundreds of colors to choose from, you need to experiment with various colors until you achieve the effect you want.

Basic Survival

Changing the Font or Size of Text

To change the look or style of your text, you change its font. Some fonts are more professional looking, such as Arial and Times New Roman. Others are purely decorative, such as Shelley Volante. Still others are more modern, and less stuffy, such as COMICS CARTOON.

Font = style of text

The font you select lets the reader see the attitude behind your words. The current font and point size is shown in the Formatting toolbar. To find out what font and point size is used in your document, click in the text and look at the Formatting toolbar. To select a new font:

1. To change the font of existing text, select it first. If you don't select text, then only the word in which the cursor is currently located will be changed.
2. Click the down arrow on the Font list Arial, located on the Formatting toolbar. A list of fonts appears.
3. Select a font by clicking on it. Fonts preceded by the letters TT are TrueType fonts, which means that they are displayed onscreen *exactly* as they will appear when printed. If you select other font types (most likely, PostScript fonts), your printed results may vary from the onscreen display.

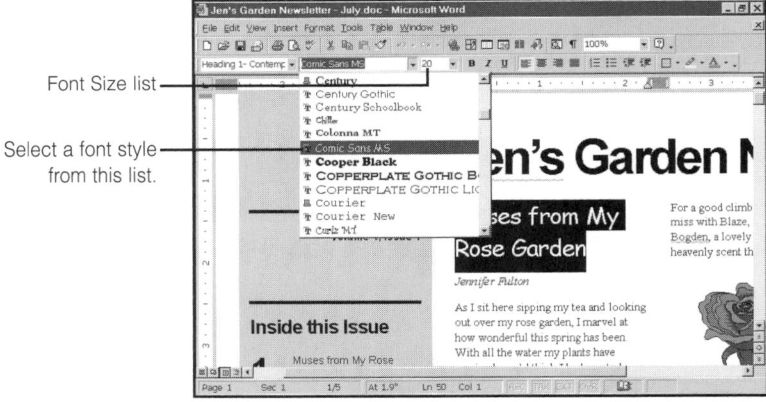

In addition to changing the style of text, you can also change its size. The size of text is measured in points. One point is equal to 1/72 of an inch. To change the size of text:

1. Select it first.
2. Click the down arrow on the Font Size list 14, located on the Formatting toolbar. A list of various point sizes appears.
3. Click the point size you want.

If you're changing text as you type, the text remains in the font you selected until you select another one. This is true of other text characteristics as well. For example, if you change to 10-point text, text remains in that size until you change to another point size.

Changing Your Text Formatting

To add emphasis to important words, add bold, italic, or underlining to your text. Follow these steps:

1. To change existing text, select it first. If you don't select text, then only the word in which the cursor is currently located will be changed.
2. Click one of the following buttons, located on the Formatting toolbar:

Bold	**B**
Italic	*I*
Underline	U

You can also use these keyboard shortcuts to change text as you type:

Turn Bold ON or OFF	Ctrl+B
Turn Italic ON or OFF	Ctrl+I
Turn Underlining ON or OFF	Ctrl+U

Remember that if you're changing text as you type, the text remains bold, italic, and so on, until you change it back to plain text. When you are typing bolded text, for example, the Bold button on the Formatting toolbar looks pushed in. To turn bold off, click the Bold button again or press Ctrl+B. You don't have to do this if you select text *first*, then make it bold, italic, and so on.

Beyond Survival

Using the Font Dialog Box to Change Text

Got a lot of changes to make to a section of text? Why not use the Font dialog box? With it, you can change your text's font and size, and add bold, italic, or underlining all at the same time. Here's how:

1. To change existing text, select it first.
2. Open the Format menu and select Font. The Font dialog box appears.

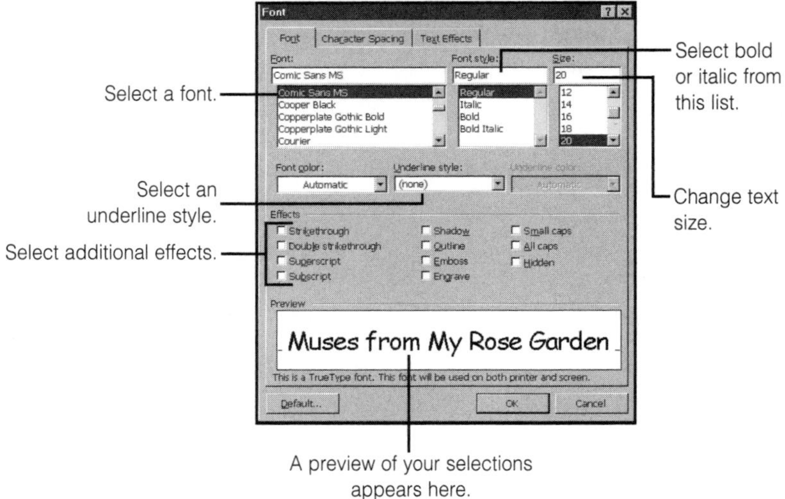

3. If needed, click the Font tab.
4. Select the font you want from the Font list.
5. Select the size text you need from the Size list.
6. To add bold, underline, or italic, select it from the Font style list. Make additional selections from the Effects area as needed.
7. Click OK when you're finished.

If you will be presenting your document onscreen or passing it to others for review, you can add animation effects. These effects appear only onscreen; *they do not print.* You can select an animation effect from the Text Effects tab in the Font dialog box.

Changing the Color of Text

When you change the color of text, you can draw attention to a quotation, an important heading, or other element in your document. The color won't actually print, however, unless you have a color printer. But even without a color printer, you can vary the gray tones in your document by adjusting the color. In addition, color can draw attention to text when presented onscreen. You might use color to guide a colleague's attention to a section of the document that needs review, for example.

Follow these simple steps to change text color:

1. If you want to change existing text, select it first. If you don't select text, then the word in which the cursor is currently located will be changed. If the cursor is not within a word, then new text will be changed to the color you select.
2. Click the down arrow on the Font Color button, located on the Formatting toolbar. A variety of colors are displayed. (If you want to use the color already displayed on the button, just click the Font Color button without opening its drop-down list.)
3. Click a new color or click on More Colors and select a color from the colors pallette, then click OK.

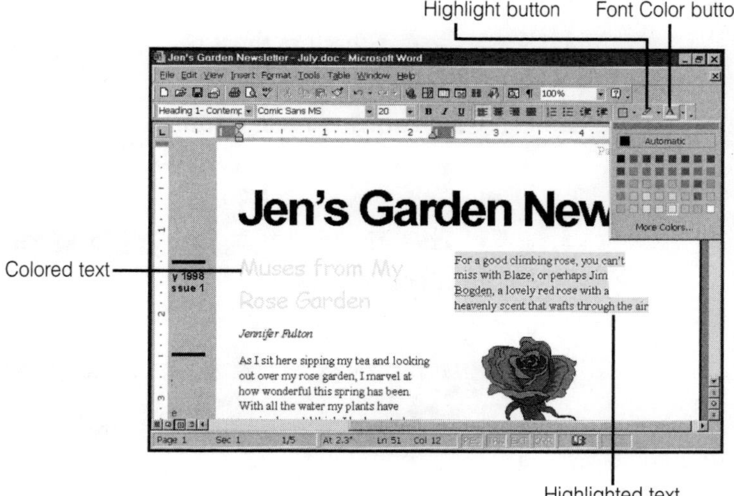
Highlight button
Font Color button
Colored text
Highlighted text
Jen's Garden Newsletter - July.doc - Microsoft Word
Jen's Garden New
Muses from My Rose Garden
Jennifer Fulton
For a good climbing rose, you can't miss with Blaze, or perhaps Jim Bogden, a lovely red rose with a heavenly scent that wafts through the air
As I sit here sipping my tea and looking out over my rose garden, I marvel at how wonderful this spring has been. With all the water my plants have
Automatic
More Colors...

You can also highlight text, if your desire is to draw attention to it during a proofreading review. To highlight text:

1. If you want to change existing text, select it first.
2. Click the down arrow on the Highlight button, located on the Formatting toolbar. A variety of colors are listed. (If you want to use the color already displayed on the button, you can click the Highlight button rather than opening the drop-down list.)

3. Click on the color you want to use. To remove highlighting, click on None.

If you selected a color *and have not yet selected any text,* the mouse pointer changes to a highlighter pen. Drag the mouse pointer over the text you want to change or, double-click on a word to highlight it; Ctrl+Click to highlight a sentence; triple-click to highlight a paragraph.

To turn off the highlighting function, click the Highlight button again or press Esc.

Copying Text Formatting

After making all your formatting selections for a section of text, it's an easy process to copy that same formatting to other bits of text as well. Copying formatting saves you the trouble of having to select new text and then make the same choices. Here's how to copy text formatting:

Great time saver!

1. Select the text that has those characteristics you want to copy.
2. Click the Format Painter button, located on the Standard toolbar. The mouse pointer changes to a paintbrush.
3. Drag your "paintbrush" over the text to which you want to copy your formatting.

Copy the formatting of this heading...

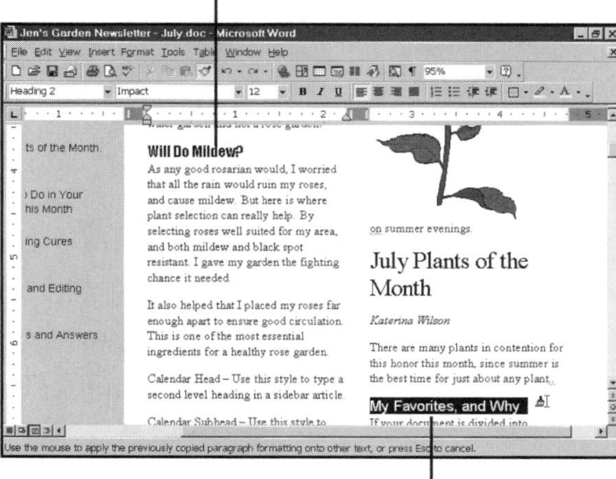

...to this heading, with the Format Painter.

If you want to copy formatting to several sections of text, double-click the Format Painter button. You can then drag the mouse pointer over several bits of text. When you're finished, click the Format Painter button again, or press Esc. The mouse pointer returns to normal.

Cheat Sheet

Aligning Text and Justifying Paragraphs

1. Click in the paragraph you want to change or select several paragraphs.
2. Click the appropriate button:

   Align Left

   Center

   Align Right

   Justify

Indenting Paragraphs

1. Use the View/Ruler command to display the ruler.
2. Click in the paragraph you want to change or select several paragraphs.
3. Choose any of the following options:
   - To indent just the first line of a paragraph, drag the First Line Indent marker (the top triangle on the left) to the desired position.
   - To indent a paragraph from the left, drag the Left Indent marker (the bottom square on the stack of three markers at the left) to the desired position.
   - To indent all the lines of a paragraph *except the first line* (to create a hanging indent), drag the Hanging Indent marker (the bottom triangle on the left) to the desired new position.
   - To indent a paragraph from the right, drag the Right Indent marker (the triangle on the right) to the desired position.

Changing Line and Paragraph Spacing

1. Click in the paragraph you want to change or select several paragraphs.
2. To change line spacing, press one of the following (or select Format, Paragraph and make the desired line spacing changes).
3. To change paragraph spacing, select Format, Paragraph and type an amount in the Before or After text box.
4. Click on OK.

17

Changing How Paragraphs Look

Now that you know how to change the look of text, you're ready for bigger game—changing how paragraphs look. In this chapter, you'll learn about the kinds of changes that affect paragraphs as a whole, such as the way a paragraph aligns against the left and right margins, whether the first line (or all the lines) of a paragraph is indented, and the spacing between lines and before and after a paragraph.

Basic Survival

Aligning and Justifying Paragraphs

By default, when you type text, it's left-aligned (the text along the left edge touches the margin). The right edge, on the other hand, is ragged (meaning that the lines in the paragraph end at different lengths).

When a paragraph is right-aligned, the exact opposite is true: text aligns against the right margin, and the text along the left-hand edge is ragged. When text is centered, each edge is about the same distance from the left and right margins. With justified text, extra spaces are inserted as needed, so that each line touches both the left and right margins.

To change the alignment of a paragraph:

1. Place the cursor within the paragraph you want to change. To change several paragraphs at once, select them.

2. Click the Align Left, Align Right, Center, or Justify button, located on the Formatting toolbar:

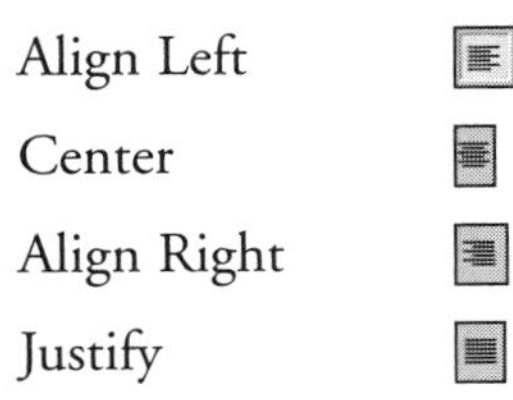

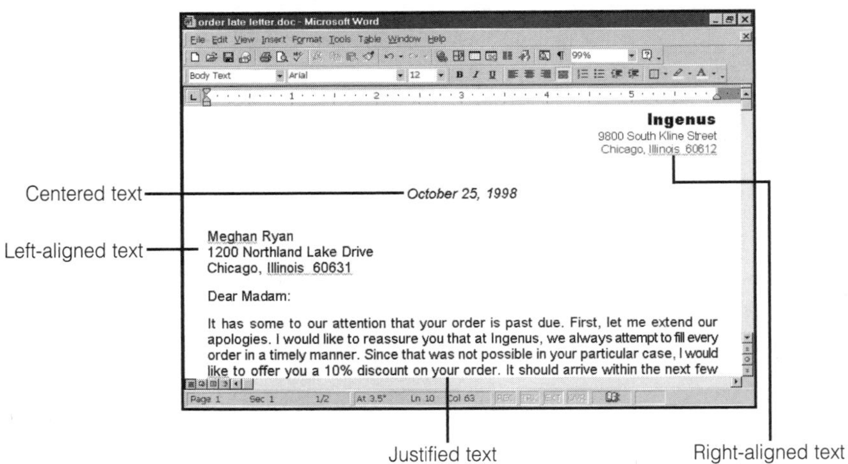

Indenting Paragraphs

An indent is a bit of extra space that's inserted between the lines of a paragraph and the margin. The most frequently used type of indent is a first line indent, where the first line of a paragraph is pushed to the right five spaces, away from the left margin.

You can also indent all the lines of a paragraph to make it stand out. You might indent a quotation, for example. You can indent a paragraph from the left, right, or from both the left and right margins. You can also create a hanging indent, in which the first line of a paragraph is outdented (moved closer to the margin). You use hanging indents in numbered and bulleted lists and bibliographies.

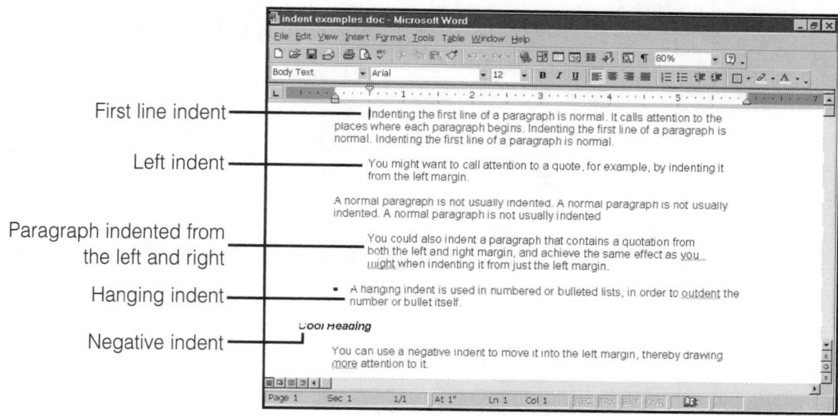

indent examples.doc - Microsoft Word
First line indent
Left indent
Paragraph indented from the left and right
Hanging indent
Negative indent
Indenting the first line of a paragraph is normal. It calls attention to the places where each paragraph begins. Indenting the first line of a paragraph is normal. Indenting the first line of a paragraph is normal.
You might want to call attention to a quote, for example, by indenting it from the left margin.
A normal paragraph is not usually indented. A normal paragraph is not usually indented. A normal paragraph is not usually indented
You could also indent a paragraph that contains a quotation from both the left and right margin, and achieve the same effect as you might when indenting it from just the left margin.
A hanging indent is used in numbered or bulleted lists, in order to outdent the number or bullet itself.
Cool Heading
You can use a negative indent to move it into the left margin, thereby drawing more attention to it.

To indent a paragraph from the left margin, use the Formatting toolbar:

1. Place the cursor in the paragraph you want to left indent, or select several paragraphs.
2. Click the Increase Indent button on the Formatting toolbar to move all the lines of the paragraph to the right, by one-half-inch increments. Click the button as many times as you need.

   To move the lines of a paragraph to the left by one-half–inch increments, click the Decrease Indent button instead.

Beyond Survival

Indenting Paragraphs with the Ruler

When you use the ruler to indent a paragraph, you can see where your indent will fall, before the paragraph is changed. Using the ruler is quicker and more visual, but it can also be a bit of a challenge. Follow these steps:

1. Display the ruler if needed by opening the View menu and selecting Ruler.
2. Click within the paragraph you want to change, or select several paragraphs.
3. Choose any of the following options:

- To indent just the first line of a paragraph, drag the First Line Indent marker (the top triangle on the left) to its new position.
- To indent a paragraph from the left, drag the Left Indent marker (the bottom square on the stack of three markers at the left) to its new position.
- To indent all the lines of a paragraph except the first line (to create a hanging indent), drag the Hanging Indent marker (the bottom triangle on the left) to its new position.
- To indent a paragraph from the right, drag the Right Indent marker (the triangle on the right) to its new position.

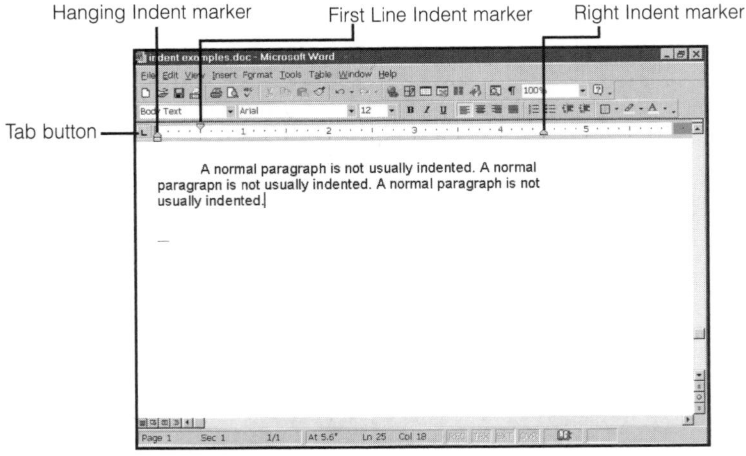
Hanging Indent marker
First Line Indent marker
Right Indent marker
Tab button
A normal paragraph is not usually indented. A normal paragrapn is not usually indented. A normal paragraph is not usually indented.

Use the right marker.

Selecting the correct marker can be challenging (see the figure). If you have trouble identifying the right marker, you can click the tab button several times until the First Line Indent or Hanging Indent button appears. Click on the ruler to set the indent marker.

If the ruler proves too frustrating at first (it won't later on, after you get the hang of it), just skip it for now. Instead, use the Format/Paragraph command to display the Paragraph dialog box, where you can type the indent measurements you want to use.

Changing Line Spacing

Normally, the paragraphs you type are single-spaced. You can increase the space between lines to leave room for an editor's comments, or to make your document easier to read. Follow these steps:

1. Click within the paragraph you want to change, or select several paragraphs.
2. Open the Format menu and select Paragraph. The Paragraph dialog box appears.
3. Open the Line spacing drop-down list box and select the option you desire:
   - Single. Single spacing
   - 1.5 Lines. 1 and 1/2 line spacing
   - Double. Double spacing
   - Exactly. Specifies the exact spacing between lines, in points. The tops of characters are truncated if they are too large.
   - At Least. Specifies a minimum height for the space between lines, in points. If a line contains text that is too large for this space, the distance between lines is adjusted appropriately.
   - Multiple. Changes the space between lines by the factor you indicate. A factor of 2 is the same as double spacing.

To use the keyboard for quick line spacing changes, press Ctrl+1 for single spacing, Ctrl+2 for double spacing, or Ctrl+5 for one and a half line spacing.

Changing Paragraph Spacing

Normally, when you type a paragraph, you must press Enter twice to insert a blank line between it and the next paragraph. In addition, the line you insert is the same size as the text of the preceding paragraph.

Add Sp. before/after para.

Sometimes, you may want to have more or less space between paragraphs than a single line. For example, after typing a heading, you may want to add more space to visually separate it from the paragraph that follows it. Follow these steps:

1. Click within the paragraph you want to change, or select several paragraphs, if you like.
2. Open the Format menu and select Paragraph. The Paragraph dialog box appears.
3. To add space before the paragraph(s), type an amount (in points) in the Before text box.

   To add space after the paragraph(s), type an amount in the After text box.
4. Click OK.

Cheat Sheet

Setting Tabs with the Ruler

1. Display the ruler, if needed, by opening the View menu and selecting Ruler.
2. Select the paragraphs to which you want to add tabs.
3. At the left end of the ruler, select the tab type you want to set.
4. Point to the place on the ruler where you want to set the tab.
5. Click the ruler and drag the tab marker left or right to adjust the tab.
6. When you've placed the tab marker where you want it, release the mouse button to set the tab.
    - To remove a tab, drag the tab off of the ruler.

Setting Tabs with a Dialog Box

1. Select the paragraph whose tabs you want to set.
2. Open the Format menu and select Tabs. The Tabs dialog box appears.
3. Type the position at which you want to set a tab in the Tab stop position text box.
4. Select the type of tab you want from the Alignment area.
5. If you want to add a tab leader, select that option from the Leader area.
6. Click Set. Repeat steps 3–6 to add more tabs.
    - To remove all tabs from a paragraph, click the Clear All button.
    - To remove a single tab, select it from the Tab stop position list, then click Clear.

18

Setting Tabs

Tabs are used to align columns of data, such as a price list, an address list, or a phone list. When typing such a list, you press Tab between each column of data. This tells Word to insert a tab and move the cursor to the next tab stop.

By default, tabs are set at intervals 1/2-inch apart. You can remove these tabs and set your own using the ruler or the Tab dialog box.

Basic Survival

Tab Types

You can set various types of tabs:

- **Left-aligned tab** The left-hand edge of the data is aligned with the tab stop.
- **Right-aligned tab** The right-hand edge of the data is aligned with the tab stop.
- **Centered tab** The data in the column is centered under the tab.
- **Decimal tab** The decimal points in a column of numbers are aligned under the tab.
- **Bar tab** Inserts a vertical line at the tab stop. Data is not aligned at this tab, so you must use it with other tab types. The vertical line runs through the paragraph it is set within.

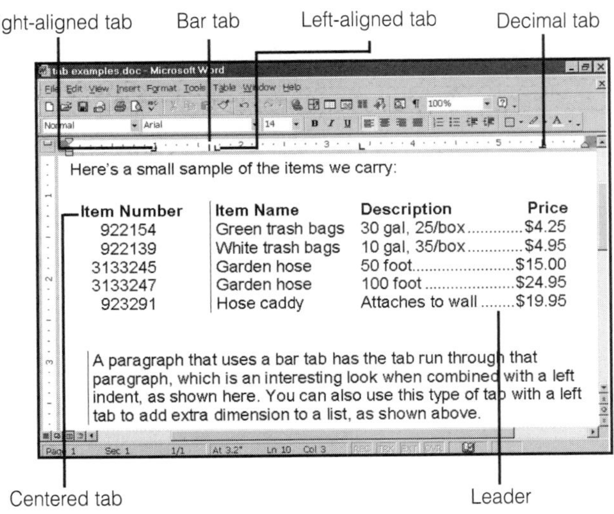

Leader = dots or dashes between tab stops

When setting a tab, you can add a *leader*. A leader is a series of dots or dashes that helps the reader scan across a long line of data.

Setting Tabs with the Ruler

If you want to set tabs quickly, use the ruler. Not only is it convenient, but it also provides a visual aid in proper tab placement. Here's how to use the ruler to set tabs:

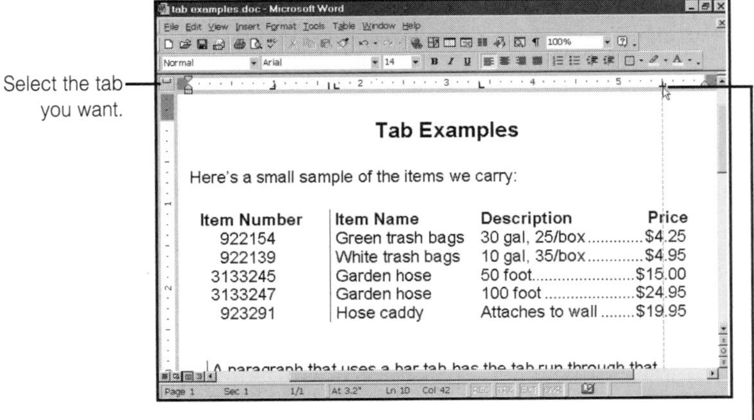

Use ruler to set tabs!

1. Display the ruler by opening the View menu and selecting Ruler.
2. Select the paragraphs to which you want to add or move tabs.
3. At the left end of the ruler, select the tab type you want to set.
4. Point to the place on the ruler where you want to set the tab.
5. Click the ruler and hold the mouse button down; this enables you to drag the tab marker left or right to adjust the tab as needed. As you drag, a dashed vertical line appears, showing you the location of the tab in relation to your text.
6. When you've placed the tab marker where you want it, release the mouse button to set the tab.

Delete tab: drag it off ruler

If you accidentally place a tab in the wrong spot, you can move it by dragging it to its new location. To remove a tab completely, drag it down and off the ruler.

Beyond Survival

Setting Tabs with a Dialog Box

If you don't like using the ruler to set tabs, you don't have to. Instead, you can enter your tab stops manually through the Tabs dialog box:

1. Select the paragraph(s) in which you want to set or edit tabs.
2. Open the Format menu and select Tabs. The Tabs dialog box appears.
3. Type the position at which you want to set a tab in the Tab stop position text box.
4. Select the type of tab you want from the Alignment area.
5. If you want to add a tab leader, select that option from the Leader area.
6. Click Set. Repeat steps 3–6 to add more tabs.

You can remove all tabs from a paragraph by clicking the Clear All button in the Tabs dialog box. You might want to do this, for example, to remove the default tabs prior to setting your own custom tabs for a paragraph.

To remove a single tab, select it from the Tab stop position list, then click Clear.

Cheat Sheet

Creating a Numbered List

1. Click the Numbering button on the Standard toolbar.
2. Type the first item and press Enter.
3. Type the next item and press Enter. Continue adding items as needed.
4. When you reach the end of the list, press Enter again to end the list.
   - If the text already exists, select it, then click the Numbering button to add numbers.

Creating a Bulleted List

1. Click the Bullets button on the Standard toolbar.
2. Type the first item and press Enter.
3. Type the next item and press Enter. Continue adding items as needed.
4. When you reach the end of the list, press Enter again to end the list.
   - If the text already exists, select it, then click the Bullets button to add bullets.

Customizing a Numbered or Bulleted List

1. Select the paragraphs containing the bullets or numbers to be changed.
2. Right-click on the highlighted text and select Bullets and Numbering.
3. To customize bullets, select the Bullets tab and make a choice from those shown, or, click the Customize button. Click the Bullet tab and choose a new character from the symbol chart, then click OK until you return to the document.
4. To customize numbers, select the Numbered tab and make a choice from those shown. Or, click the Customize button and make choices as needed. Click OK until you return to the document.

19

Creating Numbered and Bulleted Lists

One way to set off important information within a document is to present it in a list. Word provides two types of automatically formatted lists: numbered lists and bulleted lists.

num list = steps
bullet list = any items

Typically, you use numbered lists for presenting the steps in a procedure or for enumerating the items in a long list, such as a top ten list. Bulleted lists are used when presenting items that do not need to appear in any particular order. When you create a numbered or bulleted list using Word, each item in the list appears with its own number or bullet. You can change the style of the default number or bullet easily by following the steps at the end of this chapter.

Basic Survival

Creating a Numbered List

When you type a numbered list, each item is automatically assigned a number. If you add items to the list later, those items are automatically renumbered. This is one of the reasons why using Word to create a numbered list is so easy. Follow these steps:

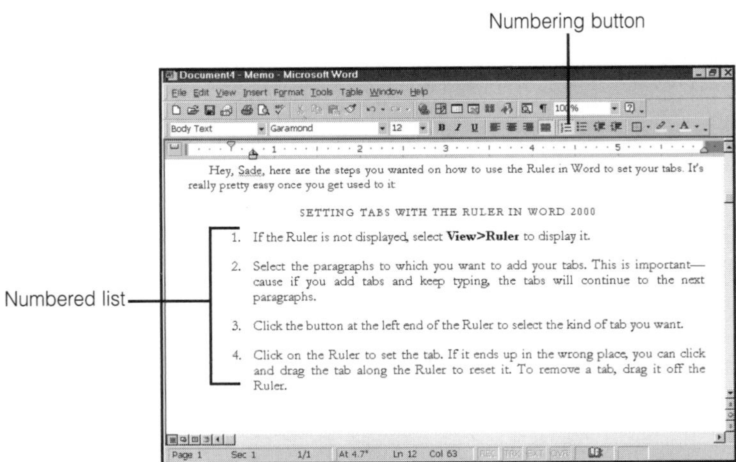

1. Click the Numbering button on the Standard toolbar.
2. The number "1." automatically appears. Type the first item and press Enter.
3. The number "2." appears. Type the next item and press Enter. Continue adding items as needed.
4. When you reach the end of the list, press Enter twice to end the list.

You can create a numbered list from existing text by selecting it first, then clicking the Numbering button. Each paragraph is treated as a separate item in the list.

To add items to an existing list, place the cursor at the end of the item after which you want to add the new item. For example, to add something after item 2, place the cursor at the end of item 2. Press Enter and add the item. Items in the list that follow the new item are automatically renumbered.

To add a blank line beneath a numbered item, place the cursor at the end of a numbered item and press Shift+Enter. This allows you to add text without a number.

If you don't like this automatic numbering business, you can turn it off by opening the Tools menu, selecting AutoCorrect, and clicking the AutoFormat As You Type tab. Then select Automatic numbered lists to turn that option off. (You can turn off automatic bullets as well.) Click OK.

Creating a Bulleted List

Creating a bulleted list is similar to creating a numbered list. Once again, Word does the work for you:

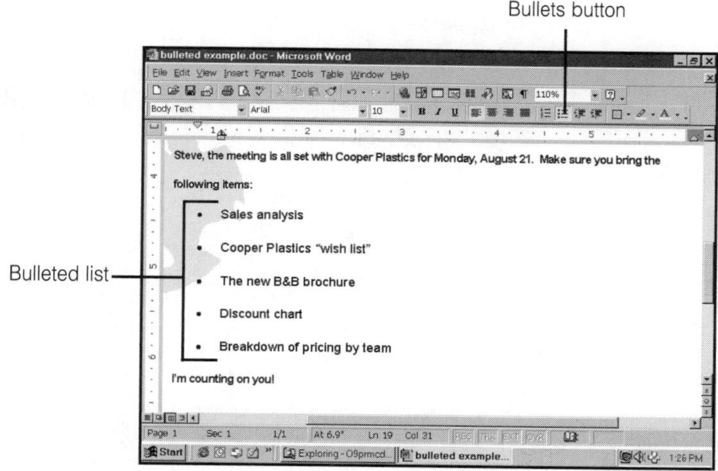

1. Click the Bullets button on the Standard toolbar.
2. A bullet (a dot) appears. Type the first item and press Enter.
3. Another bullet appears. Type the next item and press Enter. Continue adding items as needed.
4. When you reach the end of the list, press Enter again to end the list.

To create a bulleted list from existing text, select the text and then click the Bullets button. To add items to an existing list, place the cursor at the end of the item that appears above the item you want to add, then press Enter. A blank line appears with a bullet. Type the new item on this line.

Beyond Survival

Changing the Number Style

When you create a list using the Numbering button, Word places a "1." in front of the first item. But what if you prefer to list your items as a, b, c rather than 1, 2, 3? Well, no problem; just change the number style used in the list. Here's how:

1. Select those items in the list with the numbering style you want to change.
2. Open the Format menu and select Bullets and Numbering. The Bullets and Numbering dialog box appears.

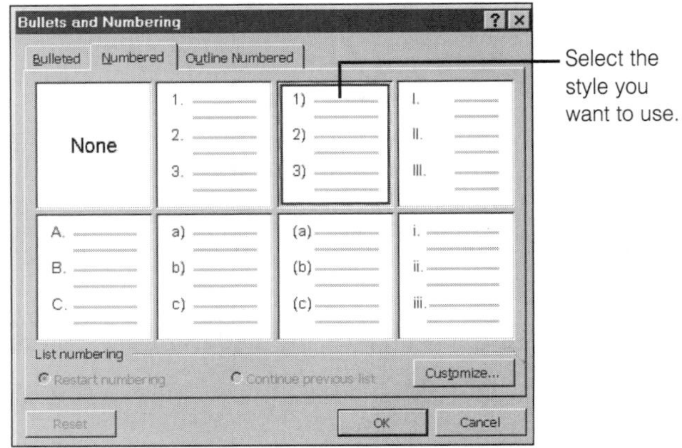

3. Select the style you want to use from those listed.
4. If you don't see a style you like, you can customize an existing style to suit your needs. Select a style that's close, and click Customize. The Customize dialog box appears. Make your changes and click OK.
   - To add text before or after the number, type it in the Number format text box. You can change the characters that follow the number as well; for example, you could type **Step 1:**.
   - Change the font by clicking the Font button and selecting a new one.

- Select the number style you want to use from the Number style list. You can change the starting number as well.
- To change the position of the number, select a different Number position or adjust the Aligned At value. You can adjust the Indent At value as well, to adjust the position of the text.

5. Click OK.

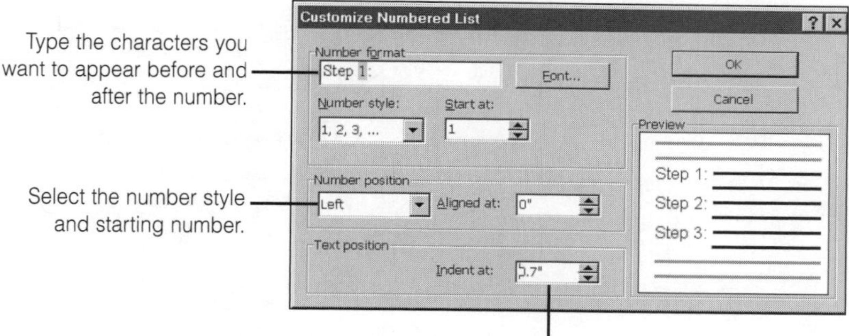

Adjust the position of the number or the text.

Changing the Bullet Style

When you create a bulleted list, Word uses a small dot as the bullet. You can change this bullet to something else, and add pizzazz and style to your document. Follow these steps:

1. Select the bulleted list with the style you want to change.
2. Open the Format menu and select Bullets and Numbering. The Bullets and Numbering dialog box appears.
3. Select the style you want to use from those listed.
4. If you don't see a style you like, you can replace an existing style with a custom bullet style. Click Customize. The Customize dialog box appears. Keep the following ideas in mind:
   - Click on a bullet character you don't like (because that style will be replaced by the new bullet you select), then click Bullet to see the entire symbol set.

- When you're selecting your custom bullet, the Symbol font is used. If you have another font that contains characters you want to use as bullets (such as WingDings or WebDings), select that font from the Font list.
- Select a character from a symbol set.

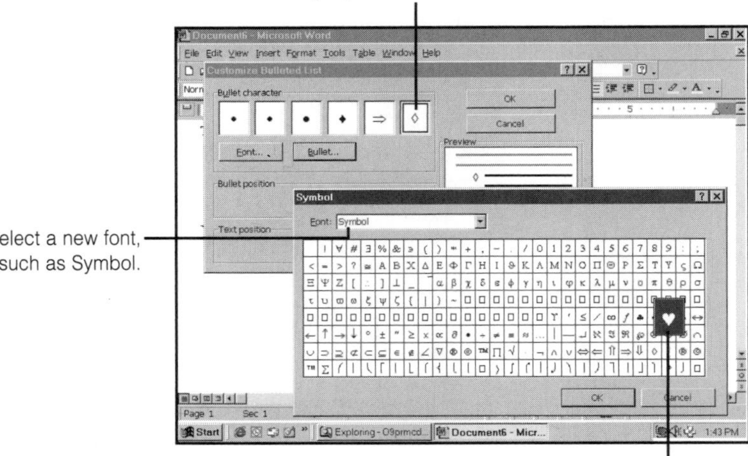

Select a style you don't like, then click Bullet.
Select a new font, such as Symbol.
Select a new bullet style.

5. Click OK.

You can also create a bullet using a graphic. This is especially effective for documents you plan on publishing to the Web.

1. Select the bulleted list with the style you want to change.
2. Open the Format menu and select Bullets and Numbering. The Bullets and Numbering dialog box appears.
3. Click Picture.
4. Select a bullet style you like and click OK. You can also import a graphic you like by clicking Import Clips.

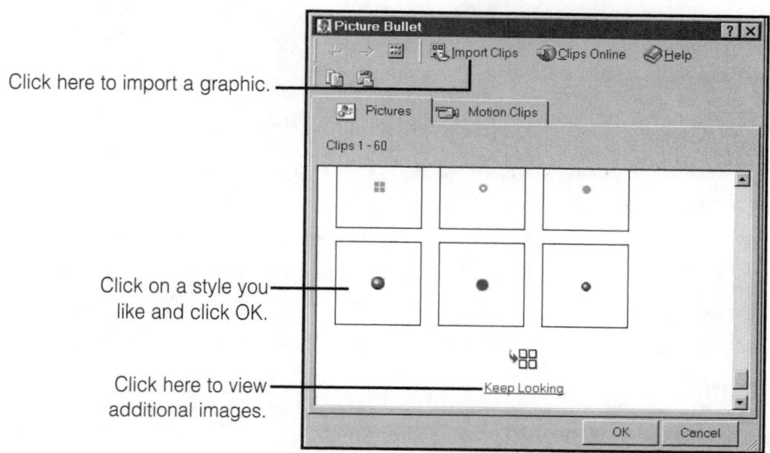
Picture Bullet
Import Clips
Clips Online
Help
Click here to import a graphic.
Pictures
Motion Clips
Clips 1 - 60
Click on a style you like and click OK.
Click here to view additional images.
Keep Looking
OK
Cancel

Cheat Sheet

Creating a Header or Footer

1. Open the View menu and select Header and Footer.
2. To create a footer, click the Switch Between Header and Footer button on the Header and Footer toolbar.
3. Type the text you want into the dashed area. Use the Header and Footer toolbar to insert special text, such as page numbers, date, time, and filename.
4. Click the Close button on the Header and Footer toolbar when you're done.

20

Adding a Header or a Footer

A header is text that prints at the top of each page in a document. A footer is text that prints at the bottom of each page. For example, in this book, the header tells you which part and which chapter you're reading. The footer tells you the page you're on.

header = top
footer = bottom

You can add headers and footers to your documents to do the same thing. For example, your header might contain your company's name, the document name, or something similar. The footer might contain the page number, date, filename, and even your name, if you like. When you create a header or footer, you type the basic text you want, then Word recreates it for you on each page in the document.

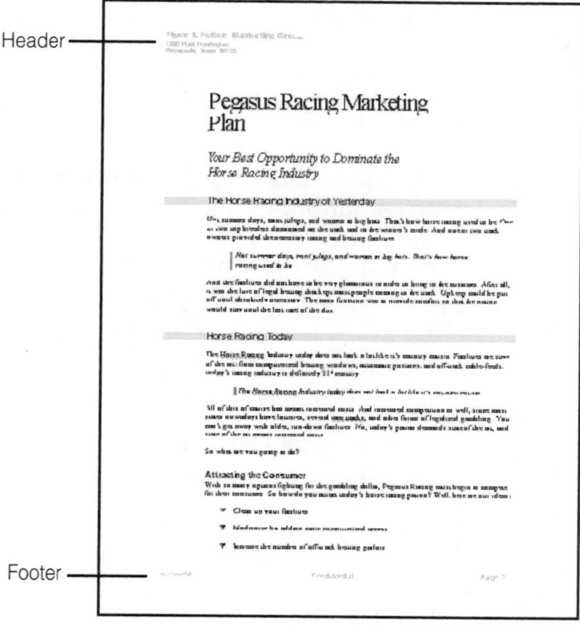

Pegasus Racing Marketing Plan

Your Best Opportunity to Dominate the Horse Racing Industry

The Horse Racing Industry of Yesterday

Horse Racing Today

Attracting the Consumer

Basic Survival

Creating a Header or a Footer

Remember that a header appears at the top of each page in the document. To print something at the bottom of each page, create a footer instead. Follow these steps:

1. Open the View menu and select Header and Footer. Word displays the Header and Footer toolbar and switches you to Page Layout view.

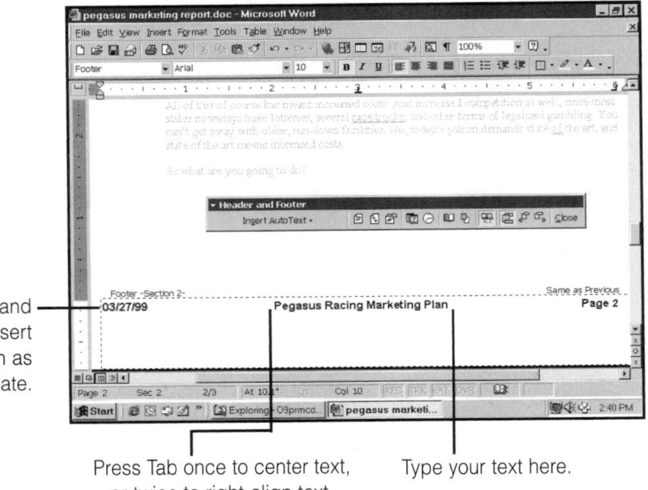

Use the Header and Footer toolbar to insert special items, such as today's date.

Press Tab once to center text, or twice to right-align text.

Type your text here.

2. To create a footer, click the Switch Between Header and Footer button on the Header and Footer toolbar.
3. Type the text you want into the dashed area. You can use the Formatting toolbar to format your text as needed. To center the text, press Tab once and then type. To right-align text, press Tab twice. If you want to add a graphic to the footer, use the Insert/Picture command to insert it.
4. Click the Close button Close on the Header and Footer toolbar when you're finished.

Use the Header and Footer toolbar to insert special text such as page numbers, the filename, and so on. See the next section for more information.

Using the Header and Footer Toolbar

Most headers and footers contain the same kind of text: your company name, the current date, the page number, and so on. You can type your company's name easily enough, but how do you insert the current date? Do you have to keep changing it each time you open the document? And what about the page number? Do you have to type the actual number on each page?

With the help of the Header and Footer toolbar, you can insert a date that changes automatically, a page number that reflects the actual page in the document, and more, as shown in this table:

Button	Description
 Insert AutoText ▾	Inserts your choice of several standard entries, such as the filename, or Page X of Y.
	Inserts the page number.
	Inserts the total number of pages.
	Enables you to format the page number.
	Inserts the current date.
	Inserts the current time.
	Provides access to page setup so you can create odd/even page headers and footers, change the margins, and other things.
	Displays/hides the document text.
	Makes this header or footer the same as the previous one.
	Switches you between editing the header and the footer.
	Displays the previous header or footer, if there's more than one.

continues

continued

Button	Description
[Next button]	Displays the next header or footer, if there's more than one.
Close	Removes the Header and Footer toolbar and returns you to the document text.

Beyond Survival

Creating a Different First Page or Odd and Even Headers or Footers

If you're creating a report, you may not want the page number or date to appear on the cover or first page. Or you may want different information to appear on the first page than on the rest of the pages in the report. For this, you need to create a different first page header/footer than the one that prints on the rest of the pages in your document.

If your document is going to be bound like a book, you may want to use different headers and footers for your odd and even pages. For example, in this book, the even pages display the part number and title. The odd pages display the chapter name and title. The page numbers are left-aligned on the even pages, and right-aligned on the odd, so that they appear on the outer corners of this book.

Do this for unique first pg hdr/ftr.

If you want to create a header or footer that's different for the first page or for even pages than the header or footer that's used in the rest of the document, follow these steps:

1. Open the View menu and select Header and Footer.
2. If you're entering a footer, click the Switch Between Header and Footer button on the Header and Footer toolbar.
3. Click the Page Setup button on the Header and Footer toolbar. The Page Setup dialog box is displayed.
4. Select the Different first page option to create a unique first page header/footer, or select the Different odd and

even option to create odd and even page headers and footers. Click OK.

5. If needed, click the Show Previous button on the Header and Footer toolbar to move to the first page, or to an odd page if you're creating odd/even headers and footers.
6. Create the header or footer as previously described. If you don't want the first page (or odd pages) to actually have a header or footer, skip this step.
7. Click the Show Next button on the Header and Footer toolbar.
8. Create either the even page header/footer or the header/footer you want to use for the rest of the document.
9. Click the Close button Close on the Header and Footer toolbar.

Removing a Header or Footer

To remove a header (or footer):

1. Open the View menu and select Header and Footer.
2. To remove a footer, click the Switch Between Header and Footer button on the Header and Footer toolbar.
3. Select all the text in the header or footer and press Delete.
4. If there are more than one Header or Footer that was created with odd/even headers and footers, click the Show Next or Show Previous buttons on the Header and Footer toolbar, then repeat step 3.
5. Click the Close button Close on the Header and Footer toolbar.

PART 3

Excel 2000

If you like playing with numbers, you'll love Excel. With it, you can organize, analyze, and chart all sorts of financial data. You can even use Excel to organize textual data, such as address lists, phone lists, and so on.

Part 3 covers the following topics:

- Taking a Look Around
- Entering Data
- Selecting a Range
- Copying, Moving, and Deleting Data
- Viewing a Worksheet
- Working with Worksheets
- Changing How Numbers Look
- Changing How Text Looks
- Changing the Alignment of Data
- Changing How Cells Look
- Inserting and Removing Cells, Rows, and Columns
- Changing the Size of Cells
- Creating Formulas
- Copying Formulas
- Using Functions in Your Formulas
- Printing a Workbook
- Creating a Chart

Cheat Sheet

Moving Within a Worksheet

Press this	To move here
← → ↑ ↓	One cell in the direction of the arrow.
Ctrl+↑, Ctrl+↓	To the top or bottom of the data region (the area of the worksheet that actually contains data).
Ctrl+←, Ctrl+→	To the leftmost or rightmost cell in the data region.
Page Up, Page Down	Up or down one screen.
Home	To the leftmost cell in a row (column A).
Ctrl+Home	Upper-left cell in the worksheet.
Ctrl+End	Last cell in the data region.
End+↑, End+↓, End+←, End+→	If the active cell is empty, then this moves you in the direction of the arrow to the first cell that contains data. If the active cell contains data, then this moves you in the direction of the arrow to the last cell that contains data.

Moving from Worksheet to Worksheet

- Click the tab of the worksheet to which you want to go. If you can't see the tab of the worksheet you want, use the tab scroll buttons to display it.
- Press Ctrl+Page Up to move to the next worksheet, or Ctrl+Page Down to move to the preceding one.

21

Taking a Look Around

When you start Excel, it presents you with a blank worksheet in which you can start entering data and formulas. Before you jump in, however, it's a good idea to get an overview of the program as a whole.

Many elements of the Excel window are already familiar to you, such as the Minimize, Maximize/Restore, and Close buttons, among other things. However, some elements of the Excel window are unique to Excel itself; this chapter examines these more closely.

Basic Survival

Understanding the Excel 2000 Screen

Before you begin using Excel, you should become familiar with the purpose of each of its screen elements:

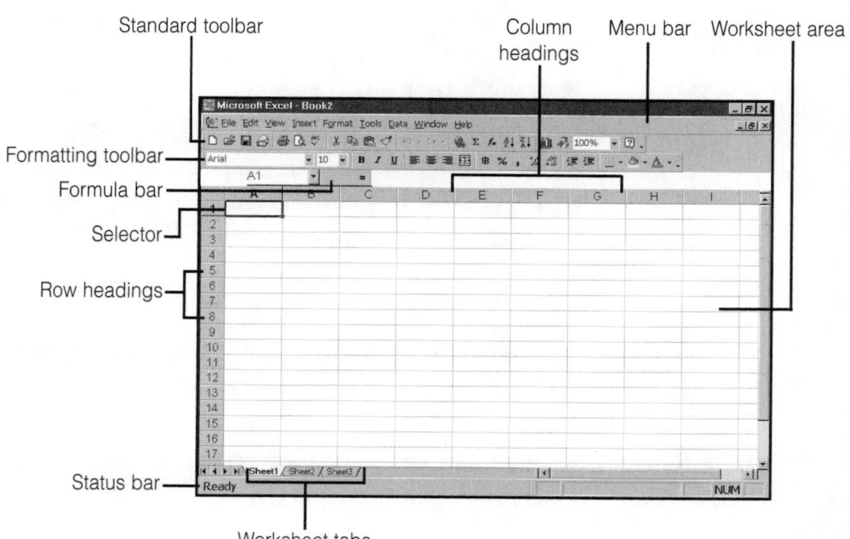

- **Menu bar** This bar contains the Excel menus. To open a menu, click on it. For example, to open the File menu, click on the word *File*. A list of commands appears—to select one, click on it. Only the commands you use the most often appear on the menus. To display all the commands on a menu, click the down arrow at the bottom of the menu.
- **Toolbars** Excel has many specialized toolbars that you can use to accomplish specific tasks. Initially, the Standard and Formatting toolbars are displayed. To display other toolbars, open the View menu, select Toolbars, and then select the one you want to display. The toolbar that is already displayed appears with a check mark in front of its name. If a button you want does not appear on a toolbar, click the More Buttons button, located at the right end of the toolbar and select the button you want from the list that appears.
- **Formula bar** Information that you type into each cell appears here first. You also see the cell location of the selector displayed in a name box.
- **Column and row headings** The column headings (letters) appear across the top of the worksheet, and they help you identify in which column you are. The row headings (numbers) appear down the left side of the worksheet; they help you identify in which row you are.
- **Worksheet area** This is the area into which you type your data and formulas. The selector (the dark outline that appears around the current cell) marks the cell into which data is being placed when you begin typing.
- **Worksheet tabs** To the left of the horizontal scrollbar are the worksheet tabs and tab control buttons, which you can use to move from worksheet to worksheet within the workbook. You'll learn more about them later in this chapter.
- **Status bar** This bar displays the status of your workbook.

Beyond Survival

Moving Within a Worksheet

selector = dark outline around active cell

When you open a workbook, the selector is placed in the first cell. You can always tell which cell is the active cell by looking for the selector (the dark outline around the current cell). To move the selector so you can enter or change data in a different cell, just click in any visible cell. You can also use the keys listed in this table:

Press this	To move here
← → ↑ ↓	One cell in the direction of the arrow.
Ctrl+↑, Ctrl+↓	To the top or bottom of the data region (the area of the worksheet that actually contains data).
Ctrl+←, Ctrl+→	To the leftmost or rightmost cell in the data region.
Page Up, Page Down	Up or down one screen.
Home	To the leftmost cell in a row (column A).
Ctrl+Home	Upper-left cell in the worksheet.
Ctrl+End	Last cell in the data region.
End+↑, End+↓, End+←, End+→	If the active cell is empty, then this moves you in the direction of the arrow to the first cell that contains data. If the active cell contains data, then this moves you in the direction of the arrow to the last cell that contains data.

To jump to any cell: type address in Name box.

Only a small portion of the worksheet is visible at any time. You can use the scrollbars to scroll to an area you want to view. Click the arrows at either end of the scrollbars, or drag the scroll box to scroll more quickly. As you drag, a small box appears, listing the current row or column to which the scroll box points. Release the scroll box when you find the location you want.

Moving from Worksheet to Worksheet

If you know the address of the cell to which you want to move, just type it in the Name box at the left end of the Formula bar and press Enter. You'll learn about cell addresses in Chapter 23.

Each workbook (or Excel file) contains several worksheets in which you can enter and organize your data. By default, each workbook contains three worksheets, but you can add or delete worksheets as needed (see Chapter 26 for help). To move from worksheet to worksheet, do one of the following:

- Click the tab of the worksheet to which you want to go. If you can't see the tab of the worksheet you want, use the tab scroll buttons to display it.
- Press Ctrl+Page Up to move to the next worksheet, or Ctrl+Page Down to move to the preceding one.

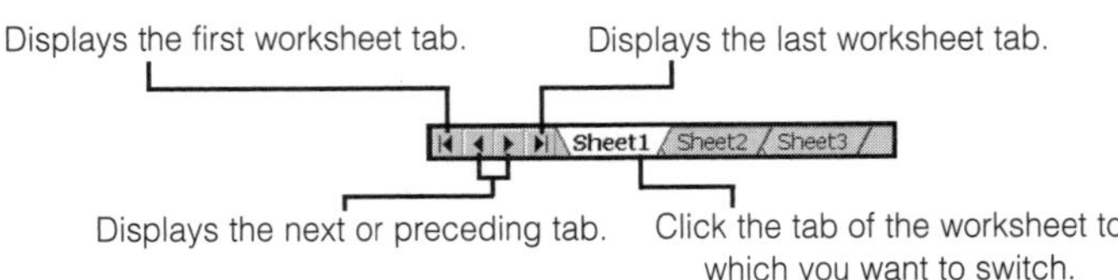
Displays the first worksheet tab.
Displays the last worksheet tab.
Sheet1
Sheet2
Sheet3
Displays the next or preceding tab.
Click the tab of the worksheet to which you want to switch.

Cheat Sheet

Entering Text, Numbers, Dates, or Times

1. Move the selector to the cell in which you want to enter the data. To enter data in a cell that's visible, click in the cell.
2. Type the data. As you do, it appears in the Formula bar. You can press Backspace as needed to erase a mistake. If you've made a mistake and you don't want to enter the data into the cell, press Esc.
3. Press Enter. You can press Tab rather than Enter to move to the next cell to the right, or press an arrow key to move in any direction.
4. To delete data after it is entered, press Delete.

Sample Entries

Data type	Entry	Appearance in cell
Text	Beth Jones	Beth Jones
	'12 West Main	12 West Main
	Quarter 1	Quarter 1
	'299-0910	299-0910
Numbers	-200	-200
	(200)	-200
	50%	50%
	.5	0.5
Dates	10-21	21-Oct
	Oct-21	21-Oct
	10/21/98	10/21/98
Times	4:21 a	4:21 AM
	16:32	16:32

22

Entering Data

After starting Excel, it opens a workbook for you that awaits the data you will add. You can enter various types of data into an Excel worksheet, including text, numbers, dates, times, and formulas. Formulas are covered later; this chapter first examines how you enter basic worksheet data.

Basic Survival

Entering Text

Text is any combination of letters, numbers, and even spaces. You typically use text to identify the columns or rows of numbers you enter into a worksheet, as shown here:

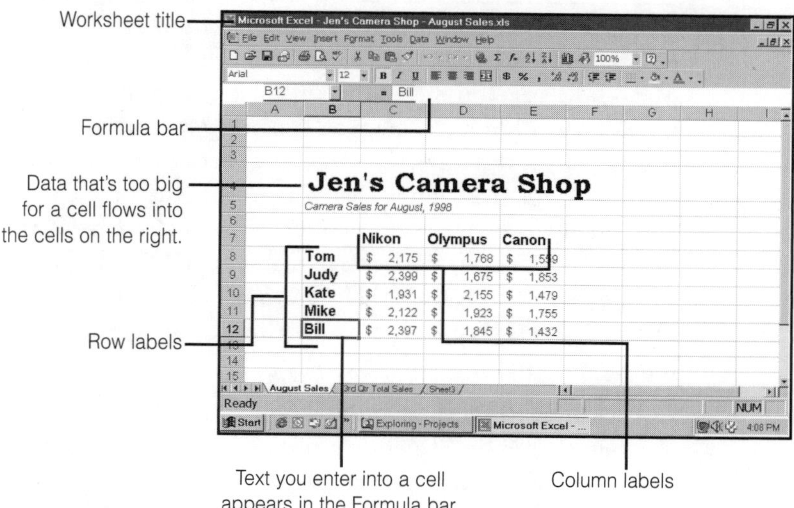

To enter text, follow these steps:

1. Move the selector to the cell in which you want to enter text. To enter text in a cell that's visible, click in the cell.

2. Type the text. As you do, it appears in the Formula bar. You can press Backspace as needed to erase a mistake. If you've made a mistake and you don't want to enter any text, press Esc.

3. Press Enter. Text appears in the cell, left-aligned. You can press Tab rather than Enter to move to the next cell to the right, or press an arrow key to move in any direction.

If you want to enter a number as text, such as a zip code or a phone number, type an apostrophe and then the number, and it will be left-aligned like other text. Former Lotus 1-2-3 users are already familiar with using an apostrophe to denote numbers that should be treated as text and not as part of a formula.

Text too big flows into next cell.

If you enter text that's too big for the column's width, then only part of the text shows (unless the cell to the right is empty, in which case the text flows into that cell). To change the width of a column so that its data automatically fits, double-click the right-hand border of the column heading. You'll learn more about adjusting column width in Chapter 32.

Entering Numbers

When you enter numbers, you can type commas, decimal points, dollar signs, percent signs, and other characters as well—however, you may not want to. The reason is that after typing in a column of data, you can easily format it so that the numbers look the way you want. And, because it's just the formatting of the data you're changing (rather than the data itself) you can change your mind as often as you like (or as often as the boss makes you). So, rather than type $1234.50, just type 1234.5, and then format the number as a dollar value with two decimal places. (See Chapter 27 for help.) To enter numbers, follow these steps:

Don't enter . , $, or %

1. Move the selector to the cell in which you want to enter your number. To enter a number in a cell that's visible, click in the cell.

2. Type the number, leaving out the commas, dollar signs, and percent signs. To enter a negative number, press – and then type the number. To enter a fraction, type **0** then the fraction, as in **0 1/2**.

3. Press Enter. The number appears in the cell, right-aligned. You can press Tab rather than Enter to move to the next cell to the right, or use an arrow key to move in any direction.

Pound signs means column not wide enough.

If you enter a number that's too big for a cell, it appears as ########. This doesn't affect your formulas, but prevents you from seeing or printing the formula. To display the number, widen the column (see Chapter 32 for more information). To change the width of a column so your data fits automatically, double-click the right-hand border of the column heading.

Entering Dates and Times

Dates and times can be entered in a variety of ways:

Date/time format	Example date/time
M/D	8/16
M/YY	8/98
MM/DD/YY	8/16/98 or 04/08/58
MMM-YY	Aug-98
MMMMMMMMM-YY	August-98
MMMMMMMMM DD, YYYY	August 16, 1998
DD-MMM-YY	16-Aug-98
DD-MMM	16-Aug
HH:MM	18:52
HH:MM:SS	18:52:08
HH:MM AM/PM	6:52 PM
HH:MM:SS AM/PM	6:52:08 PM
MM/DD/YY HH:MM	8/16/98 18:52

As you probably noticed in the table, Excel assumes that you're using a military 24-hour clock, unless you add the AM/PM designation.

When you enter a date or time, Excel converts it to a number. This enables you to change the date or time format at will, and to perform calculations involving dates. To enter a date or time:

1. Move the selector to the cell in which you want to enter your date or time. To enter data in a cell that's visible, click in the cell.
2. Type the date or time, using one of the formats listed in the table. You don't actually have to type "AM" if that's the format you're using; just type an "a" or a "p" and Excel will get the idea.
3. Press Enter. The date or time appears in the cell, right-aligned. You can press Tab rather than Enter to move to the next cell to the right, or use an arrow key to move in any direction.

Uses military clock. Type a or p.

As with numbers, if the date or time format you select is too big to display in a cell, ####### appears instead. To display the date or time fully, widen the column by double-clicking the right-hand border of the column heading.

Beyond Survival

Correcting a Mistake

Excel makes it easy for you to correct mistakes in your spreadsheets:

- If you find a mistake as you're entering data, just use the Backspace key to back up and correct it.
- To correct data already entered into a cell, click on the cell. Then click in the Formula bar, make the correction, and press Enter or click the Enter button ✓.
- To correct data in the cell without jumping to the Formula bar, double-click on the cell instead.
- To delete data in a cell without replacing it, press Delete.

Just double-click in cell to edit.

- To replace a cell's data with new data, just click on the cell and begin typing. What you type replaces the old contents.

Olympus

Click here or press Enter when done.

Click here and make the correction.

Entering a Series of Years, Months, and Other Data

If you were creating a sales worksheet for the year, you might enter the column labels January, February, and so on. This sequence of months is called a *series.* Excel makes it easy to enter any series of data, such as consecutive months, days, years—even a series of numbers, such as 10, 20, 30, and so on. Follow these steps:

Remember this!

1. Enter the first item in the series.
2. With the mouse pointer, click on the fill handle.
3. Drag the fill handle downward or to the right, and the series is copied to the adjacent cells.

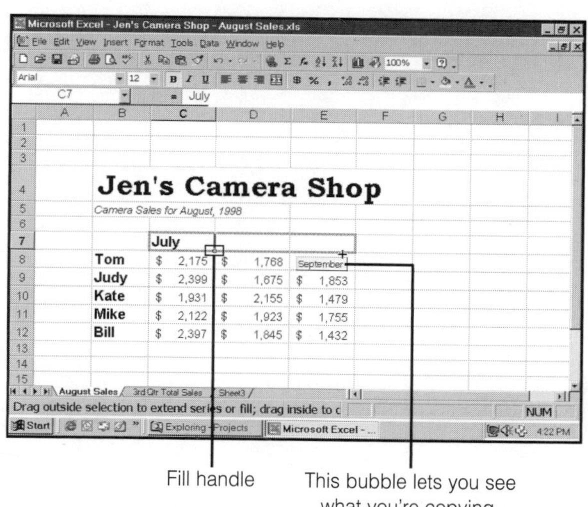

Fill handle

This bubble lets you see what you're copying.

Sometimes Excel has trouble understanding your series. For example, you want even years only, as in 1990, 1992, 1994, and so on, but Excel gives you something more like 1990, 1991, 1992, and so on. To fix the problem, enter two cells with the series data, such as 1990 and 1992. Then select both the cells (by dragging over them) and drag the fill handle as usual.

By the way, you can use this drag and fill method to copy data as well, without creating a series, as you'll learn in Chapter 24.

Cheat Sheet

Range and Cell Addresses

When typing a cell or a range address, remember these things:

- A cell address is made up of its column letter and its row number, as in cell C12.
- A range is defined by its *anchor points*—the upper-left-hand and the lower-right-hand cell in the range.
- To refer to a range, you type in the address of these two cells, separated by a colon ":", as in **C12:F14**.

Selecting a Range with the Mouse

1. Click on the upper-left-hand cell in the range.
2. Hold down the mouse button as you drag downward and to the lower-right-hand cell in the range.
3. Release the mouse button and the range is highlighted. To deselect the range, click anywhere in the worksheet.

Shortcuts for Selecting a Range

- To select several ranges, select the first range, then press and hold the Ctrl key as you select additional ranges.
- To select an entire row, click the row header. To select an entire column, click the column header.
- To select an entire worksheet, click the Select All button.
- To select a range that is not visible, click in the Name box on the Formula bar, type the range address you want to select, and press Enter.
- To select the same range on several worksheets, select the worksheets first by pressing Ctrl and clicking each tab. Then select the range you want.

23

Selecting a Range

A range may refer to a single cell, but more often it is a rectangular grouping of adjacent cells, as in this figure. You might select a range to perform some function on a group of related cells, such as copying, moving, or formatting them. You can also use ranges in formulas to perform calculations on related data, such as totaling up a column of numbers.

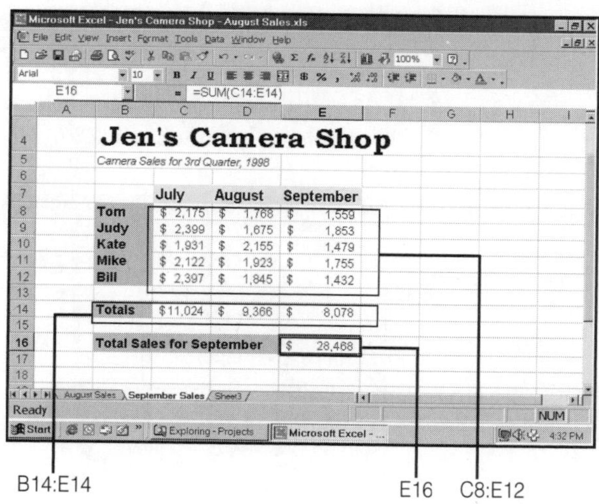

Basic Survival

Range and Cell Addresses

A range is defined by its anchor points—the upper-left-hand and the lower-right-hand cell in the range of cells. To refer to a range, type in the address of these two cells (the upper-left and lower-right), separated by a colon (:). To do that, of course, you have to know what a *cell address* is.

Cell address: upperanchor: loweranchor

A cell address is made up of the cell's column letter and row number, as in cell C12. Remember, column letters appear at the top of the worksheet, and row numbers appear along the left-hand side.

Now, to create a range address, list the two anchor cells, separating them with a colon, as in range C12:F14. The ranges in the preceding figure include C8:E12, B14:E14, and the single cell E16. Note that a single cell can also constitute a range.

Selecting a Range with the Mouse

Prior to copying, moving, or deleting the cells in a range, you must first select them. You might also select a range to indicate which cells you want Excel to use in a particular formula. To select a range with the mouse:

Drag from anchor pt to anchor pt.

1. Click on the upper-left-hand cell in the range.
2. Hold down the mouse button as you drag downward to the lower-right-hand cell in the range.
3. Release the mouse button, and the range is highlighted. To deselect the range, click anywhere in the worksheet.

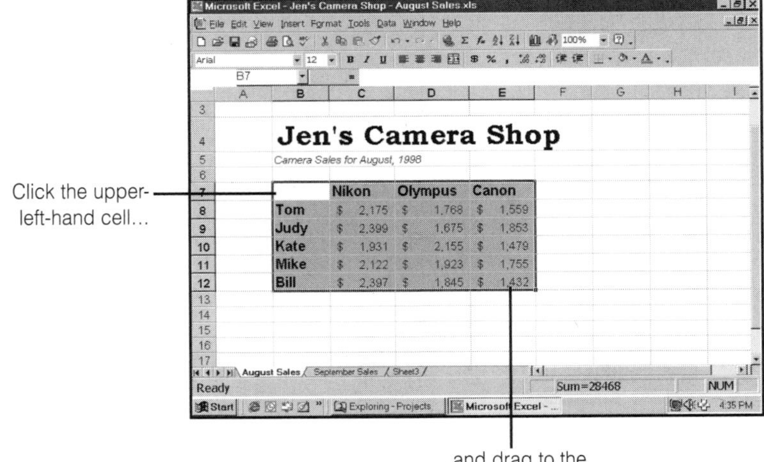

If you don't like this dragging business, you can select a range by clicking on the first anchor point, pressing and holding the Shift key, and clicking on the second anchor point.

You can use some shortcuts when selecting a range with the mouse, as listed in this table.

To select this	Perform this action
Several ranges	Select the first range, then press and hold the Ctrl key as you select additional ranges.
The same range on several worksheets	Select the worksheets first by pressing Ctrl and clicking each tab. Then select the range you want.
An entire row	Click the row header.
An entire column	Click the column header.
An entire worksheet	Click the Select All button—the gray button located to the left of the column headings, just above the row headings.
Some range that is not visible	Click in the Name box on the Formula bar, type the range address you want to select, and press Enter.

Selecting a Range with the Keyboard

Press Shift and use arrow keys to select.

If you don't like the mouse, you don't have to use it to select a range:

1. Move the selector to the upper-left-hand cell in the range you want to select.
2. Press and hold the Shift key.
3. Using the arrow keys or some other keyboard shortcut, move the selector to the lower-right-hand cell in the range. The range you select is highlighted.

Beyond Survival

Selecting a Range Within a Dialog Box

When you use a dialog box, you're asked to make certain selections. Sometimes you even need to type in information, such as a range address. Excel has designed its dialog boxes so that you can select the range you want instead of typing in its address. Follow these steps:

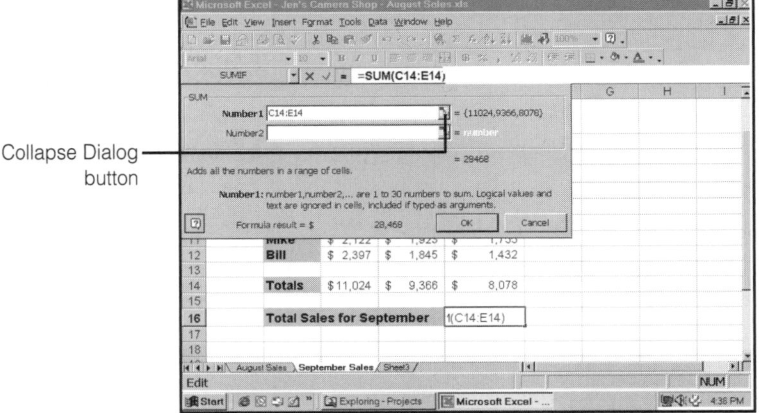

Remember this!

1. At the end of the text box in which you must enter a range address, click the Collapse Dialog button. The dialog box is reduced to just the text box, and the worksheet underneath is revealed.
2. Using the mouse, select the range you want.
3. Click the Collapse Dialog button again, and the dialog box automatically reappears, with the address of the range you selected inserted into the appropriate text box.

Naming a Range

One of the things you can do with a range after selecting it is to name it. Why name a range? Because doing so enables you to refer to that range by its name, rather than its address. It's also easier to remember the name "INCOME" than the range, B2:B18.

Naming ranges saves time.

You can use a range name anywhere you might use a cell address: in a formula, in a command (such as Print), or in a dialog box. To create a range name:

1. Select the range you want to name. Remember that a single cell can be a range, so you can name just a cell if you like.
2. Click in the Name box of the Formula bar.
3. Type the range name. The first character in a name must be a letter, but after that, you can use any combination of letters (upper- or lowercase), numbers, periods, and underscores, but no spaces. So if you want to name a range "Quarter 1," you have to use "Quarter1" or "Quarter_1." You can't use anything that looks like a cell address, such as Q1. Also, you're limited to 255 characters.
4. Press Enter.

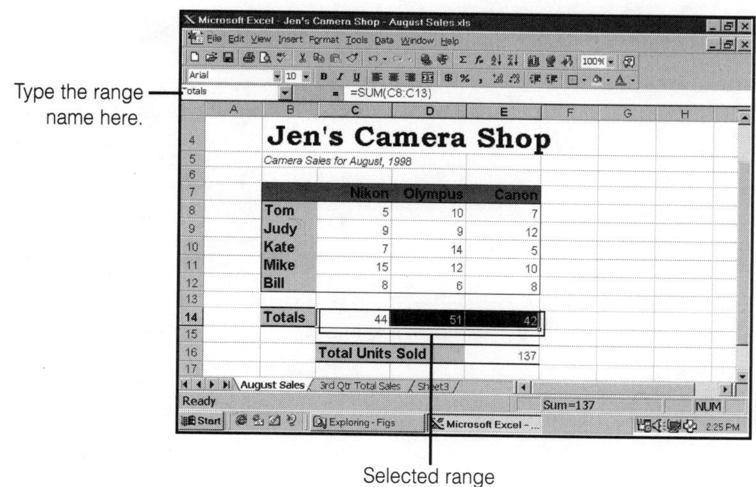

You can jump to a named range by selecting it from the Name drop-down list box.

To delete a range name, or to adjust the range to which it refers, use the `Insert/Name/Define` command. In the Define Name dialog box, select the range name you want to delete and click the Delete button. To change its range instead, click the Collapse Dialog button in the Refers to text box and select the new range.

Cheat Sheet

Copying or Moving Data Using Drag and Drop

1. Select the cell or range you want to copy or move.
2. Move the mouse pointer to the outer edge of the selected cell or range. The pointer changes to an arrow.
3. If you want to copy the data (rather than move it), press and hold the Ctrl key. Then drag the selection to its new location and release the mouse button.

Deleting Data

To remove the contents of a cell or range of cells, follow these steps (or to remove the format, contents, and/or comments, use the Edit/Clear command; to remove the cell completely, use the Edit/Delete command):

1. Select the cell or range that has the contents you want to delete.
2. Press Delete.

Copying the Same Data Over a Range of Cells

1. Click on the cell that has the contents you want to copy.
2. Click on the fill handle and drag it downward or to the right, selecting the cells to which you want to copy.
3. Release the mouse button and the data is copied to the cells you selected.

Copying or Moving Multiple Items with the Office Clipboard

1. To copy a selected item, click the Copy button.
2. To paste all the items on the Office Clipboard at the current cell, click Paste All on the Clipboard toolbar.
3. To paste a selected item from the Office Clipboard, click its icon.
4. To remove everything from the Office Clipboard, click Clear Clipboard.

24

Copying, Moving, and Deleting Data

When you copy or move data, that data is placed on the Clipboard, a temporary storage area in Windows. To complete the Copy or Move process, the data is then pasted from the Clipboard to the location you select. The data remains on the Clipboard until the next Copy or Move process; this enables you to paste the same data to several different locations.

All your programs share the Windows Clipboard, so it enables you to copy or move data between worksheets, workbooks, and even documents created by other applications.

If you're working only within Office documents to copy or move data, you can use the Office Clipboard toolbar (described in the "Beyond Survival" section). This toolbar allows you to copy or move up to 12 individual items and paste them anywhere within Office.

Basic Survival

Copying Data

When you copy data, the original data is left in place, and a copy is put on the Clipboard. You then paste this copy to a new location. Follow these steps:

1. Select the cell or range of cells with data you want to copy.
2. Click the Copy button.
3. Click the cell to which you want to copy your data. If you're copying a range, click on the upper-left-hand cell of the range to which you want the data copied.
4. Click the Paste button.

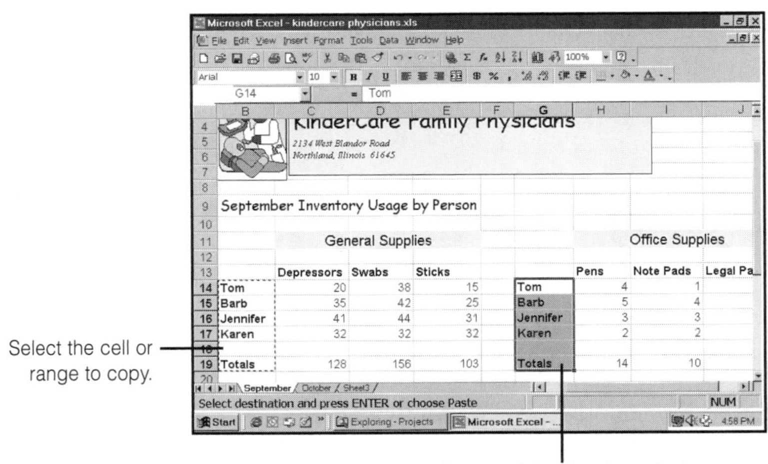

Moving Data

To move: Cut/Paste

When you move data, the original data is removed from its location, and put on the Clipboard. You then paste a copy of this data to a new location. (Remember that data remains on the Clipboard until you perform another copy or move, when it is replaced by the new data unless you use the Clipboard toolbar described later in this section.) Follow these steps to move data:

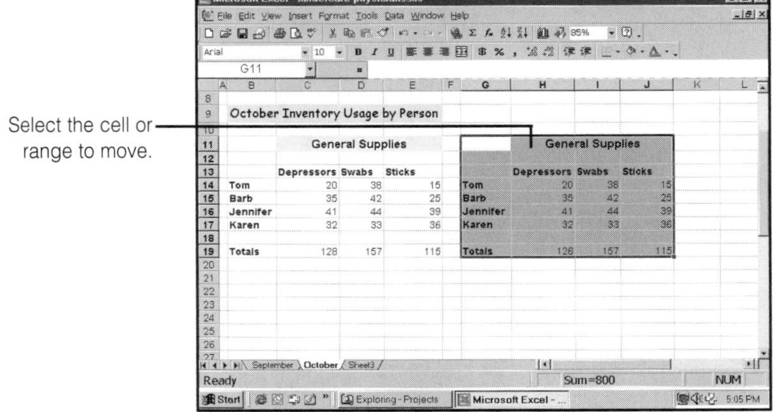

1. Select the cell or range of cells with data you want to move.

2. Click the Cut button.

3. Click the cell to which you want to move your data. If you're moving a range, click on the upper-left-hand cell of the range to which you want the data moved.

4. Click the Paste button.

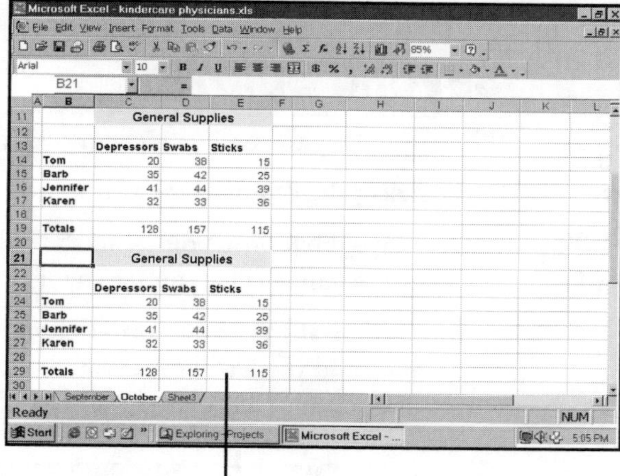

The data is pasted to the new location.

Deleting Data

To remove the contents of a cell or range of cells, you delete them. Follow these steps:

1. Select the cell or range that has contents you want to delete.

2. Press Delete.

Delete removes data, not formatting.

When you use Delete, it removes only the contents of the selected cells, not the formatting. If you want to remove the formatting and any attached comments as well (or if you want to remove only the formatting), you use the Clear command:

1. Select the cell or range you want to clear.

2. Open the Edit menu and select Clear.

3. Select the option you want from the cascading menu that appears:

All. Clears the contents, formatting, and comments from the cell.

Formats. Clears only the formatting from the cell.

Contents. Clears only the cell contents; this is the same as using Delete.

Comments. Clears only the attached notes.

Beyond Survival

Copying or Moving Data Using Drag and Drop

The easiest way to copy or move data is to use drag and drop:

1. Select the cell or range you want to copy or move.
2. Move the mouse pointer to the outer edge of the selected cell or range. The pointer changes to an arrow.
3. If you want to copy the data (rather than move it), press and hold the Ctrl key. Then drag the selection to its new location and release the mouse button.

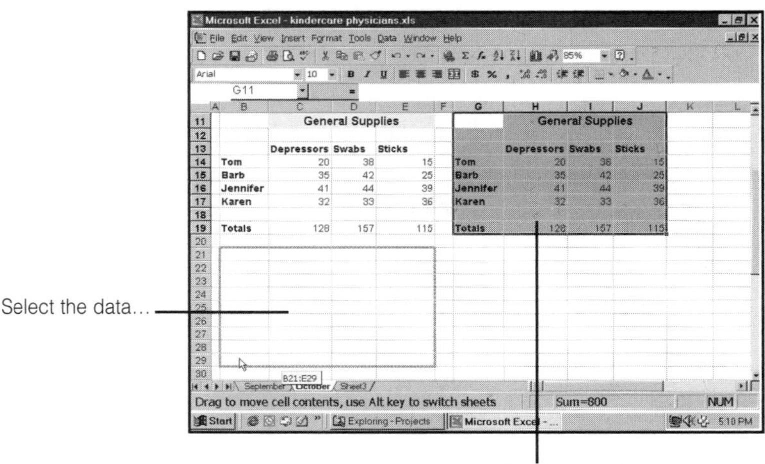

If you're copying data, you see a small plus sign near the mouse pointer as you drag. You must, by the way, hold the Ctrl key down until you release the mouse button, or Excel thinks you are still trying to move the data.

Copying the Same Data Over a Range of Cells

Drag fill handle to copy data across or down.

If you need to copy the same data to adjacent cells, there's a quick way to do it—one that's even faster than drag and drop! Copying data in this manner is especially useful when working with formulas. Here's what you do:

1. Click on the cell that has the contents you want to copy.
2. Click on the fill handle and drag it downward or to the right, selecting the cells to which you want to copy.
3. Release the mouse button, and the data is copied to the cells you selected.

Double-click the fill handle to automatically copy down.

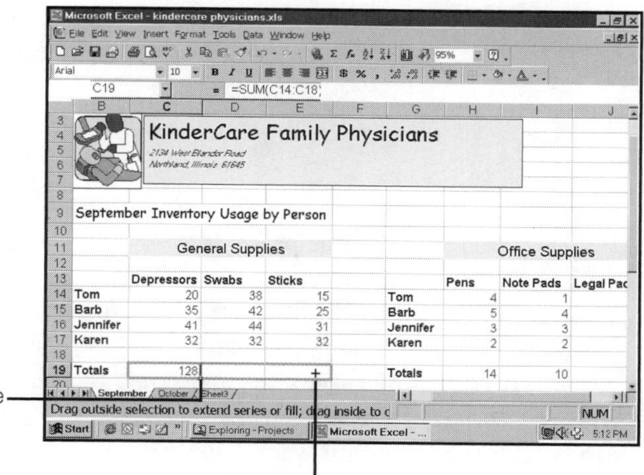

If the data in the original cell is something that looks as if it might be a series, such as January, February, and so on, then Excel tries to create that series when you drag the fill handle. If you don't want to create a series and you just want to copy data, press and hold the Ctrl key as you drag.

Removing Cells

Sometimes, rather than delete the contents of some cells, you want to *remove* them completely. When you remove cells, the data in the worksheet is shifted upward or to the left to fill the gap. You might want to do this when you no longer need the data in a group of cells. Follow these steps to remove cells.

1. Select the cells you want to remove.
2. Open the Edit menu and select Delete. The Delete dialog box appears.

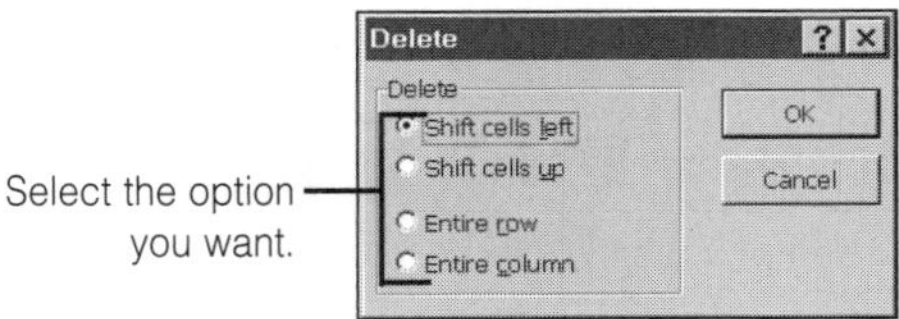
Delete
Delete
Shift cells left
Shift cells up
Entire row
Entire column
OK
Cancel
Select the option you want.

3. Select the option you want: Shift Cells Left or Shift Cells Up.
4. Click OK.

You can remove entire columns and rows if needed—see Chapter 31 for help.

Copying or Moving Multiple Items with the Office Clipboard

Office clpbd, Office use only

With the Office Clipboard, you can copy or move multiple items in one step—to any Office document. You don't have to perform any extra steps to activate the Office Clipboard—just select an item, and copy or cut it as usual. After you've selected all the items you want, use the Office Clipboard toolbar to paste them into a document.

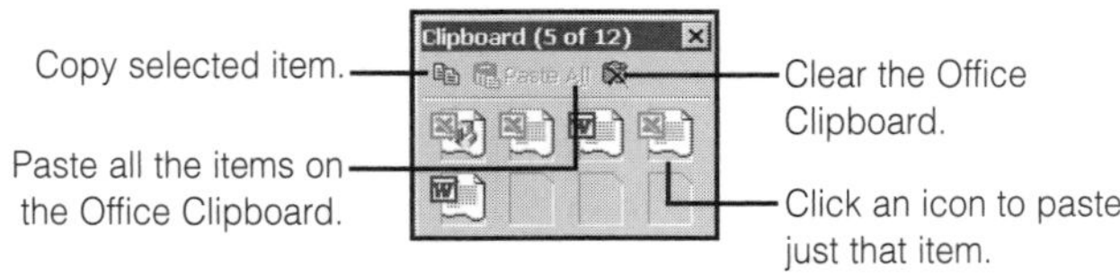
Clipboard (5 of 12)
Paste All
Copy selected item.
Paste all the items on the Office Clipboard.
Clear the Office Clipboard.
Click an icon to paste just that item.

Perform any of the following:

- To copy a selected item, you can click the Copy button on the Office Clipboard, or the Copy button on the Standard toolbar. They're the same.
- To paste all the items on the Office Clipboard at the current cursor location, click Paste All. You will not be able

to choose Paste All while in Excel if the Office Clipboard contains a combination of graphic images and text. Instead, to paste all the items on the Office Clipboard, paste each one individually.

- To paste a selected item from the Office Clipboard, click its icon. If you're not sure which icon you want, move the mouse pointer over it, and a ScreenTip appears, displaying a description of the item's contents.
- To remove everything from the Office Clipboard, click Clear Clipboard. This also clears the Windows Clipboard, which contains the last item you cut or copied.
- To remove the Office Clipboard from the screen, click its Close button. The Office Clipboard will normally reappear when needed, but if you want to display it, choose View, Toolbars, Clipboard.

Cheat Sheet

Zooming a Worksheet

1. Click the down arrow on the Zoom button 100% .
2. Select the zoom percentage you want, or
3. Click inside of the Zoom button and type a specified amount, then press Enter.

Freezing Columns and Row Labels

1. Click in the cell *to the right* of the row labels and/or *below* any column labels you want to freeze.
2. Open the Window menu and select Freeze Panes.
3. When you're ready to unlock the labels, open the Window menu and select Unfreeze Panes.

Splitting the Screen

1. Click on either the vertical or the horizontal split box.
2. Drag the split down or to the right to split the window into two panes.
3. When you're finished, double-click on the split bar to return to a one-pane window.

Hiding Columns and Rows

1. Click on the column or row label for the column or row that you want to hide.
2. Open the Format menu and select Row or Column, then select Hide.
3. To redisplay the hidden rows or columns, select the rows or columns surrounding the hidden ones, then open the Format menu, select Rows or Columns, then select Unhide.

25

Viewing a Worksheet

You can view your worksheet in many ways. For example, you can zoom in on a particular area of the worksheet, or zoom out to view a large worksheet in its entirety. You can "freeze" row or column labels so you don't lose track of what you're looking at when you scroll through a large worksheet. And you can split the screen to see two parts of the worksheet at the same time. You'll learn how to do all this and more in this chapter.

Basic Survival

Zooming a Worksheet

When you want to see more or less of your worksheet, you adjust the zoom:

1. Click the down arrow on the Zoom button 100%.
2. Select the zoom percentage you want. The view is automatically adjusted.

Zoom out to view a large worksheet in its entirety.

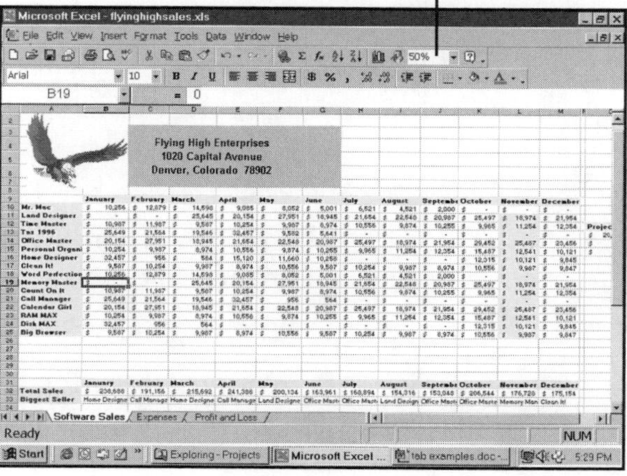

If you like, you can select an area of the worksheet on which you'd like to concentrate, and then choose Selection from the Zoom list to zoom in on that area. You can also click in the Zoom button [100%] and type a custom percentage.

Full Screen: no toolbars, formula bar, status bar.

Another way to see as much of the worksheet as possible is with the View/Full Screen command. When you do, Excel removes the toolbars, Formula bar, and the status bar from the screen. To return to normal view, click the Close Full Screen button that appears or select View, Full Screen from the menu.

Freezing Column and Row Labels

When you're working on a large worksheet, it's easy to get a bit lost, especially when you find yourself in a sea of numbers, with nary a column or row label in sight. To get your bearings, freeze the row or column labels (or both), and then scroll to the data you want to view. With your labels in sight, you can easily understand the meaning of the numbers you see.

With a large worksheet, freeze the labels!

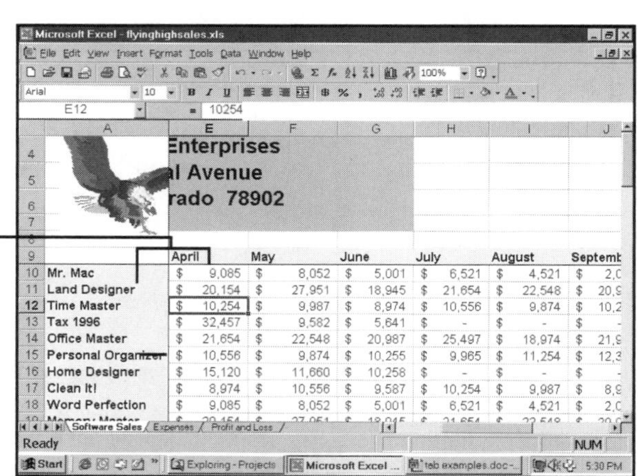

When you freeze your labels, you can view data more easily in a large worksheet.

To freeze row or column labels, follow these steps:

1. Click in the cell to the right of the row labels and/or below any column labels you want to freeze.
2. Open the Window menu and select Freeze Panes.
3. Move the selector to the cells you want to view. As you do, the row and/or column labels remain as they were, enabling you to associate them with your data.

4. When you're ready to unlock the labels, open the Window menu and select Unfreeze Panes.

Beyond Survival

Splitting the Screen

Another way to deal with a large worksheet is to split the window in two and view different parts of the worksheet in each pane. Follow these steps:

1. Click on either the vertical or the horizontal split box.

Drag split bar to split screen in 2.

2. Drag the split bar down or to the right to split the window into two panes.
3. Click in the pane in which you want to work. You can scroll each pane independently.
4. When you're finished, double-click on the split bar or drag it back to its home to return to a one-pane window.

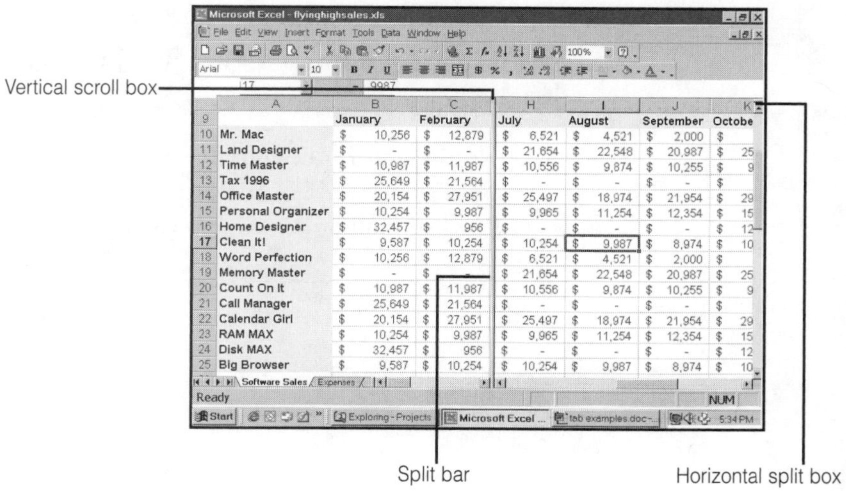

Hiding Columns and Rows

If certain columns or rows contain sensitive data, or data you don't want to print or display right now, you can hide them.

Hidden data doesn't print.

Private information, such as the phone numbers in column E, can be hidden from view.

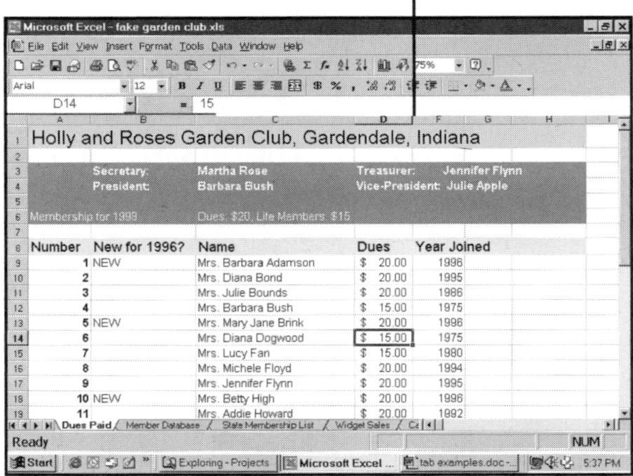

1. Click on the column or row heading for the column or row that you want to hide. To select several rows or columns, drag over the headings you want to select.
2. Open the Format menu and select Row or Column, then select Hide.

To redisplay the hidden rows or columns, select the rows or columns surrounding the hidden ones, then open the Format menu, select Rows or Columns, and select Unhide.

Cheat Sheet

Selecting Worksheets

- To select one worksheet, click its tab.
- To select adjacent worksheets, click the first tab, press and hold the Shift key, and click the last tab in the group.
- To select nonadjacent worksheets, press and hold the Ctrl key as you click each tab.
- To ungroup a set of worksheets you've selected, click on the tab of any one of the worksheets in the group, or click the tab of a worksheet *not in the group.*

Adding a Worksheet to a Workbook

1. Click the tab of the worksheet *in front of which* you want the new worksheet inserted.
2. Open the Insert menu and select Worksheet.

Changing a Worksheet's Name

1. Double-click the tab of the worksheet you want to change. The cursor appears in the tab.
2. Type a new name for the worksheet and press Enter. The new name appears on the worksheet tab.

Removing Worksheets from a Workbook

1. Select the worksheet(s) you want to remove.
2. Open the Edit menu and select Delete Sheet. A dialog box appears, asking you to confirm the deletion.
3. Click OK, and the worksheet(s) are removed.

26

Working with Worksheets

When you open a new workbook in Excel, it includes three separate worksheets. You can use these different worksheets to organize your data logically. For example, on one worksheet, you could list your income. On the second, you could list your expenses. And on the third, you could list your net worth. In this chapter, you'll learn how to add worksheets when needed, and how to delete them as well. You'll also learn any additional skills you need to know to work in a multiple-worksheet file.

Basic Survival

Selecting Worksheets

You can copy, move, and delete worksheets, but to do so, you must first select the worksheets you want to use. Here's how:

Shift = select adjacent worksheets Ctrl = select any worksheet

- To select one worksheet, click its tab.
- To select adjacent worksheets, click the first tab, press and hold the Shift key, and click the last tab in the group.
- To select nonadjacent worksheets, press and hold the Ctrl key as you click each tab.

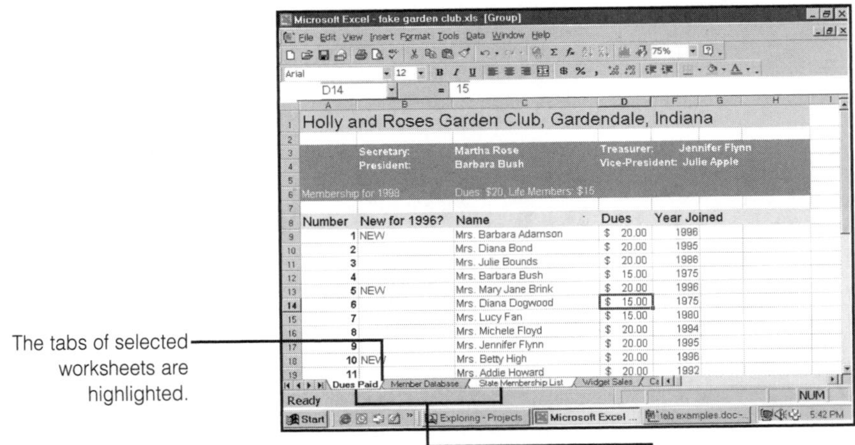

Press Shift and click tab to ungroup wksheets

If you select more than one worksheet, they begin to act as a group until you ungroup them. Text or formatting that is done in one worksheet will be done in all selected worksheets. There are several ways in which you can do that:

- Press and hold the Shift key as you click on the tab of any one of the worksheets in the group.
- Right-click on the tab of one of the worksheets in the group, and select Ungroup Sheets from the shortcut menu that appears.
- Click on the tab of a worksheet in the group or one that is not in the group.

Adding a Worksheet to a Workbook

If you find that you need more worksheets in your workbook than Excel has provided, here's how to add them:

1. Click the tab of the worksheet in front of which you want the new worksheet inserted. For example, if you select Sheet 3, the new worksheet will be inserted in front of Sheet 3.
2. Open the Insert menu and select Worksheet.

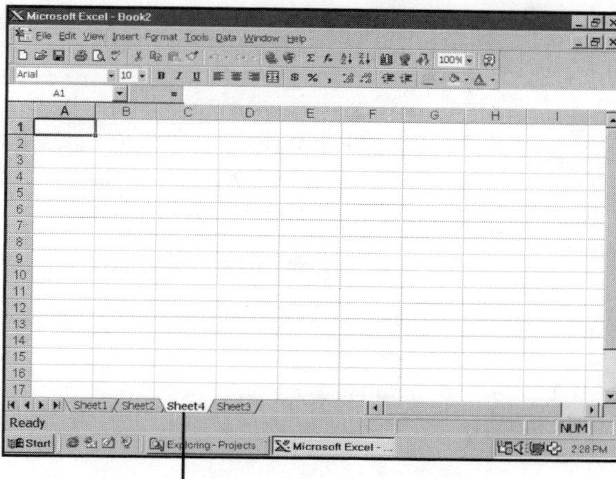

The new worksheet is inserted in front of Sheet 3.

Worksheets are added in front of the one you select.

If you want to start out *all* your new workbooks with more (or less) than three worksheets, you can change the default by opening the Tools menu, selecting Options, and clicking the General tab. Change the number that appears under Sheets in New Workbook, and click OK.

Changing a Worksheet's Name

It can be confusing to work in a workbook that has multiple worksheets, because "Sheet 2" doesn't identify a particular worksheet as the one that contains your sales data for April 1999. So rather than just live with the generic names that Excel gives each worksheet, why not change them to something more descriptive? Here's how:

Double-click the tab to change worksheet name.

1. Double-click the tab of the worksheet you want to change. The cursor appears in the tab field.
2. Type a new name for the worksheet and press Enter. The new name appears on the worksheet tab.

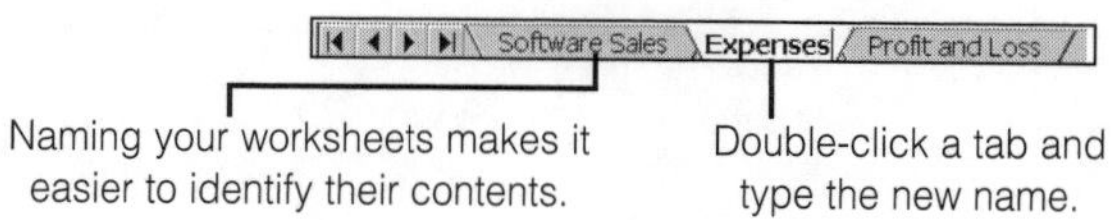

Naming your worksheets makes it easier to identify their contents.

Double-click a tab and type the new name.

Beyond Survival

Removing Worksheets from a Workbook

If you know that you won't need the extra worksheets that Excel provides, you can remove them from the workbook. Doing so makes the workbook file a bit smaller and easier to use. Follow these steps:

1. Select the worksheet(s) you want to remove.
2. Open the Edit menu and select Delete Sheet. A dialog box appears, asking you to confirm the deletion.
3. Click OK, and the worksheet(s) is removed.

You can remove a worksheet that contains data, although you probably shouldn't. The confirmation box that appears in step 2 is the only thing that stops you from doing that, so be careful when using the Edit/Delete Sheet command.

Moving a Worksheet

After entering data on several worksheets, you may decide later on that you don't like the order in which they appear. No problem; you can reorder the worksheets to suit your taste. Follow these steps:

1. Select the worksheet(s) you want to move.
2. Press and hold the mouse button as you drag the tab to its new location in the workbook. The mouse pointer changes to an arrow with a small sheet attached, to indicate that you are dragging a worksheet.
3. As you drag, a small down arrow appears, marking the place to which the worksheet(s) will be moved. When this marker is in the correct spot, release the mouse button, and the worksheet is moved to the place you indicated.

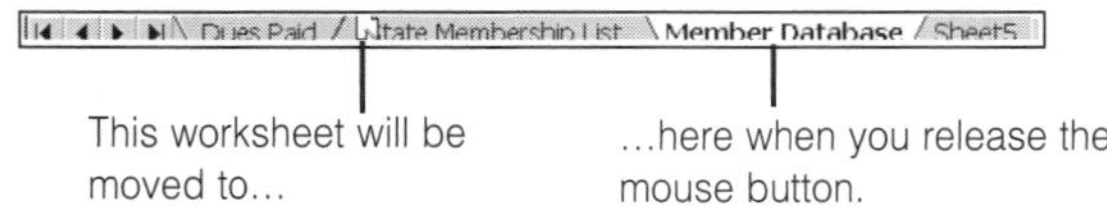

Move = just drag tab

You can move the worksheet into another open workbook if you like, although it takes a bit more work:

1. Select the worksheet(s) you want to move.
2. Open the Edit menu and select Move or Copy Sheet. The Move or Copy Sheet dialog box appears.

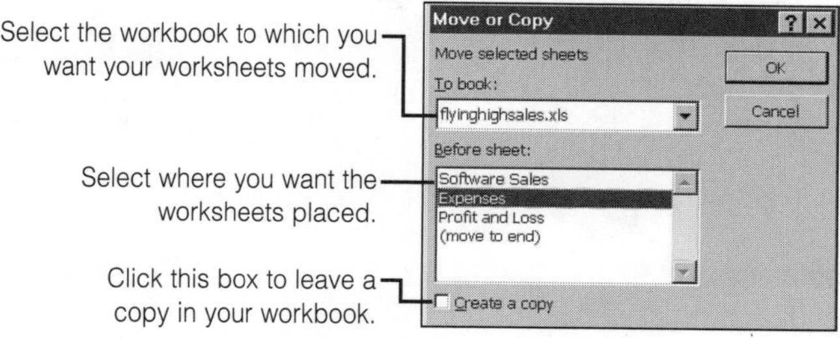

3. Select the name of the open workbook to which you want to move your worksheet(s) from the To book: drop-down list, or select new book to place it in a new file.
4. Select the sheet in front of which you want your worksheet(s) moved from the Before sheet: list.
5. Click OK.

Copying a Worksheet

Copy = press Ctrl and drag tab

After you spend a long time formatting and perfecting a particular worksheet, why start over from scratch when you need to create a worksheet that's similar? Instead, just copy it and change the necessary data. Follow these steps:

1. Select the worksheet(s) you want to copy.
2. Press and hold the Ctrl key as you drag the tab to its new location in the workbook. The mouse pointer changes to an arrow with a small sheet attached. The small plus sign indicates that you are copying a worksheet.
3. As you drag, a small down arrow appears marking the place to which the worksheet will be copied. When the marker is in the right spot, release the mouse button, and the worksheet(s) is copied to the place you indicated.

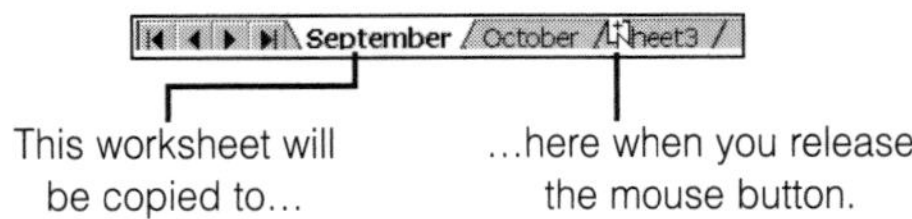

September
October
Sheet3
This worksheet will be copied to...
...here when you release the mouse button.

You can copy the worksheet into another workbook, using the Move or Copy Sheet command described earlier, but make sure you select the Create a Copy option.

Cheat Sheet

Using the Style Buttons to Format Numbers

1. Select the cell(s) you want to format.
2. Click the appropriate button on the Formatting toolbar.

Currency Style	$	$1,200.90, $(450.00)
Percent Style	%	11%, –15%
Comma Style	,	1,200.90

To increase/decrease the number of decimal places, click the appropriate button as many times as necessary:

Increase Decimal	+.0 .00
Decrease Decimal	.00 +.0

Using the Format Cells Dialog Box to Format Numbers

1. Select the cell(s) you want to format.
2. Open the Format menu and select Cells. The Format Cells dialog box appears.
3. Click the Number tab.
4. Select the format you want to use from the Category list. The default format style for that category is displayed in the Sample area.
5. Adjust the number of decimal places with the Decimal Places spin box.
6. If you want to include commas, select the Use 1000 separator option.
7. Select the style you want to use for negative values from the Negative Numbers list.
8. Click OK.

Using the Keyboard to Format Numbers

Currency with two decimals Style	Ctrl+Shift+$
Percent Style	Ctrl+Shift+%

27

Changing How Numbers Look

A number's appearance tells us a lot about its meaning. A number that's preceded by a dollar sign means *money*, while a number that's followed by a percent sign means *a percentage of something else.* Excel provides many number formats so that you can be sure the values in your worksheet tell the story you want them to.

In Chapter 22, you learned that you should enter numbers into the worksheet without any particular formatting. In this chapter, you'll learn how to format the numbers so they will look the way you want.

Basic Survival

Using the Style Buttons to Format Numbers

Some number formats seem to be used over and over, so Excel has provided quick access to them through the Style buttons on the Formatting toolbar:

Currency Style	$	$1,200.90, $(450.00)
Percent Style	%	11%, –15%
Comma Style	,	1,200.90

The quick way to format numbers!

To format your numbers, you can follow these steps before or after you enter the values into the cells:

1. Select the cell(s) you want to format. You can select multiple worksheets and select a range to format that same in all worksheets. See Chapter 26 for selecting multiple worksheets.
2. Click the appropriate button on the Formatting toolbar.

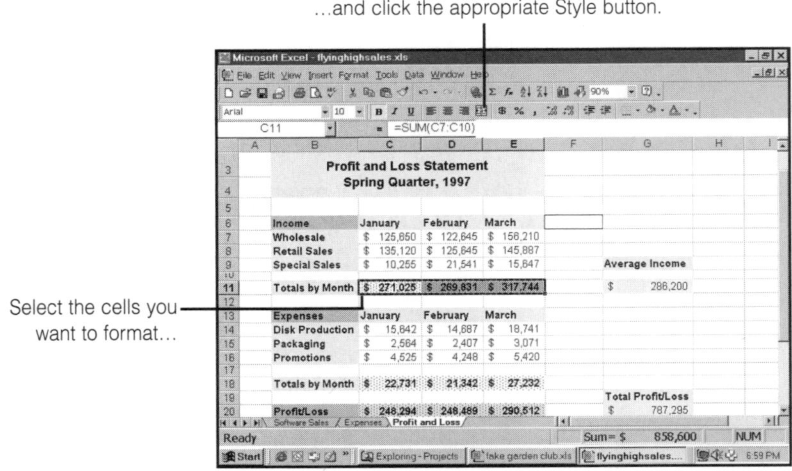

Notice that with the Currency and Comma styles, negative numbers are shown in parentheses. If you'd like to highlight them in red, or use a negative sign, use the Format Cells dialog box, as described in the "Beyond Survival" section.

Both the Currency and the Comma styles include two decimal places. To increase/decrease the number of decimal places, click the appropriate button as many times as necessary:

Increase Decimal	+.0 .00
Decrease Decimal	.00 +.0

Double-click the right side of column header to widen.

Remember as you're playing around with decimal places, that if a value is too large to be displayed within a cell, ###### is displayed instead. To widen a column to fit the data it contains, double-click on the right side of the column's header.

You can copy formatting from one cell to another as needed; see Chapter 30 for help. You'll also learn other nifty tricks in that chapter, including how to apply conditional formatting, so that, say, sales over 1,000 are highlighted.

Beyond Survival

Using the Format Cells Dialog Box to Format Numbers

If you want to use a format that's different than the standard Currency, Percent, and Comma styles, you need the help of the Format Cells dialog box. Follow these steps:

1. Select the cell(s) you want to format.
2. Open the Format menu and select Cells. The Format Cells dialog box appears.

Total control over how numbers look!

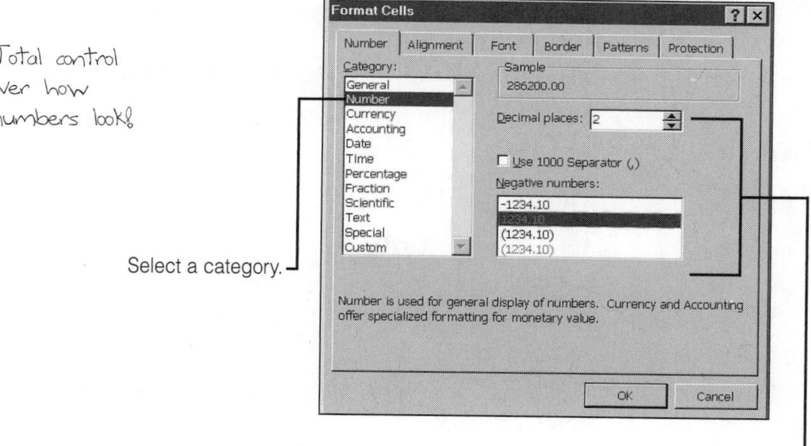

Crtl+Shift+ = formats currency at 2 decimals.

3. Click the Number tab.
4. Select the format you want to use from the Category list. The default format style for that category is displayed in the Sample area.
5. Adjust the number of decimal places with the Decimal Places spin box.
6. If you want to include commas, select the Use 1000 separator option.
7. Select the style you want to use for negative values from the Negative Numbers list.
8. Click OK.

Ctrl+Shift+% formats percent style.

Cheat Sheet

Changing the Font or Size of Text

1. Select the cell you want to change.
2. Select the font you want from the Font drop-down list [Arial] on the Formatting toolbar.
3. Select the size you want from the Font Size drop-down list [14].

Making Text Bold, Italic, or Underlined

1. Select the cell you want to change.
2. Click the appropriate button on the Formatting toolbar, or use the appropriate keyboard shortcut.

Bold	B	Ctrl+B
Italic	I	Ctrl+I
Underline	U	Ctrl+U

28

Changing How Text Looks

A worksheet isn't all about numbers; it's about text, too. So, after entering your data and formatting your numbers, you want to make your text look good as well. This gives your worksheet a professional look.

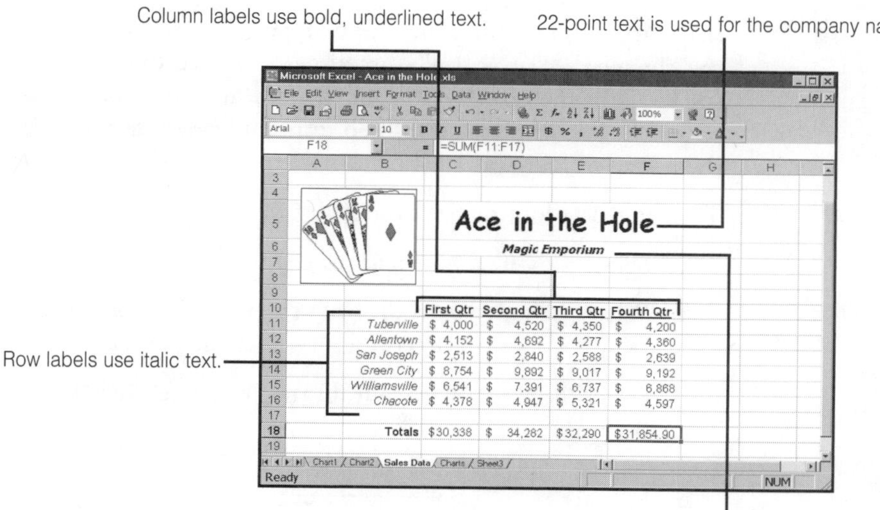

You can do a lot of things to change the look of text. You can change the font (typeface) and the text size, and add other attributes such as bold, italic, or underline. You can even change the color of text. You'll learn how to make all these changes in this chapter.

Basic Survival

Changing the Font or Size of Text

font = typeface

A font or typeface is a set of characters with a similar style. The type of font you choose tells your reader a bit about your attitude—a font can say “professional,” or “fun and carefree.” The figure shows a sample font you might try.

The fonts your system has depends on the applications you’ve installed. Office 2000 comes with a series of fonts, but you can use fonts from other applications as well. Each application contributes its own fonts to the Windows “pool.”

One point = 1/72 inch

In addition to changing the font or typestyle of your text, you can change the size as well. Sometimes you need to change the size to make the text readable, or to cram more data onto a page. The size of text is measured in points; one point is equal to 1/72nd of an inch.

To change the font or size of text:

1. Select the cell(s) you want to change.
2. Select the font you want from the Font drop-down list Arial on the Formatting toolbar.
3. Select the size you want from the Font Size drop-down list 14 .

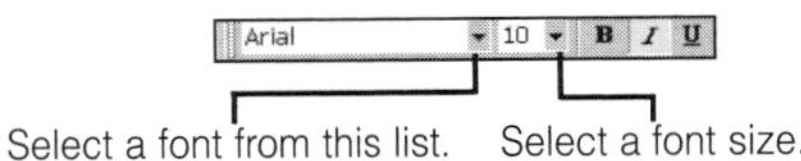

Select a font from this list. Select a font size.

After formatting some text, you can copy the formatting to other cells; see Chapter 30 for help.

You can change the default font.

When you type text into a cell, it’s normally formatted in Arial font, 10-point type. To change this default, select Tools, Options and click the General tab. Select a standard font and font size to be used as your default for every new spreadsheet you create. Click on OK and exit Excel. When you re-enter Excel, all new spreadsheets you create are formatted with the new settings.

Making Text Bold, Italic, or Underlined

Another way you can change how text looks is to add text attributes such as bold, italic, or underline. Follow these steps:

1. Select the cell(s) you want to change.
2. Click the appropriate button on the Formatting toolbar:

Bold	B
Italic	I
Underline	U

You can also use the following keyboard shortcuts to add text attributes:

Bold	Ctrl+B
Italic	Ctrl+I
Underline	Ctrl+U

The underline style you get when you use the Underline button is the standard, single underline. If you want to use double-underline or an accounting underline style (which leaves more space between the text and the underline), then you need the help of the Format Cells dialog box, described in the "Beyond Survival" section.

Beyond Survival

Using the Format Cells Dialog Box to Change Text

If you need to make several changes to text, why not make them in one simple step? It's easy with the Format Cells dialog box:

1. Select the cell(s) you want to change.
2. Open the Format menu and select Cells. The Format Cells dialog box appears.
3. Click the Font tab.

Format/Cells: do everything in 1 step!

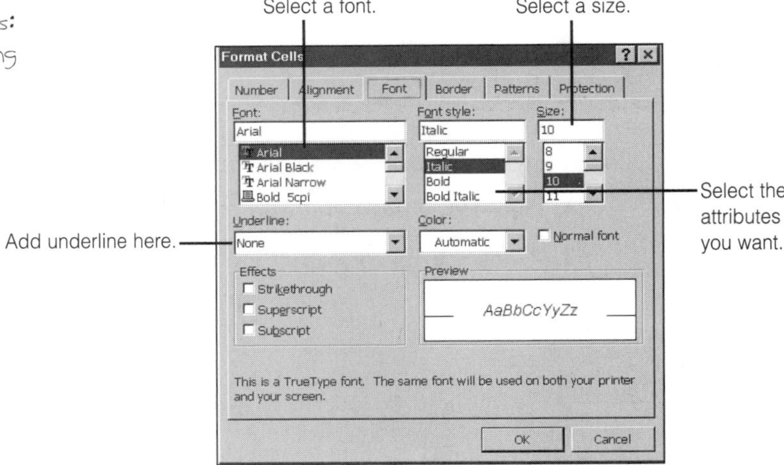

4. Make your selections. To change the font, select one from the Font list. To change the size of text, select a size from the Size list. Select the attributes you want from the Font style list. You can add different types of underline by selecting a style from the Underline drop-down list.

5. Click OK.

You can use the Font tab to apply other attributes as well, such as strikethrough, superscript, and subscript. You can even apply color to text if you like.

You probably also noticed that the Format Cells dialog box has a lot of tabs, which you can use to change your cells in other ways, such as when adding a border or shading. You'll learn how to do these things in upcoming chapters.

Changing the Color of Text

One neat thing you can do to text to make it look more attractive is to colorize it. Of course, if you don't have a color printer, the color only appears onscreen. It may, however, affect the shade of gray that's used when printing, so even without a color printer, color is fun to play around with:

Try this!

1. Select the cell(s) you want to change.
2. Click the down arrow on the Font Color button on the Formatting toolbar and select the color you want to apply. (If the toolbar is absent, select View, Toolbars, Formatting.)

After changing the color of text in a cell, you may also want to change the color of the background. Excel calls this *cell shading*, and you'll learn how to apply it in Chapter 30.

Cheat Sheet

Changing Data Alignment

1. Select the cell you want left-aligned, right-aligned, or centered.
2. Click the appropriate button on the Formatting toolbar:

   Align Left

   Center

   Align Right

Merging Text Across Columns

1. Select the cell that contains the data, *and* the cells over which you want the data centered.
2. Click the Merge and Center button on the Formatting toolbar.

Rotating Data and Changing Its Vertical Alignment

1. Select the cell you want to change.
2. Open the Format menu and select Cells. The Format Cells dialog box appears.
3. Click the Alignment tab.
4. To slant text, drag the pointer in the Orientation display box.
5. To change the vertical alignment of the data, select the option you want from the Vertical drop-down list.
6. Click OK.

29

Changing the Alignment of Data

Normally, when you type text into a cell, Excel aligns it to the left side of the cell. Numbers, on the other hand, are normally aligned to the right. You can realign your data to the left, right, or center, as needed. For example, you might want to center your column labels and right-align your row labels. You can even center a label (such as a worksheet title) across several cells. And, when needed, you can slant data (such as labels) to make more data fit in a tighter space.

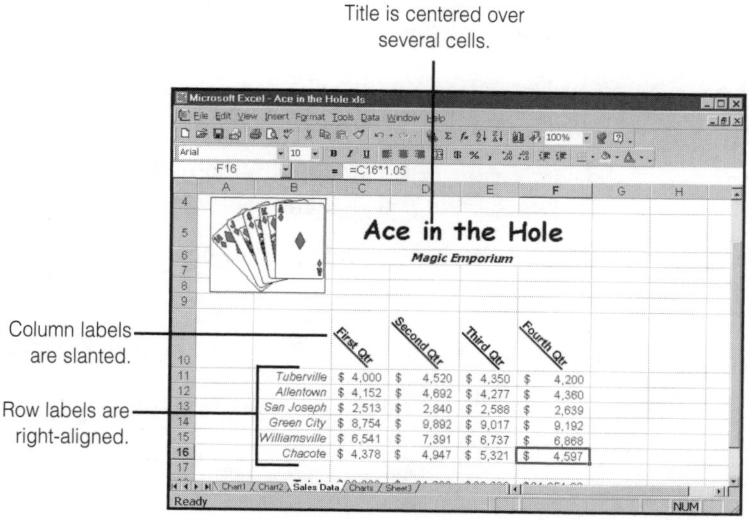

Text is left-aligned; numbers are right-aligned.

Title is centered over several cells.

Column labels are slanted.

Row labels are right-aligned.

Microsoft Excel - Ace in the Hole.xls

Ace in the Hole

Magic Emporium

	First Qtr	Second Qtr	Third Qtr	Fourth Qtr
Tuberville	$ 4,000	$ 4,520	$ 4,350	$ 4,200
Allentown	$ 4,152	$ 4,692	$ 4,277	$ 4,360
San Joseph	$ 2,513	$ 2,840	$ 2,588	$ 2,639
Green City	$ 8,754	$ 9,892	$ 9,017	$ 9,192
Williamsville	$ 6,541	$ 7,391	$ 6,737	$ 6,868
Chacote	$ 4,378	$ 4,947	$ 5,321	$ 4,597

Basic Survival

Changing Data Alignment

To change the alignment of data in cells, use the buttons on the Formatting toolbar:

1. Select the cell(s) you want to left- or right-align or center. If you want to center a title over several cells, see the next section for help.
2. Click the appropriate button on the Formatting toolbar:

   Align Left

   Center

   Align Right 

If you want to slant text or change its vertical alignment, see the "Beyond Survival" section for help. In addition, you can add an indent to text in a cell, if you like. This might be helpful if you have a list of items beneath a heading. Indenting the items can help give order to the list. To add the indent, select the cell and click the Add Indent button. To remove the indent, click the Decrease Indent button instead.

Merging Text Across Columns

If you have a title you want to center across your columns of data, you can, but it takes a bit more work:

1. Select the cell that contains the data, and the cells over which you want the data centered.
2. Click the Merge and Center button on the Formatting toolbar.

Try this with all worksheet titles!

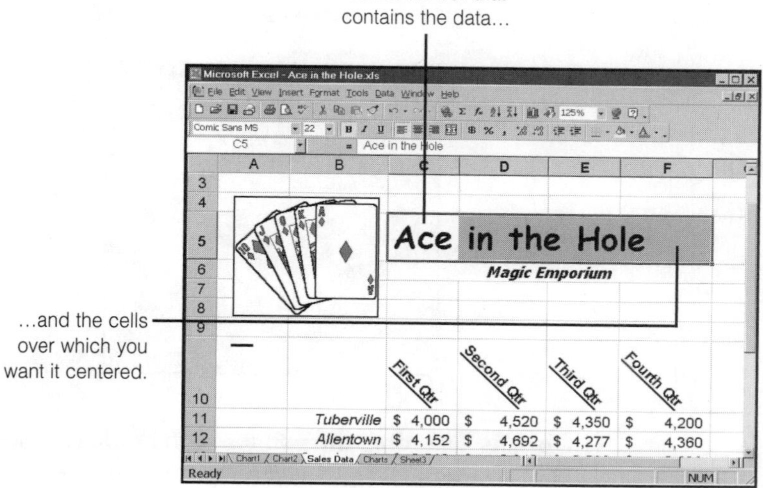

Beyond Survival

Rotating Data and Changing Its Vertical Alignment

Slanting text is relatively easy, and it can add a new dimension to your worksheet labels. Another effect you might want to try is changing the vertical alignment of text. Normally, text is aligned at the bottom of the cell, but you can center it or place it at the top of the cell if you like. Here's how to slant text or change its vertical alignment:

Cool effect!

1. Select the cell(s) you want to change.
2. Open the Format menu and select Cells. The Format Cells dialog box appears.
3. Click the Alignment tab.

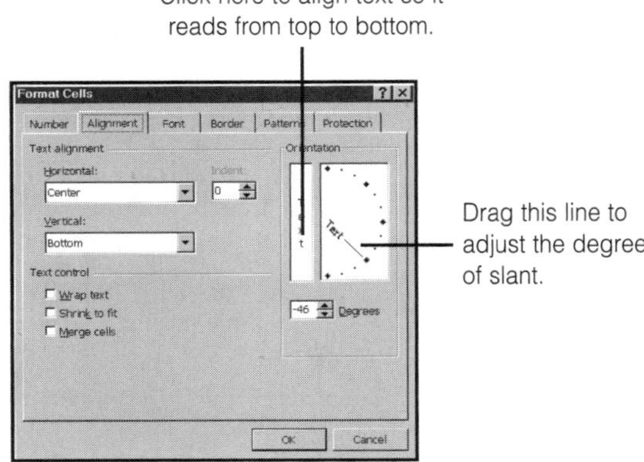

4. To slant text, drag the pointer in the Orientation display box, or use the Degrees spin box to enter the degree of slant you want. To align text so that it reads from top to bottom, click the vertical text box to the left of the Orientation display.
5. To change the vertical alignment of the data, select the option you want from the Vertical drop-down list.
6. Click OK.

You might be curious about some other options in the Format Cells dialog box. Use the Wrap text option when typing a lot of text (such as a paragraph) into a single cell. Use the Shrink to fit option to adjust the size of text so that it fits exactly in the cell, even if the cell's width is later adjusted. Use the Merge Cells option to merge the data in the first selected cell with the other selected cells (provided those cells are blank).

Cheat Sheet

Adding Borders to Cells

1. Select the cell around which you want to place a border.
2. Open the Format menu and select Cells. The Format Cells dialog box appears.
3. Click the Border tab.
4. Select the border style (and color) you want.
5. Click inside the border area to draw the borders you want.
6. Click OK.

Adding Shading to Cells

1. Select the cell you want to shade.
2. Open the Format menu and select Cells. The Format Cells dialog box appears.
3. Click the Patterns tab.
4. Select the color you want from the Color area.
5. If desired, select a pattern from the Pattern drop-down list.
6. Click OK.

Removing All Borders

1. Select the cell around which you want to remove a border.
2. Press Ctrl+Shift+_.

30

Changing How Cells Look

So far, you've learned how to change the appearance of your data—how to change the format of numbers and text to suit your needs. In this chapter, you'll learn how to change the look of the cell itself—the cell's outline (border) and its fill color (shading).

Basic Survival

Adding Borders to Cells

Gridlines don't print unless you request them to print.

As you enter data into a worksheet, each cell is defined by a faint gray line. These gridlines, as they are called, do not print; they are there to help you enter data into each individual cell. (Actually, you *can* print the gridlines if you want, but they don't appear very dark, and they print everywhere—even in areas that do not contain data.)

If you want to highlight certain areas of your worksheet, you can place a border around them. Here's how:

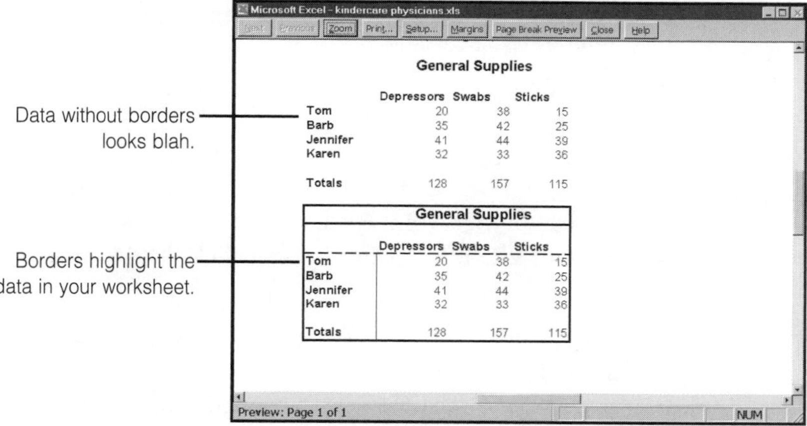

Data without borders looks blah.

Borders highlight the data in your worksheet.

1. Select the cell(s) around which you want to place a border.
2. Open the Format menu and select Cells. The Format Cells dialog box appears.

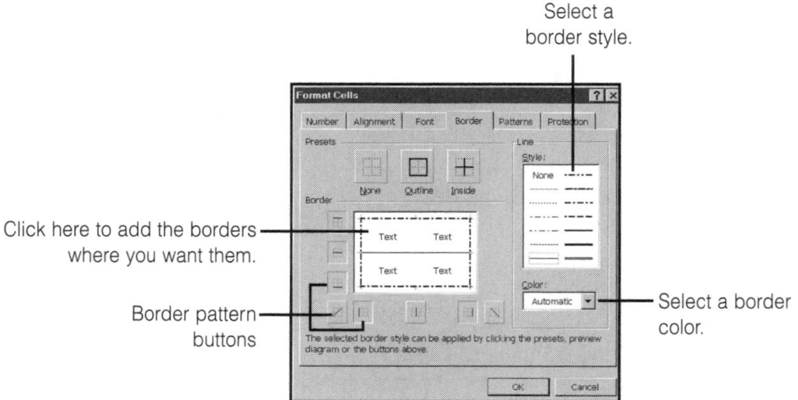

3. Click the Border tab.
4. First, select the border style you want from the Style box. If you want to add a colored border, select the color you want.
5. Then click inside the Border area to draw the borders you want. You can save time by clicking on a border pattern button. To remove a border line that appears in the Border area, just click it.
6. Click OK.

Remove all borders by pressing Ctrl+Shift+_.

You can use the Borders button on the Formatting toolbar to add certain border patterns quickly. Try it and see! For example, to remove borders from a cell or group of cells, click the down arrow on the Borders button and click the "No Border" pattern.

To see what your worksheet will look like when printed, you can click the Print Preview button, or turn off gridlines from the display by opening the Tools menu, selecting Options, clicking the View tab, and unchecking Selecting the Gridlines option.

Adding Shading to Cells

Choose the best shading.

If you want to really set off a group of cells, fill them with a pattern (shading). This shading prints in various shades of gray, unless you use a color printer. Cells can be filled with color at full or partial strength, so you can achieve the exact effect you desire.

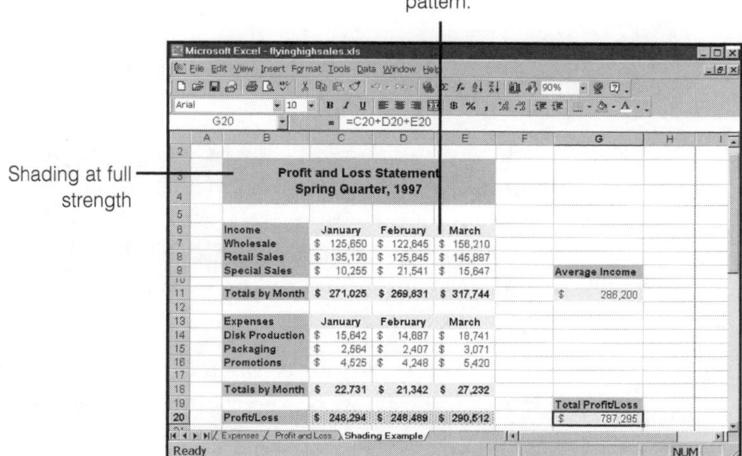

To add shading to your cell(s), follow these steps:

1. Select the cell(s) you want to shade.
2. Open the Format menu and select Cells. The Format Cells dialog box appears.

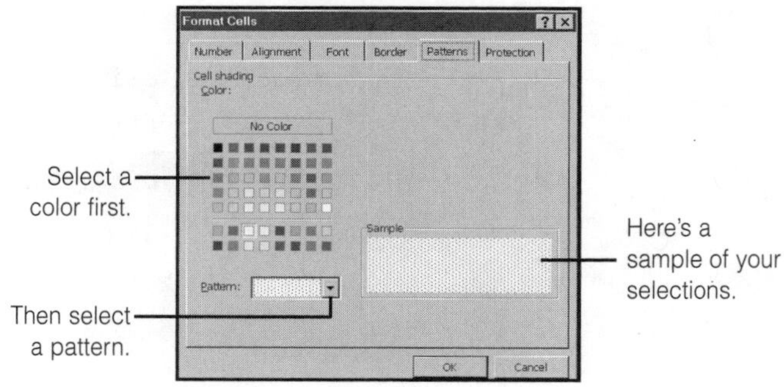

3. Click the Patterns tab.
4. Select the color you want from the Color area. A sample is displayed in the Sample area.
5. If you don't want to add the color you selected in step 4 at full strength, select the pattern you want to use from the Pattern drop-down list. This pattern is drawn on top of your initial color by using the color black; if you want the pattern to have a color (to achieve a more subtle effect), select it from the Pattern drop-down list as well.
6. Click OK.

You can add shading more quickly by using the Fill Color button on the Formatting toolbar. Click the arrow on this button and select a color from the list to add that color at full strength. To remove a color, choose the No Fill option. If you want to add the color shown on the button, just click the button itself.

After adding shading to your cells, you may want to adjust your text color. Click the arrow on the Font Color button and select the color you want.

Beyond Survival

Using AutoFormat

If trying to select your own border and shading patterns seems a bit too much to handle, why not let Excel make the selections for you? With AutoFormat, it's easy:

1. Select the cell(s) that contain the data you want to format.

Let AutoFormat do the work.

2. Open the Format menu and select AutoFormat. The AutoFormat dialog box appears.
3. Select the format you want to apply from those samples shown. Scroll down to see all the AutoFormat samples.

4. If you want to exclude certain elements of the table format you selected, click Options. The AutoFormat dialog box expands.
5. Select the options you want to exclude by clicking them to turn them off.
6. Click OK to apply the formats to the selected cells.

If you decide you hate the AutoFormat you just applied, click the Undo button to remove it. You can also select the same area as before and use the Format/AutoFormat command to remove it; just select None from the AutoFormat list.

Removing Formatting

You've learned a lot about how to change the look of cells (and your data) in the last few chapters. Here's how to get rid of your changes without deleting the data itself:

1. Select those cells that have formats you want to remove.
2. Open the Edit menu and select Clear.
3. Select the option you want from the cascading menu that appears:
    - All. Removes the data and the formats (and any comments) from the cell.
    - Formats. Removes only the formats from the cell.
    - Contents. Removes the data from the cell.
    - Comments. Removes any attached notes from the cell.

Copying Formats

After you get a cell looking exactly the way you want, you can copy its formatting to other cells and save yourself some time. You can copy the number and text formats as well as borders and shading. Follow these steps:

Use this to copy formats!

1. Click the cell that contains the formats you want to copy.
2. Click the Format Painter button .
3. Drag over the cells to which you want to copy. The cells are automatically reformatted to match the formats of the original cell.

If you want to copy the formats of your cell to several *groups* of cells, double-click the Format Painter button in step 2. Then click on or drag over as many groups of cells as you like. When you want to turn Format Painting off, click the Format Painter button again.

Cheat Sheet

Inserting Rows and Columns

1. To insert a single row, click in the row *below* where you want the new row inserted.

   To insert a new column, click in the column to the *right* of where you'd like the new column to appear.

   To insert multiple rows or columns, select the number of rows or columns you want to insert.
2. Open the Insert menu and select Rows or Columns.

Removing Rows and Columns

1. Select the rows or columns you want to remove.
2. Open the Edit menu and select Delete.

Inserting Cells

1. Select the range of cells you want to shift.
2. Open the Insert menu and select Cells.
3. Select Shift Cells Right or Shift Cells Down.
4. Click OK.

Wrapping Text in Cells

1. Type the first line of text into a cell. Press Alt+Enter and type a second title line.
2. Press Enter to insert the text into the cell.

Merging Cells Using Formats

1. Select the title cell and the surrounding cells in which you want your title placed.
2. Open the Format menu and select Cells.
3. Click the Alignment tab.
4. Click the Merge Cells option. Select any additional options.
5. Click OK.

31

Inserting and Removing Cells, Rows, and Columns

What happens if you enter two columns of data, only to find that you need to insert a new column between them? Do you need to move one column of data over to the next column? Or do you have to start over completely?

Neither, as it turns out. With Excel, you can insert additional columns or rows at any time. When you do, Excel automatically shifts the appropriate data downward or to the right to make room for the new column or row. In addition, formatting from the row or column you select initially is copied to the inserted rows/columns. Also, cell references in your formulas are automatically adjusted whenever you add or remove rows or columns (unless they are absolute references, which you'll learn about in Chapter 34).

Basic Survival

Inserting Rows and Columns

You can insert a single row or column, or multiple rows/columns, in one step. When inserting a column, the new column is placed to the left of the column you select; when inserting a row, the new row is placed above the row you select. Follow these steps to insert a new column or row:

New column on left, new row above.

1. To insert a single row, click in the row below which you want the new row inserted. To insert a new column, click in the column to the right of where you'd like the new column to appear.

   To insert multiple rows or columns, select the number of rows or columns you want to insert. For example, if you select rows 3 and 4, then two new rows will be inserted above row 3. To select multiple rows or columns, click and drag over their row/column headings.

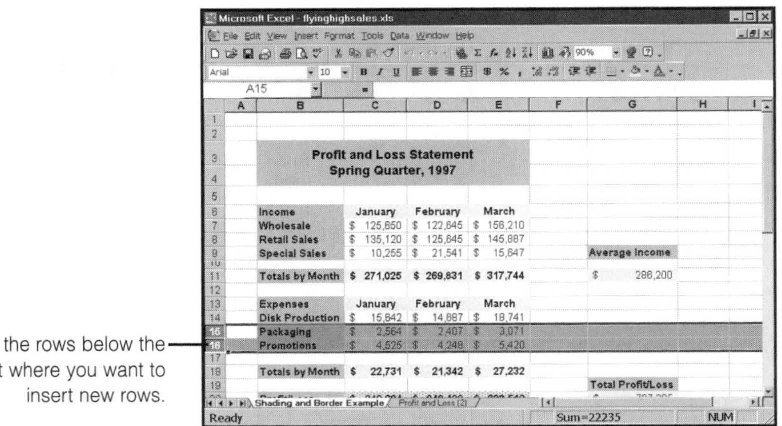

Select the rows below the point where you want to insert new rows.

2. Open the Insert menu.
3. Select Rows or Columns.

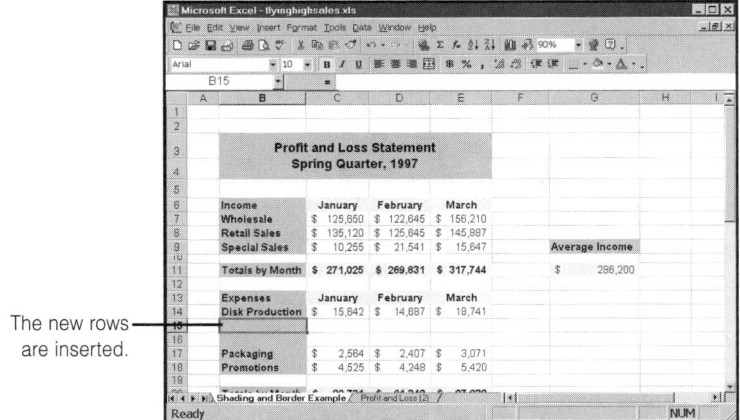

The new rows are inserted.

Beyond Survival

Removing Rows and Columns

Be careful when removing rows or cols.

When you remove rows or columns, the data in those rows/columns is removed as well, so be careful when performing this task. After a row is removed, data is shifted up to fill the gap. If a column is removed, then data is shifted to the left. Follow these steps:

1. Select the rows or columns you want to remove.
2. Open the Edit menu and select Delete. Excel removes the rows/columns you selected and shifts the data to fill the gap.

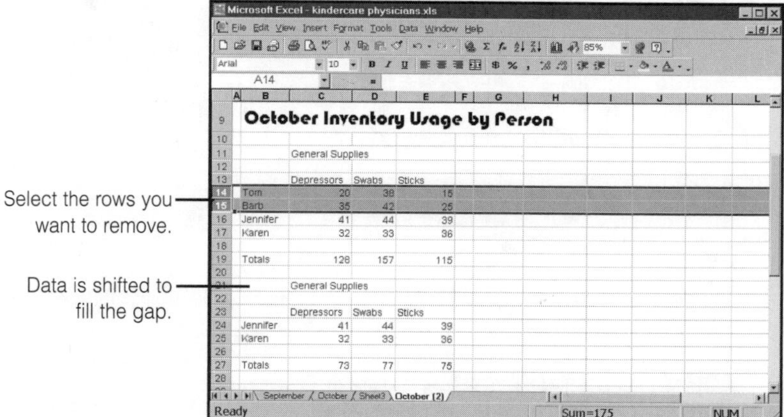

Inserting Cells

Inserting cells shifts existing data.

Besides inserting rows or columns, you can also insert cells. You might do this if you started entering data in the wrong cells, for example. When you insert cells into a worksheet, data is shifted downward or to the right to make room for the new cells. Follow these steps:

1. Select the range of cells you want to shift.
2. Open the Insert menu and select Cells. The Insert dialog box appears.

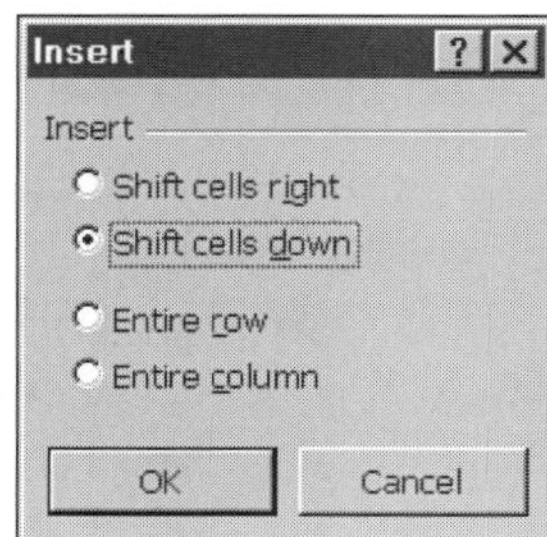

3. Select Shift Cells Right or Shift Cells Down.
4. Click OK.

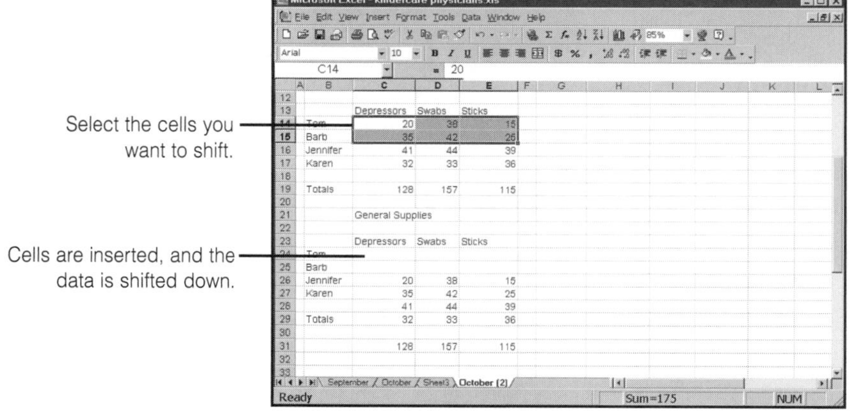

Merging Cells

If you like, you can merge the data in one cell with surrounding blank cells, forming one big cell with which you can work. You might do this when creating a two-line title for your worksheet, as shown in the figure. With the single merged cell, you can quickly change the font, point size, fill, border, and other attributes of the cell. You can also change the alignment of your title, centering it within the large, merged cell. Here's how to merge cells:

Merging cells is good for worksheet titles.

1. Type the first line of data you want to use as a title into a cell.
2. If you want a two-line title, press Alt+Enter to move to the second line. Now type the second line of text.

3. Press Enter to place the two lines of text into one cell.
4. Select the title cell and the surrounding cells in which you want your title placed.
5. Open the Format menu and select Cells. The Format Cells dialog box appears.
6. Click the Alignment tab.
7. Click the Merge Cells option. Select any additional options you want, such as adjusting the Vertical alignment.
8. Click OK.

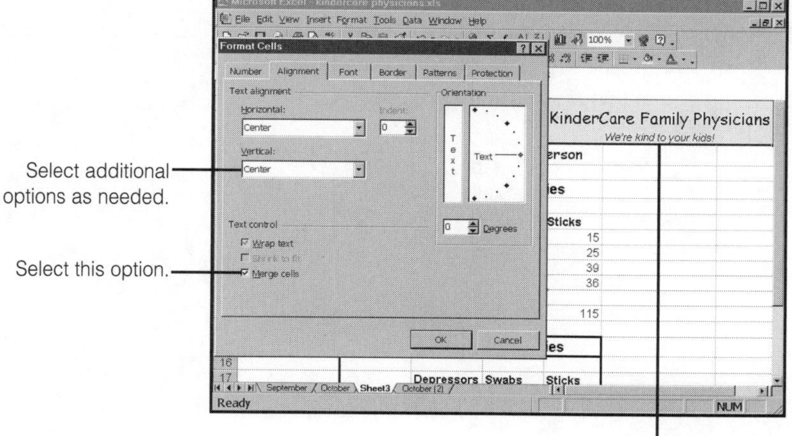

To format each line of the title separately as shown in the figure, format the cell as usual, making the selections you want for the top line. Then click in the merged cell and select the text for the bottom line. Choose the font, point size, and other attributes you want.

If you want to merge your title into surrounding cells and center it at the same time, you can do that quickly by selecting the cells you want to use, and clicking the Merge and Center button, as explained in Chapter 29.

Cheat Sheet

Changing Column Width and Row Height

1. To adjust the width/height of several columns/rows, select the columns or rows you want to change.
2. Move the mouse pointer to the edge of the column or row heading until the mouse pointer changes to an arrow.
3. Drag the mouse to adjust the size of the row or column.
4. Release the mouse button.

Adjusting Cells to Fit Their Data

1. To adjust the width of several columns, select them now.
2. Move the mouse pointer to the right edge of the last column heading until the mouse pointer changes to an arrow.
3. Double-click the mouse button.

32

Changing the Size of Cells

#######
means that the column isn't wide enough.

When you enter data into the worksheet, the width of the cells does not automatically adjust to fit that data. As a result, some of your longer text labels may be cut off; large numbers are replaced with #######. In such cases, you need to adjust the width of your cells manually.

The height of a cell is adjusted automatically.

If text can't fit in a cell, it's cut off.

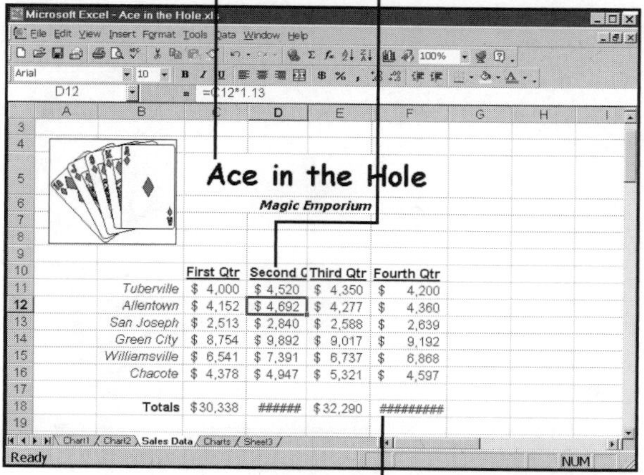

If a number can't fit, pound signs are displayed instead.

It's rare that you'll need to adjust the height of a cell, because it's automatically adjusted to fit the point size of your data. However, if you adjust the height manually, you can add additional whitespace between rows of data as needed.

Basic Survival

Changing Column Width and Row Height

You can change the width of one or more columns in a few simple steps:

1. If you want to adjust the width of several columns so that they are all the same, select those columns by dragging over their headings.
2. Move the mouse pointer to the right edge of the last column heading of the selection. The mouse pointer changes to a two-headed arrow with a line through it.

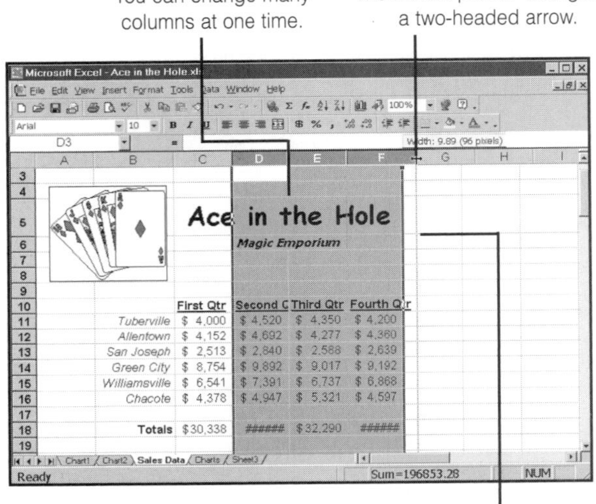
You can change many columns at one time.
The mouse pointer changes to a two-headed arrow.
Drag the edge of the column to change its size.
Ace in the Hole
Magic Emporium

3. Drag the mouse to the right to make the column wider; drag to the left to make the column smaller. As you drag, a small box appears, displaying the exact width of the column, in standard-sized characters.
4. Release the mouse button, and the column are adjusted.

To adjust the row height instead, follow these same steps, but place the mouse pointer at the bottom edge of the last row heading in the selection. Drag downward to make the row taller, or upward to make them skinnier.

You can quickly size a column (or columns) so that the width is the exact size of your data. For more information, see the next section.

Beyond Survival

Adjusting Cells to Fit Their Data

Double-click edge of column to make your column wide enough!

Instead of manually adjusting the widths of your columns, you can have Excel adjust them for you so that your data fits just right. Here's how:

1. If you want to adjust the width of several columns so that they are all the same, select those columns now by dragging over their headings.
2. Move the mouse pointer to the right edge of the last column heading of the selection. The mouse pointer changes to a two-headed arrow with a line through it.
3. Double-click the mouse button, and the columns you selected are automatically adjusted.

Cheat Sheet

Entering Formulas

1. Click the cell in which you want the result to appear.
2. Type an equal sign (=).
3. Begin typing the formula. When you need to enter the address of a cell, click the cell.
4. Press Enter or click the Enter button ✓.

Editing a Formula

1. Click the cell that contains the formula you want to edit.
2. Click Edit Formula button =. The Formula bar expands.
3. Make your change and click the Enter button ✓ or press Enter when you're through.

Calculating a Quick Sum Without Entering a Formula

1. Drag over the cells that contain the numbers you want to add.
2. The total of the values in the cells you selected appears in the status bar at the bottom right of your screen. To display the average, minimum, maximum, or count, right-click the status bar and select the option you want from the shortcut menu.

Other Formula Tricks

- To view formulas rather than results, press Ctrl+` (the accent key next to the 1 key).
- To stop formulas from recalculating automatically, open the Tools menu and select Options. Click the Calculation tab. Select the Manual option and click OK. When you're ready to recalculate your formulas, press F9.

Creating Formulas

After entering all your data, you're probably anxious to start analyzing it. One way you might do that is with formulas. For example, if you want to see whether you sold more widgets in April than in March, you can compare the totals of both columns. To calculate each column total, you enter a formula that adds up the values of the cells in that column. The total then appears in the cell, rather than the formula you typed. The formula appears in the Formula bar when the selector is in the cell.

Result—not formula—appears in cell.

The formula you enter is displayed in the Formula bar.

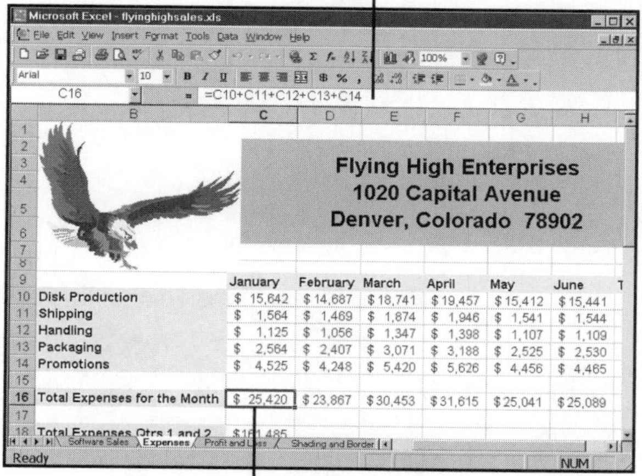

The result of the formula is displayed in the cell.

Basic Survival

What Is a Formula?

A formula is a calculation that computes a value. You can use formulas to compute all sorts of things, from sales totals to expenses to income to net profit. A simple formula begins with

Formulas begin with =.

an equal sign (=), followed by a cell address and a mathematical operator, and another cell address, like this:

=C2+B2

Valid mathematical operators include:

Operator	Example	Description
+	=C2+B2	Adds the values in cells C2 and B3.
–	=C2-B3	Subtracts the value in cell B3 from the value in cell C2.
*	=C2*B3	Multiplies the value in cell C2 by the value in cell B3.
/	=C2/B3	Divides the value in cell C2 by the value in cell B3.
^	=C2^3	Raises the value in cell C2 to the 3rd power.

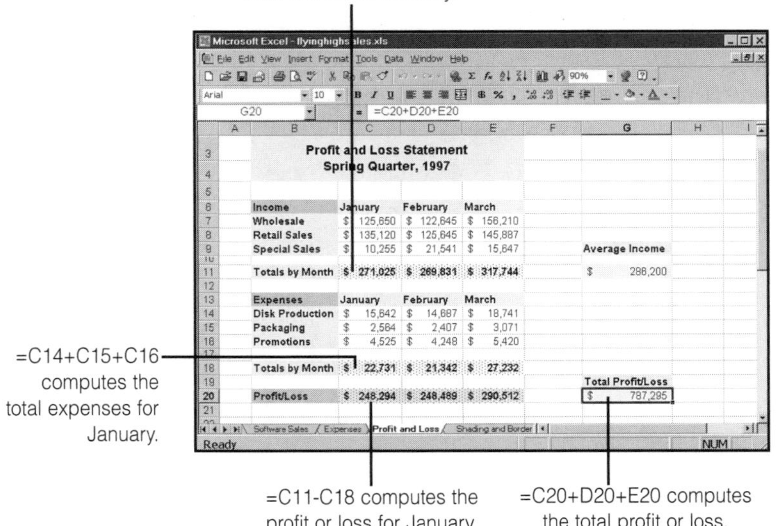

=C7+C8+C9 computes the total income for January.
=C14+C15+C16 computes the total expenses for January.
=C11-C18 computes the profit or loss for January.
=C20+D20+E20 computes the total profit or loss.
Profit and Loss Statement
Spring Quarter, 1997

You should keep several things in mind when using formulas:

- Formulas are recalculated automatically. If you change the value in a cell that's used in a formula, the result of the formula is recalculated for you.
- Even if you set up a cell to display only two decimal places, the result of a formula may contain more decimal places than what's displayed. If you were to total up such a column, you might be off by a penny or more because of undisplayed decimal places. To display the decimal places so your total will match what's displayed, click the Increase Decimal button as needed.
- Another way to fix the problem of undisplayed decimal places is to use a function (utility) to round the values displayed in the column to two decimal places. For example, you could round 146.9875 to 146.9900, and 345.9876 to 345.9900, then display just the values 146.99 and 345.99. This way, what's displayed (146.99 and 345.99) is equal to the values that are being added by the computer (146.9900 and 345.9900), so your totals won't be off.
- Do not refer to the cell in which you type the formula in the formula itself. For example, in cell C2, do not type the formula =C2+C3=C4. This is called a *circular reference*, and it prevents the formula from being calculated.
- If an error message appears in a cell, make sure that you have not tried to divide by zero or a blank cell.
- If you plan on referring to the same cell in several formulas, give that cell a range name, as explained in Chapter 23. You can then use the name in the formula, as in **=INCOME*.90**.
- You can use your row and column labels to enter formulas. For example, if you have several columns, beginning with January, February, and so on, and the row labels Wholesale and Discounted Sales, then you can enter a formula, such as **=January Wholesale+February Wholesale**. In order to use labels in your formulas, you must turn that option on. Choose Tools, Options, then

on the Calculation tab, select the Accept Labels in Formulas option.

- You can display the same information in two places using a simple formula. For example, type **=C12** in any cell to display the contents of cell C12.
- Arguments in parentheses are calculated first (basic rules of mathematics apply here, too). For example, the formulas (2+4)/2 and 2+4/2 return different results because the formula in the second example divides 4 by 2 (for a result of 2) rather than the sum of 2+4 by 2 (for a result of 3). Be careful to use parentheses to tell Excel which action (or argument) to perform first to ensure that your calculations are correct.
- Formulas are calculated in a particular order (based on the operators you use). Exponential calculations are performed first, then multiplication and division, and finally addition and subtraction. Excel uses the same order of operations you learned in your mathematics classes.

Entering Formulas

You can enter a formula in one of two ways. You can type the whole thing, cell addresses and all, or you can use the mouse to help you select the cell references you need.

To enter a formula manually:

1. Click the cell in which you want the result to appear.
2. Type an equal sign (=).
3. Type the formula. As you do, it appears in the Formula bar. You should keep several things in mind:
   - Don't use spaces in formulas.
   - Don't use commas in formulas, either.
   - Be sure to close all parenthetical references, meaning that each time you type an open parenthesis (you must close with the close parenthesis) .
4. Press Enter or click the Enter button. If you want to cancel the formula while you're entering it, click the Cancel button or press Esc.

Click a cell to add it to a formula.

To enter a formula using the mouse, follow these steps:

1. Click the cell in which you want the result to appear.
2. Type an equal sign (=).
3. Begin typing the formula. When you need to enter the address of a cell, click the cell instead, and Excel enters the address into the formula for you. If you want to enter the address of a cell that's in another worksheet, change to that worksheet and click the cell.
4. Press Enter or click the Enter button. If you want to cancel the formula while you're entering it, click the Cancel button or press Esc.

Beyond Survival

Editing a Formula

To make changes to a formula, follow these steps:

1. Click the cell that contains the formula you want to edit.
2. Click Edit Formula button [=]. The Formula bar expands.
3. Make your change and click the Enter button [✓] or press Enter when you're finished.

Double-click to edit a formula.

To edit the formula quickly, just double-click the cell.

Controlling When Formulas Are Calculated

Normally, formulas are recalculated when you change the data to which they refer. If you have a lot of formulas in a worksheet and you're updating a lot of data, you may want to turn this option off, and then recalculate the formulas one time, after you've made your changes. Follow these steps:

1. Open the Tools menu and select Options. The Options dialog box appears.
2. Click the Calculation tab.
3. Select the Manual option and click OK.

Remember this!

When you're ready to recalculate your formulas, press F9.

Cheat Sheet

Copying Formulas with Relative Addresses

When formulas are copied, cell references are automatically adjusted, based on the column or row to which they are copied. (This is known as relative addressing.) For example, if you copy the formula =(D11+D12)-D14 from cell D15 to cell F15, Excel automatically adjusts the formula to =(F11+F12)-F14, because you copied the formula from column D to column F.

Relative addressing automatically updates row and column references for you, which is a useful tool if you want to sum several columns of numbers. Rather than create a new formula for each column, create the first formula, then copy it to the remaining columns.

Absolute Versus Relative Cell References

If you don't want a cell reference to be adjusted when you copy a formula, insert dollar signs into the cell address or press F4 to make it an absolute cell reference. Absolute addressing forces that part of a formula to remain unchanged when it is copied from one location to another.

For example, if you want to create a formula that refers to Total Income, and you do not want that cell address to change based on the formula's location in the worksheet, you enter the formula as follows:

=F20/$F$22

Now, if you copy this formula to a new location, the portion of the formula that contains the absolute cell reference is not changed to reflect its new position in the worksheet. For example, if you copy this formula to a neighboring cell in column G, it is changed to:

=G20/$F$22

34

Copying Formulas

Formulas, just like other data in your worksheet, can be copied. For example, suppose you had just entered a formula for calculating the sales total for the first quarter. You could then copy the formula to other cells and calculate the totals for the second, third, and fourth quarters without manually recreating the same formula for each of the columns containing your quarterly sales data.

Basic Survival

Copying Your Formulas to Another Location

When you copy a formula, Excel automatically adjusts the cell references so that the new formula makes sense. This is known as relative addressing. For example, suppose you have this formula in cell B14:

=B10+B11+B12

If you copy the formula to cell C14 (same row, different column), it is changed to:

=C10+C11+C12

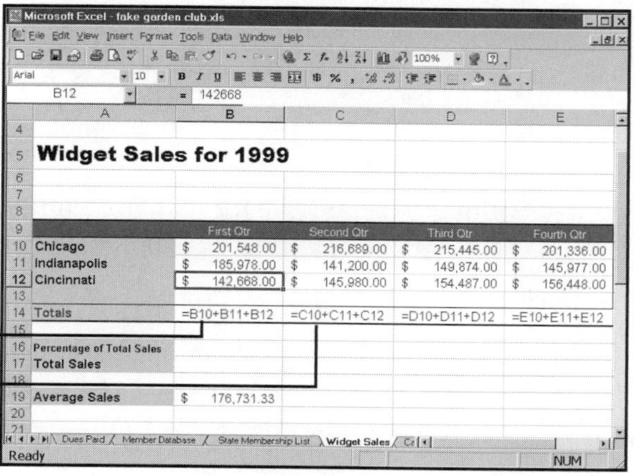

Original formula

When you copy the formula in cell B14, cell references are adjusted automatically.

The formula is adjusted to fit column C, where it has been copied. If you had copied the formula to a different row, such as cell B16, then the formula would have been changed to this:

=B12+B13+B14

Notice how the cell references were adjusted by two rows, because the formula was copied two rows down, from B14 to B16.

Beyond Survival

Absolute Versus Relative Cell References

Earlier in this chapter, you learned that when you copy a formula, the cell references in that formula are automatically adjusted. For example, if you copy a formula from cell B20 to C20, the formula is adjusted by one column:

Original formula: B12/B21

Copied formula: C12/C21

The reason the formula is adjusted is because it uses relative cell references—cell references that are relative to the particular row or column in which they appear. When relative cell references are copied, they are adjusted to fit their new column or row.

To stop cell addressing from being adjusted, use absolute cell references.

Sometimes when you copy a formula, you don't want a particular cell reference to be adjusted because it refers to a *specific* cell, column, or row. For example, suppose you want to compute the percentage of the total sales for each quarter in 1999. If cell B14 contains the total sales for quarter 1, and the total sales for the year is in cell B17, you might use this formula to compute your percentage:

=B14/B17

But if you copy the formula to column C (to compute the percentage for quarter 2) you end up with this formula:

=C14/C17

Because the total sales amount is stored in cell B17 (and cell C17 is blank), the formula would result in an error. But Excel is *supposed* to adjust formulas automatically, using *relative cell references* (cell addresses that are adjusted relative to the row or column to which they are copied).

So how do you get Excel to stop the automatic adjustment? By using absolute cell references. Absolute cell references are references that Excel does not adjust when you copy them to a new location. To make a cell reference absolute, you add a dollar sign ($) in front of the row and/or column heading, as in:

Use $ in absolute cell references.

=B14/$B$17

You can type the dollar signs yourself, or just press F4 after entering the cell address into the formula. When you copy your new formula to cell C16, it becomes:

=C14/$B$17

Press F4 to make a cell absolute.

Only the first cell reference is adjusted, because it is the relative cell reference. And this is exactly how you want the formula to be adjusted—you want to take the total sales for the second quarter (in cell C14) and divide it by the total sales for the year (in cell B17). Copy the formula to cell D16, and it becomes:

=D14/$B$17

Once again, only the first cell reference is adjusted, so this formula will take the sales total for quarter 3 and divide it by total sales for the year.

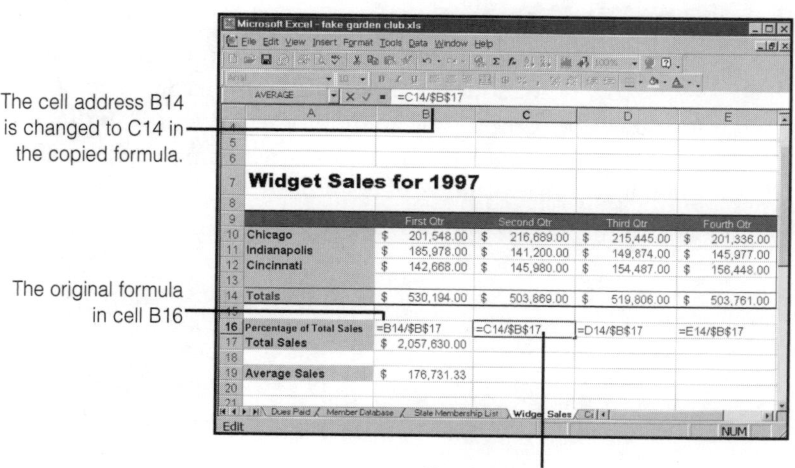

Sometimes you need to use a mixed cell reference, which combines relative and absolute cell references in one cell address, as in:

=$B4*2.14

Because the dollar sign $ is in front of only the column letter, only that part of the cell address will be adjusted if you copy the formula to some other cell. For example, if you enter the original formula into cell B6 and then copy it to cell C10, it is changed to:

=$B8*2.14

Why? Well, because of the dollar sign, the column letter B is not adjusted. But the row number (4 in the original formula) is adjusted by four rows, because you copied the formula to a cell four rows down. So row 4 in the original formula becomes row 8 in the copied formula. *The formula was adjusted to the row to which it was copied, but not the column (column C)*. If you use this original formula in cell B6 instead:

=B$4*2.14

and copy it to cell C10, it is changed to:

=C$4*2.14

In this case, because the $ appears in front of the row number, the row is not adjusted, but the column is. So, because you copied the formula one column over, column B in the original formula becomes column C. The row number (4) stays the same, because of the $ in front of it.

Cheat Sheet

Entering a Function with the Function Wizard

1. Click the cell in which you want to enter the function.
2. Click the Edit Formula button [=].
3. Select the function you want to enter from the Functions list. For a more complete list, select More Functions.
4. Enter the arguments required by the formula.

Using AutoSum

1. Click the cell in which you want to enter the =SUM() function.
2. Click the AutoSum button [Σ].
3. AutoSum inserts the =SUM() function, using the range of the cells closest to the cell you picked in step 1. If AutoSum has guessed wrong, you can select the range you really want by dragging over it.
4. Press Enter.

35

Using Functions in Your Formulas

Functions are ready-made formulas. For example, rather than enter this formula to compute a sum:

=C2+D2+E2+F2

Ranges are shown using a colon.

You can use this function:

=SUM(C2:F2)

Each function begins with an equal sign, just as any other formula, followed by the name of the function, and then parentheses. Inside the parentheses are the function's arguments (the information the function needs to perform its calculation). If a function uses more than one argument, they are separated by commas. Most functions, however, need only the address of a group of cells as an argument, which you type as a range address, like this:

=AVERAGE(B10:B22)

In this case, the function AVERAGE computes the average of the values in the range B10 to B22. Now, rather than actually type the range B10:B22, you can type a range name such as FEB_SALES, like this:

=AVG(FEB_SALES)

If the range B10 to B22 had been given the name FEB_SALES, then both these formulas would do the same thing. It's just that remembering and using range names is a lot easier than typing range addresses. (See Chapter 23 for more info on how to name a range.)

Some functions require something other than a range address or a range name. In addition, some functions take more than just one argument. For example, the function, PMT (), calculates the amount of a loan payment based on the total amount borrowed, the number of payments over the life of the loan, and the interest rate. Don't worry about having to know everything about each and every function. If you're having trouble entering a particular function (or you're not even sure which function to use), you can get help from the Function Wizard, as explained in the "Basic Survival" section.

Basic Survival

Common Functions

Here's a list of the more common functions (actual cell references, such as C2:E2, are used for example purposes only):

Function	Example	Description
AVERAGE	=AVERAGE (C2:E2)	Computes the average of the values in cells C2 through E2.
COUNT	=COUNT (C2:E2)	Counts the number of cells in the range C2 to E2 that contain numbers and not text.
COUNTA	=COUNTA (C2:E2)	Counts the number of cells in the range C2 to E2 that contain numbers or text.
IF	=IF(C2>= 500,C2*.2,0)	Calculates a 20% bonus only if the value in cell C2 is greater than or equal to $500.
MAX	=MAX (C2:E2)	Finds the maximum value in the range C2:E2.
MIN	=MIN(C2:E2)	Finds the minimum value in the range C2:E2.

Function	Example	Description
PMT	=PMT(.0725/ 12,360,225000)	Calculates the monthly payment on a 30-year loan of $225,000 at 7.25%.
	=PMT(.0525/ 12,60,,15000)	Calculates the monthly deposit needed to save $15,000 in five years (60 payments) with an interest rate of 5.25%.
SUM	=SUM(C2:E2)	Calculates the total of the values in the range C2:E2.

Entering a Function with the Function Wizard

To enter a function, follow these steps (don't worry, the Function Wizard will help you):

1. Click the cell in which you want to enter the function.
2. Click the Edit Formula button [=].
3. Select the function you want to enter from the Functions list. For a more complete list, select More Functions.
4. Enter the arguments required by the formula. (Required arguments appear in bold type.) To select a range of cells, click the Collapse Dialog button, select the range, then click the Collapse Dialog button again. If you need help with a function, click the Office Assistant button.

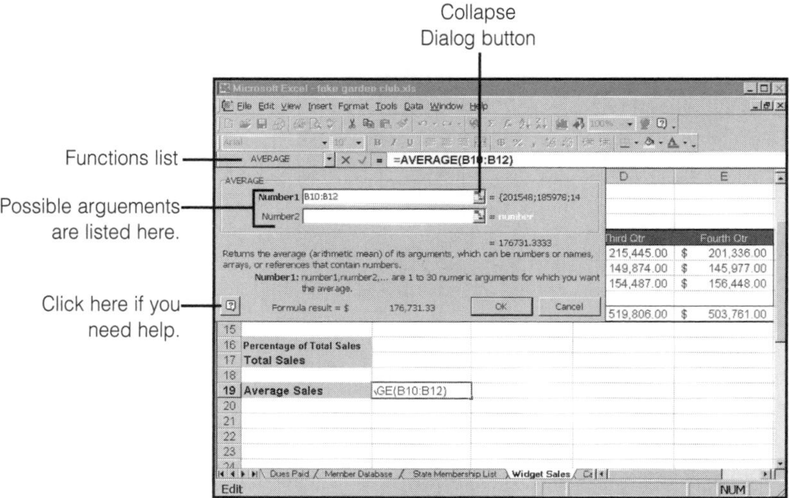

Beyond Survival

Using AutoSum

One of the functions you'll use most often is =SUM(), which calculates the total of the values in a particular range. Excel knows this, so it has provided a quick and easy way for you to enter a =SUM( ) function. Follow these steps:

Use the AutoSum button to enter = SUM() function.

1. Click the cell in which you want to enter the =SUM( ) function.
2. Click the AutoSum button [Σ].
3. AutoSum inserts the =SUM() function, using the range of the cells closest to the cell you picked in step 1. If AutoSum has guessed wrong, you can select the range you really want by dragging over it.
4. Press Enter.

If you don't think you'll have to correct the range address that AutoSum uses, you can bypass that step by double-clicking the AutoSum button in step 2. You don't need to press Enter or anything else; AutoSum enters the complete =SUM( ) function for you.

Cheat Sheet

Printing Column and Row Labels

1. Open the File menu and select Page Setup.
2. Click the Sheet tab.
3. To repeat column labels, click the Collapse Dialog button in the Rows to repeat at top text box, then select the rows that contain the column labels you want to repeat.

   To repeat row labels, click the Collapse Dialog button in the Columns to repeat at left text box, then select the columns that contain the row labels you want to repeat.
4. After making your selection, click the Collapse Dialog button again.
5. Click Print.

Adjusting Page Breaks

1. Open the View menu and select Page Break Preview.
2. Perform any of the following:
   - To move a break, drag it to its new location.
   - To remove a break, drag it off the screen.
   - To insert a new break, place the cursor in the proper cell, then open the Insert menu and select Page Break.
3. After making your changes, open the View menu and select Normal.
4. Click the Preview button, and if everything looks okay, click Print to print it.

36

Printing a Workbook

Back in Chapter 7, you learned how to print any Office document, including Excel workbooks. However, when dealing with a large workbook, there is some additional information you should know. For example, Excel enables you to choose which columns in your spreadsheet you want print on each page.

Basic Survival

Printing Column and Row Labels

Column labels are printed on page one, so if your worksheet is long, you may not know what each column of data represents on succeeding pages. The same thing happens if your worksheet is very wide; without the row labels, you can't tell what each row of data represents on page 2. So, how do you solve this problem? Simple. Just tell Excel to reprint the column and/or row labels on each page. Follow these steps:

1. Open the File menu and select Page Setup. The Page Setup dialog box appears.
2. Click the Sheet tab.
3. To repeat column labels at the top of every page (and the worksheet title, if you like), click the Collapse Dialog button in the Rows to repeat at top text box, then select the rows that contain the column labels you want to repeat.

   To repeat row labels along the left-hand side of every page, click the Collapse Dialog button in the Columns to repeat at left text box, then select the columns that contain the row labels you want to repeat.
4. After making your selection, click the Collapse Dialog button again. You're returned to the Page Setup dialog box.
5. Click Print.

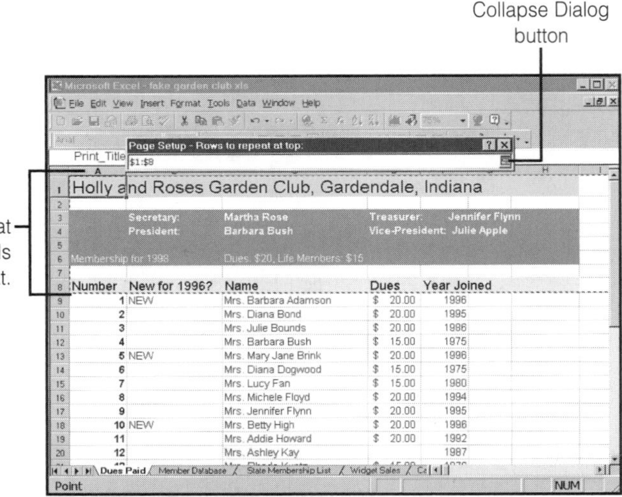

Don't repeat anything that's already part of the print area.

If the rows or columns you select to be printed on each page are also part of the designated print area, then they will print twice on each page. Because this is not exactly the effect you were looking for, you should redefine the print area so that these rows or columns that are repeated *are not* included. See the "Beyond Survival" section for help.

Adjusting Page Breaks

Normally when you print a worksheet, Excel determines where the page breaks should go. (A page break marks the end of one page and the beginning of another.) You can adjust these page breaks so that they occur in preferred places and your worksheet looks better when printed. Follow these steps:

Do this to adjust what prints on each page.

1. Open the View menu and select Page Break Preview. A welcome dialog box may appear; if it does, click OK to continue. (To fix it so this dialog box does not appear again, click the Do not show this dialog again option before you click OK.)
2. Your worksheet is displayed with the automatic page breaks. (They appear as dashed lines.) To adjust the breaks, perform any of the following:
   - To move a break, drag it to its new location.
   - To remove a break, drag it off the screen.

- To insert a new break, place the cursor in the proper cell, then open the Insert menu and select Page Break. When inserting a horizontal break between rows, move the cursor to column A, in the row below where you want the break to occur. To break the page between rows 21 and 22, click in cell A22. When inserting a break between columns, move the cursor to row 1, in the column to the right of the place where you want the break to occur. To break the page between columns L and M, then click in cell M1.

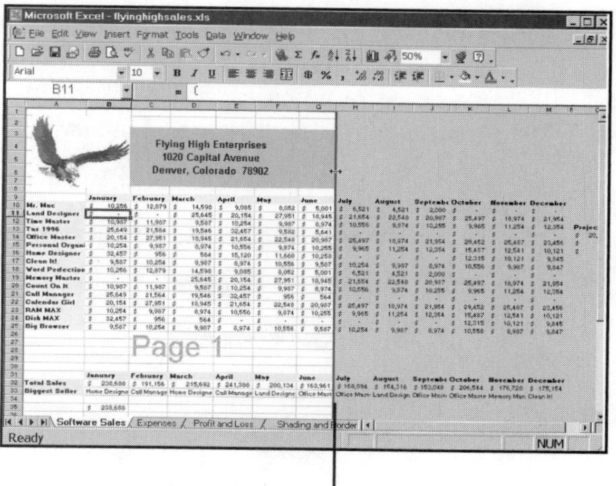

Drag the page break to change where it falls.

3. After making your changes, open the View menu and select Normal.
4. Click the Print Preview button, and if everything looks OK, click Print to print it.

Of course, there are other things you can do to affect the number of columns or rows that appear on each page of your worksheet. For example, you might want to adjust the column widths and page margins, print the worksheet in landscape orientation, and/or adjust the size of your data page exactly. (See the "Beyond Survival" section for help on this last one.)

Beyond Survival

Selecting a Print Area

Normally, when you print a worksheet, Excel prints the entire thing. When you issue the print command, Excel determines the *print area* (the data to be printed) by locating the cells that contain data and drawing a rectangle around them. You can adjust the print area as needed to print only the data you want.

If printing labels on each page, do this, too!

For example, if you opt to repeat the row or column labels on every page, you should redefine the print area so that these row and column labels are not included and therefore do not print twice.

In addition, when working with a large worksheet, you may decide to print only part of it. For example, if you're tracking expenses for an entire year, you might want to print just the figures for the first quarter: January, February, and March.

Follow these steps to change the print area:

1. Select the area of the worksheet you want to print.
2. Open the File menu and select Print Area.
3. Select Set Print Area.
4. Click the Print Preview button, and if you like what you see, click Print to print it.

If you decide later that you want to print the entire worksheet again, then follow these steps to remove the print area you defined:

1. Open the File menu and select Print Area.
2. Select Clear Print Area.

Adjusting a Worksheet to Fit a Page

If you're previewing a worksheet and you discover that it *almost* fits on a single page (or two, or three, and so on) you can tell Excel to shrink the text just a little, so that it fits the number of pages you specify—*exactly*. Follow these steps:

Cool idea!

1. Open the File menu and select Page Setup. The Page Setup dialog box appears. (If you're in Print Preview, click the Page Setup button to display the dialog box.)

2. Click the Page tab.

3. Enter the number of pages you want to print in the Fit to XX pages(s) wide by XX tall text boxes.

4. Click Print Preview.

5. If everything seems okay to you, then click Print to print the worksheet. If not, click Page Setup to return to the dialog box so you can make adjustments.

Cheat Sheet

Creating a Chart

1. Select the data you want to chart, and the column and row labels.
2. Click the Chart Wizard button on the Standard toolbar.
3. Select a Chart type, then a Chart sub-type. Click Next>.
4. In step 2, you can adjust the data range if needed, and change the data series from columns to rows. Click Next>.
5. In step 3, you make changes to the chart options such as adding a chart title, removing gridlines, and adding data labels. Go from tab to tab selecting the options you desire, then click Next> to continue.
6. Lastly, in step 4, you select where you want the chart to appear. Select the option you want and click Finish.

When to Use the Various Chart Types

Column Use this type of chart to compare the values of various items at a specific point in time.

Bar Similar to a column chart; use this type to compare values at the same point in time.

Line Use this type of chart to analyze trends, or values that change over time.

Area Similar to a line chart; use this type to emphasize the amount of change over time.

Pie Use this chart to show the relationship between categories.

37

Creating a Chart

After entering your data into the worksheet, you may decide to simply print it out. Or you may decide that, to better analyze its meaning, you need to chart your data.

A chart displays your data in a graphic format, which makes it easier (in theory, at least) to understand. There are many chart types you can use, from pie charts to column charts. In this chapter, you'll learn which chart type best fits your needs, and how to create it.

Basic Survival

The Parts of a Chart

Most charts have these things in common:

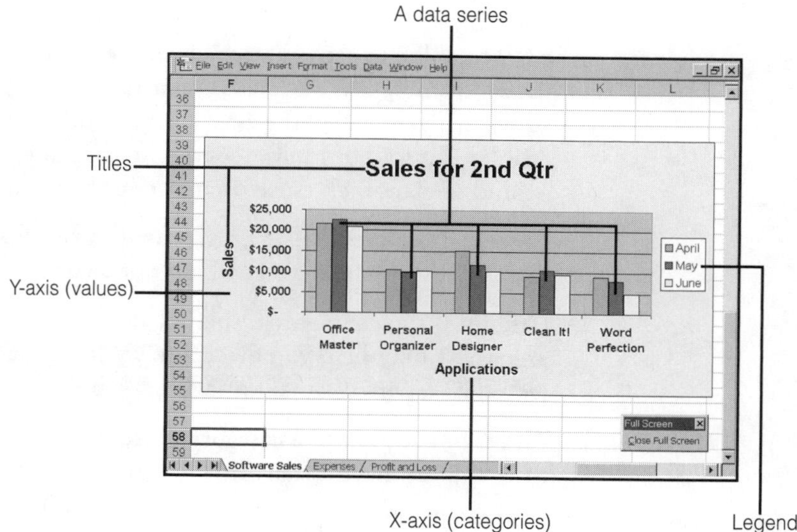

Data series apply to columns; categories apply to rows.

- Data series. Typically, each column in your worksheet represents a different data series. For example, if you have a column in your worksheet for 1997, 1998, and 1999 sales data, then you'll have three data series in your chart. Each data series is represented by a different color line, bar, or column in your chart. (If you use a pie chart, you can only have one data series.)
- Categories. Typically, each row in your worksheet corresponds to a different category. Using the earlier example of a worksheet with 1997, 1998, and 1999 sales data, you might break that down further into the categories: Eastern, Western, Midwestern, and Southern divisions. Each of these categories (or sales divisions, if you prefer) would be listed in a separate row in your worksheet. You can, by the way, change this logic and represent your data series in rows, and your categories in columns.
- Axis. A two-dimensional chart has two axes: the vertical or y-axis, and the horizontal or x-axis. Along the x-axis, you'll find your categories. (If your chart has more than one data series, they will be grouped together by category.) The value of each category is plotted against the scale shown in the y-axis. A three-dimensional chart has one additional axis, called the z-axis. The third dimension enables you to plot multiple series in each category behind one another, rather than group them side by side.
- Legend. Describes the data series used in the chart. You don't have to include a legend in your chart.
- Gridlines. Typically only displayed along the y or value axis, these lines help you determine the exact value represented by a particular column, line, or bar.
- Titles. In addition to a category (x-axis) and value (y-axis) title, you can have a chart title as well.

When to Use the Various Chart Types

The chart type you should select depends on the kind of data you're trying to graph, and the way in which you want to represent it. Here's a list of the major chart types Excel offers:

Column Use this type of chart to compare the values of various items at a specific point in time.

Each chart also can appear in 3D.

Bar Similar to a column chart; use this type to compare values at the same point in time.

Line Use this type of chart to analyze trends, or values that change over time.

Area Similar to a line chart; use this type to emphasize the amount of change over time.

Pie Use this chart to show the relationship between categories.

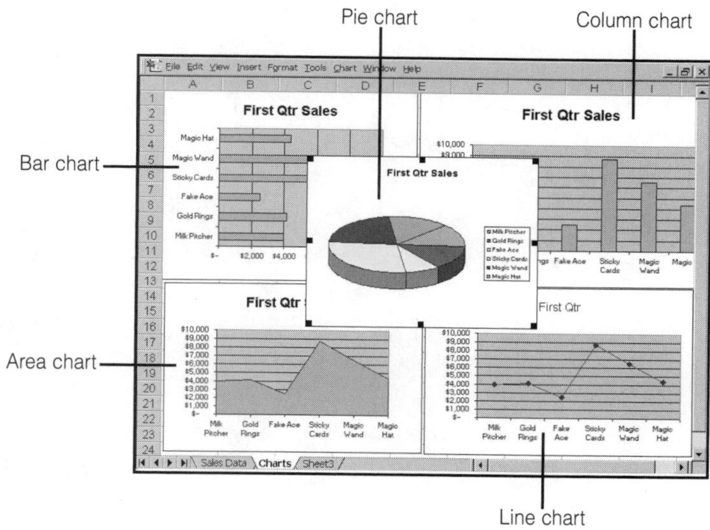

All the major chart types are available in 3D. You might prefer a 3D chart for charting data that includes several series, because the extra dimension helps your reader distinguish the difference in series values.

Creating a Chart

Charts are either embedded (treated as objects within the current worksheet), or placed on their own separate worksheets. Follow these steps to create either type:

1. Select the data you want to chart, and the column and row labels.
2. Click the Chart Wizard button on the Standard toolbar.

3. Select a Chart type, then a Chart sub-type. To preview what your selections will look like, click and hold the Press and hold to view sample button. Click Next>.

Preview the chart.

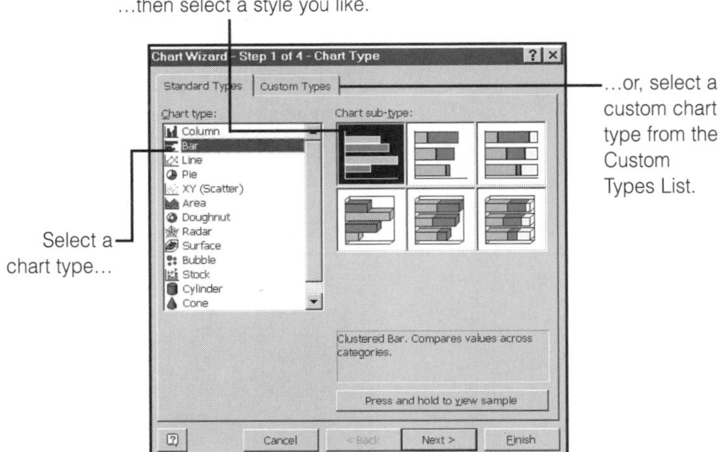

4. In step 2, you can adjust the data range if needed, and change the data series from columns to rows. The Series tab is used to input your axis labels, if for some reason they're not showing (for example, if you did not select your row and column labels when you selected your data earlier). When you finish making adjustments (if any), click Next>.

5. In step 3, you make changes to the chart options. On the Titles tab, type the titles you want to use for the chart and the x- and y-axes. The Axes tab enables you to turn off the labels for the x- or y-axes; the Gridlines tab controls the gridline display; the Legends tab controls the legend display. Data labels are text labels within the chart area itself that appear next to each column, line, or bar. A data table is a tiny worksheet that you can include with your chart to show the reader where the data is coming from. Go from tab to tab selecting the options you desire, then click Next> to continue.

6. Lastly, in step 4, you select where you want the chart to appear. If you select As new sheet, then type a name for the sheet in the text box (the new sheet is placed in front of the original Sheet 1). If you select As an object in, the chart is embedded in a spreadsheet. Select the sheet in which you want the chart placed, if different from the current sheet, then click Finish.

Now, if you don't want to customize your chart while creating it with the Chart Wizard, you can create a chart very quickly by selecting the data and pressing F11. Excel assumes that you want a column chart that appears on its own worksheet. Of course, that doesn't stop you from changing the chart type later on.

Beyond Survival

Changing How a Chart Looks

Even after you create your chart, you can still make many changes to it:

- To move an embedded chart (a chart that is on a spreadsheet), click it and handles (tiny black squares) appear. Click in a blank area of the chart and drag the chart where you want it, then release the mouse button.
- To resize an embedded chart, position the mouse pointer over a corner (it changes to a two-headed arrow). Drag the corner outward to make the chart larger, or inward to make it smaller.
- To rename a chart sheet, double-click the sheet tab, such as chart1, and type a new chart name, then press Enter.
- To make changes to the chart's appearance, use the Chart toolbar, which appears when you click once on the chart if the toolbar is missing, select View, Toolbars, Chart. Basically, you select the item you want to change by either clicking it or selecting it from the Chart Objects drop-down list. Then you click the Format Object button to display a dialog box in which you can make your changes. This table should help you out with the Chart toolbar:

Use Chart toolbar to chg parts of chart.

Button	Button Name	Description
Chart Area	Chart Objects	Lists all the objects in a chart, such as the chart title, axes, and so on.
	Format Object	Click here to format the chart part you've selected.
	Chart Type	Use this button to change the type of chart.
	Legend	This button hides/displays the legend.
	Data Table	This button hides/displays the data table.
	By Row	Use this button to select your data series by rows.
	By Column	Use this button to select your data series by columns.
	Angle Text Downward	This angles the selected text downward.
	Angle Text Upward	This angles the selected text upward.

You can also use the buttons on the Formatting toolbar to change a chart part. For example, if you select the Value Axis, you can click one of the Style buttons (such as the Comma Style button) to change the format of the numbers used on the y-axis. If you select the Category Axis, you can use the Formatting toolbar to change the color, font, and size of the x-axis labels, among other things.

Remember that each part of a chart is treated as an object, which means that it acts independently from the others. This enables you to format each part differently. It also enables you to move each part by dragging it to the desired location. For example, you can click and drag the chart title, legend, and even the entire plot area to adjust their positions.

When you click on any data series in an embedded chart, Excel's Range Finder outlines the data in the worksheet in blue, green, or purple.

If data is changed in the worksheet, all charts that use that data are automatically updated.

PART 4

PowerPoint 2000

Anyone who has ever given a talk in front of a large group of people knows how important it is to have visual aids that entice, entertain, and impress your audience. With PowerPoint, you can quickly and easily create the visual materials you need to give a professional looking presentation.

In this part, the following topics are covered:

- Taking a Look Around
- Editing the Sample Slides
- Inserting, Deleting, and Rearranging Slides
- Adding New Text to a Slide
- Changing the Look of Text
- Changing the Look of Your Presentation
- Viewing Your Slide Show

Cheat Sheet

Understanding the PowerPoint Screen

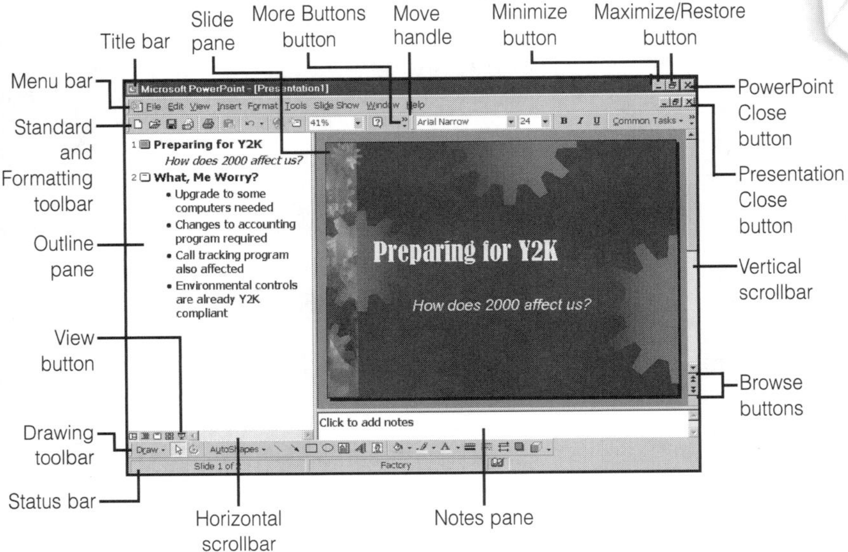

- PowerPoint has many specialized toolbars.
- The Presentation window is where you enter text and graphics.
- Use the View buttons to switch between the different views available.
- The Status bar tells you the number of the slide on which you are working.

38

Taking a Look Around

When you first start PowerPoint, it presents you with a dialog box in which you select whether you want to:

- Create a new presentation using the AutoContent Wizard. This option most often, because it enables you to select a presentation type and sit back as the AutoContent Wizard creates a complete presentation, with sample text and graphics.
- Start a new presentation by selecting a design template. You might select this option if you want to create a presentation from scratch, adding your own slides one at a time, but you'd like to select a design theme to help them all look the same.
- Start a new presentation from scratch. Selecting this option gets you a single, blank slide. Talk about work!
- Open an existing presentation. Here, you can open a presentation you've already saved and then make changes to it.

No matter which option you choose, eventually you'll be shown the PowerPoint window. Here you'll make the necessary changes to the sample text (if you used the AutoContent Wizard), add and delete slides, and perfect your presentation. In this chapter, you'll learn the basics you need to use PowerPoint: the parts of the PowerPoint window, how to get around your presentation, and how to change the display.

Basic Survival

Understanding the PowerPoint Screen

The elements of the PowerPoint screen are as follows:

- **Title bar** Displays the name of your document.
- **Window controls** With the Minimize, Maximize/Restore, and Close buttons, you can control the size of the window in which you work. The PowerPoint screen has two sets of buttons: one set controls the PowerPoint window, while the other set controls the window in which the presentation is displayed.
- **Menu bar** This bar contains the PowerPoint menus. To open a menu, click on it. For example, to open the File menu, click on the word File. A list of commands appears; to select one, click on it. Initially, only the commands you use most often are displayed. To expand the menu, click the down arrow at the bottom of the menu.

Can display more toolbars.

- **Toolbars** PowerPoint has many specialized toolbars you can use to accomplish specific tasks. Initially, the Standard, Formatting, Common Tasks, and Drawing toolbars are displayed. To display other toolbars, open the View menu, select Toolbars, and then select the one you want to display. The toolbar that is already displayed appears with a check mark in front of its name. Also, at first, the Standard and Formatting toolbars share one row. To access any button that's not displayed, click the More Buttons button. You may also want to move a toolbar onto a separate row by dragging it by its move handle.

Use browse btns to chg fm slide to slide.

- **Slide pane** This is where you enter the text, graphics, and charts that make up your presentation.
- **Outline pane** Here you can rearrange the outline of the presentation.
- **Notes pane** This is where you can enter notes for your presentation.
- **Scrollbars** Use these to scroll the onscreen contents to view data that is not currently displayed.

- **Browse buttons** The browse buttons are located under the vertical scrollbar. You can use them to quickly jump from slide to slide. You'll learn more about the browse buttons later in this chapter.
- **View buttons** To the left of the horizontal scrollbar are the view buttons, which you can use to change your view of your presentation. You'll learn more about this feature later in this chapter.
- **Status bar** This bar displays the status of your presentation. Here, you can see the number of the slide on which you're currently working, the total number of slides in the presentation, and the name of the design template (if any).

Moving from Slide to Slide

If you used the AutoContent Wizard to create your new presentation, then it contains several slides. (If you used a design template or if you started from scratch, your presentation has only one slide in it right now. To add more slides, see Chapter 40 for help.)

After your presentation contains more than one slide, you can perform any of the following to move from slide to slide (depending on the view you're using—see the "Beyond Survival" section for a description of each view):

- In the Slide pane, click the Previous Slide or the Next Slide button, located under the vertical scrollbar.
- In the Slide pane, drag the scroll box on the vertical scrollbar, and as you do, a pop-up tool tip displays the slide number. When the slide number you want appears, release the mouse button.
- In the Outline pane, click a slide's number to change to it.
- In Slide Sorter view, click on a slide or use the arrow keys to change to the slide you want. If the slide is not displayed, use the vertical scrollbar.

Beyond Survival

Changing Views

PowerPoint offers many views in which you can work on your presentation. If you've just created a new presentation, you were placed in Normal view. Normal view is best for most work since it provides three panes in which you can perform common tasks. Use the Slide pane to make changes to a slide; use the Outline pane to quickly rearrange slides; use the Notes pane to enter notes for your presentation.

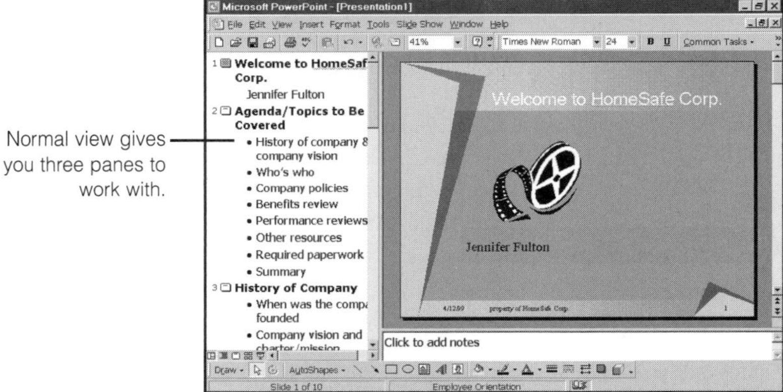

Normal view gives you three panes to work with.

To change to Normal view, click the Normal View button.

Next is Outline view. This view is best to use when organizing the content of your presentation. To switch back to Outline view at any time, click the Outline View button.

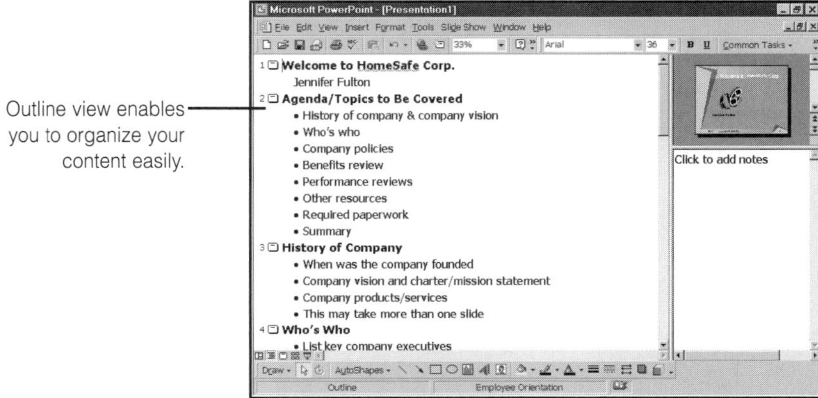

Outline view enables you to organize your content easily.

Slide view works best when you're adding or changing text, graphics, or charts on a single slide and you want to maximize the Slide window. To change to Slide view, click the Slide View button [Slide View button icon].

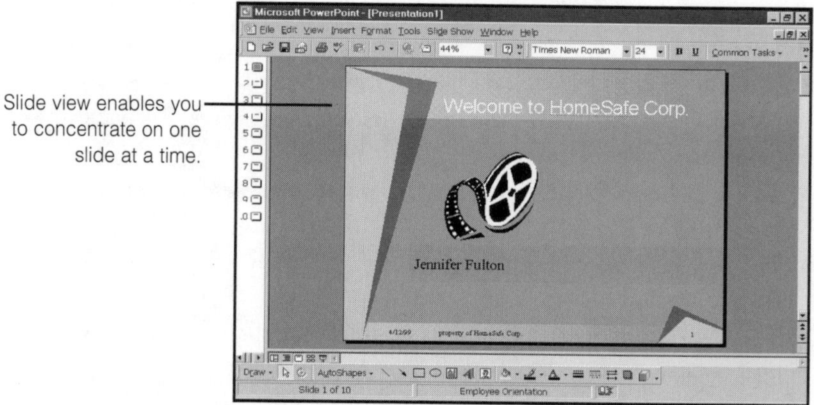

Slide Sorter view enables you to change the order of your slides easily. In this view, slides are displayed as small thumbnails, enabling PowerPoint to display nine slides at one time. To switch to Slide Sorter view, click the Slide Sorter View button [Slide Sorter View button icon].

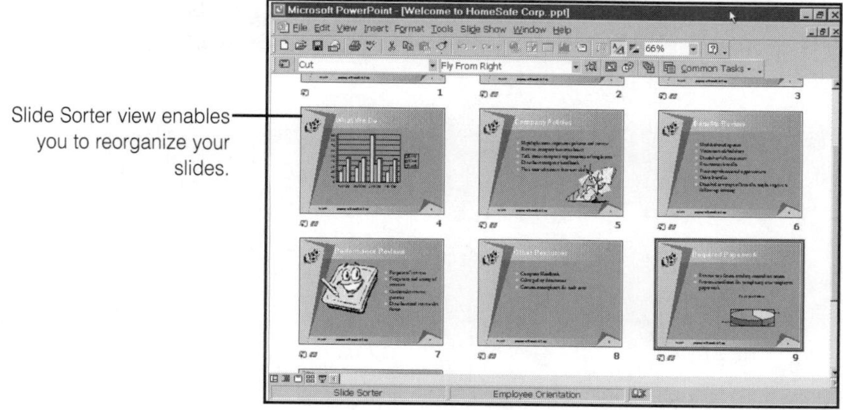

Cheat Sheet

Editing Text in Outline View

Change to Outline view by clicking the Outline View button. Display the Outlining toolbar with View, Toolbars, Outlining. Then perform any of the following:

- Click anywhere within the text to move the cursor to that spot.
- To delete text to the right of the cursor, press Delete. To back up and delete text, press Backspace.
- To select text so that you can copy, move, or delete it, drag over the text you want to select.
- To copy text, select it and click Copy. Then click where you want the text copied, and click Paste.
- To move a paragraph up within the outline, click in the paragraph and click the Move Up button.
- To move a paragraph down within the outline, click in the paragraph and click the Move Down button.

Changing the Level of Text in an Outline

- Click in the paragraph you want to change, then click Demote or press Tab to move that paragraph one level down in the outline.
- Click in the paragraph you want to change, then click Promote or Shift+Tab to move that paragraph one level up in the outline. If you move a paragraph up to slide title level, it becomes its own slide.

39

Editing the Sample and Placeholder Text

If you create your new presentation with the help of the AutoContent Wizard, you will end up with a semi-complete presentation—a large number of slides with sample text, graphics, and charts already on them. You will want to customize the text, of course, so that it fits your exact needs. The graphics and charts (if any) may also need to be changed. To make your changes, edit the sample text provided by the AutoContent Wizard.

Placeholder: holds place for text, graphics, charts.

If you create your new presentation using a design template, or you decide to go it alone, PowerPoint starts you off with a single slide that contains placeholders—small rectangles that represent where your actual text, graphics, and charts should go. In this chapter, you'll learn how to make changes to the sample and/or placeholder text in your presentation.

Basic Survival

Editing Text in Outline View

The AutoContent Wizard basically creates a complete presentation for you, with appropriate slides and sample text. You'll probably find that using Outline view is the fastest and simplest way to make changes to this text so that the presentation will start looking exactly the way you want.

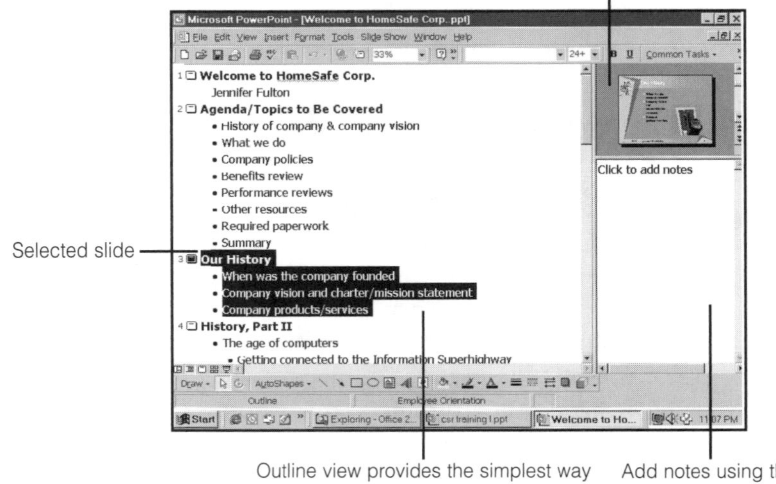

If you created your presentation using a design template or a blank slide, you may find that Slide view works best for you. Slide view enables you to edit the placeholder text on your initial slide and to add more slides easily. Editing the placeholder text in Slide view is explained in the "Beyond Survival" section.

If Using AutoContent Wizard: use Outline View to enter text.

To edit text in Outline view, first change to Outline view by clicking the Outline View button. (You can also remain in Normal view and make your changes in the Outline pane, if you want.) Next, display the Outlining toolbar with the View, Toolbars, Outlining command. Then perform any of the following:

- Click anywhere within the text to move the cursor to that spot.
- To delete text to the right of the cursor, press Delete. To back up and delete text, press Backspace.
- To select text so you can copy, move, or delete it, drag over the text you want to select. To select all the text on a slide, click the slide number. To select all the text in a bullet item, click the bullet.

- To copy text, select it and click Copy. Then click where you want the text copied, and click Paste.
- To move text, select it and click Cut. Then click where you want the text moved, and click Paste.

Another way to move text is to use the Move buttons. These buttons move whole paragraphs in one step:

- To move a paragraph up within the outline, click in the paragraph and click the Move Up button. Or, position the mouse over the bullet character and drag to a new position.
- To move a paragraph down within the outline, click in the paragraph and click the Move Down button. Or, position the mouse over the bullet character and drag to a new position.
- You can also select a paragraph and its subparagraphs and drag it up or down to move it to its desired place in the outline. To select a paragraph (and its related subparagraphs), click its bullet. Then drag the grouping wherever you like. As you drag, a horizontal line marks the group's potential placement within the outline. Release the mouse button, and the grouping is placed where indicated.

Changing the Level of Text in an Outline

When you switch to Outline view, your text is presented in a multilevel format, with lesser text indented under major text. At the top-most level is the slide title; bulleted text typically occupies the next level, with bulleted text within those bullets occupying the next level down, and so on. You can change the level of text within an outline by performing any of the following:

- Click in the paragraph you want to change, then click Demote or press Tab to move that paragraph one level down in the outline.
- Click in the paragraph you want to change, then click Promote or Shift+Tab to move that paragraph one level up in the outline. If you move a paragraph up to slide title level, it becomes its own slide.

Beyond Survival

Editing Text in Slide View

In Slide view, you can concentrate on a single slide. Slide view makes it easy to edit text this way, as well as the other elements of a slide, such as graphics and charts. Because you start out with only one slide when you create a presentation using a design template or a blank slide, you'll probably find Slide view works best in that situation.

If using a template to create presentations, use Slide View to enter text.

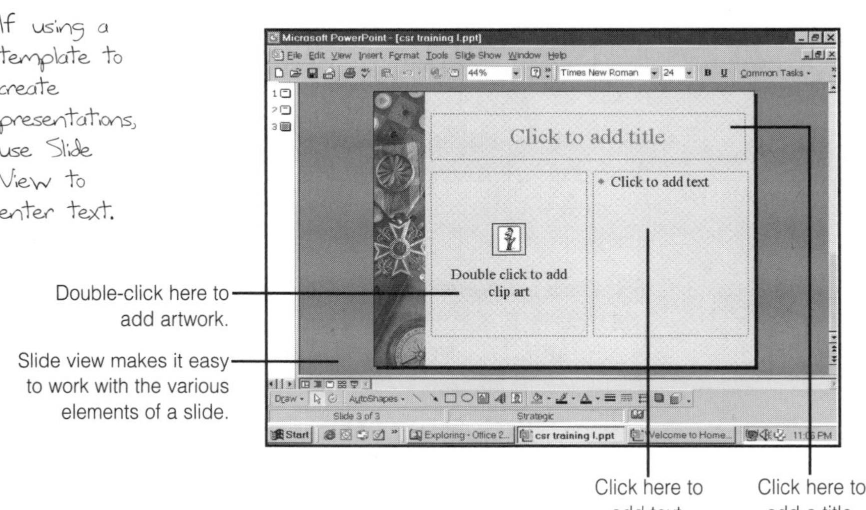
Microsoft PowerPoint - [csr training I.ppt]
Click to add title
Click to add text
Double click to add clip art
Double-click here to add artwork.
Slide view makes it easy to work with the various elements of a slide.
Click here to add text.
Click here to add a title.

When a new slide is added to a presentation, small rectangular placeholders mark the areas where text and other objects should go. If you don't use a particular placeholder, don't worry; it won't appear in your presentation unless something is in it.

To add text, click in the placeholder and type. To add other objects, double-click in the placeholder instead. For example, double-click where it says, "Double click to add chart," to add a chart to your slide. To create additional text placeholders for a slide, use a text box, as explained in Chapter 41.

Cheat Sheet

Inserting a Slide

1. Move to the slide *behind which* you want to insert your new slide.
2. Click the New Slide button.
3. Select the layout you want for the new slide, and click OK.

Selecting Slides

- If you're using Slide view or Normal view, the slide currently being displayed is considered the selected slide.
- To select a slide using Outline view, click its number. To select contiguous slides, press and hold the Shift key as you click.
- If you're using Slide Sorter view, click on a slide to select it. To select more than one slide, press and hold the Shift key as you click each slide.

Deleting Slides

1. In Slide Sorter view or Outline view, select the slide you want to delete.
2. Press Delete.

Rearranging Slides

1. Switch to Slide Sorter view.
2. Click the slide you want to move.
3. Drag the slide where you want it to go and release the mouse button.

40

Inserting, Deleting, and Rearranging Slides

When you create a presentation using a design template or a blank slide, you begin with only the initial slide. To complete your presentation, you need to add slides. As your presentation progresses, you may find that you'd like to remove a slide you no longer need, or rearrange the slides so that they appear in a more logical order.

If you created your presentation using the AutoContent Wizard, then you already have quite a few slides in your presentation. However, you probably have other slides you want to add. In addition, you may want to remove some of the slides that AutoContent provided. You may also want to rearrange the slides.

Basic Survival

Inserting a Slide

You can insert a new slide into the presentation at any time, using any view. When you do, you get the opportunity to select the layout you want for the new slide. Follow these steps:

1. Move to the slide behind which you want to insert your new slide.
2. Click the New Slide button on the Standard toolbar. The New Slide dialog box appears.

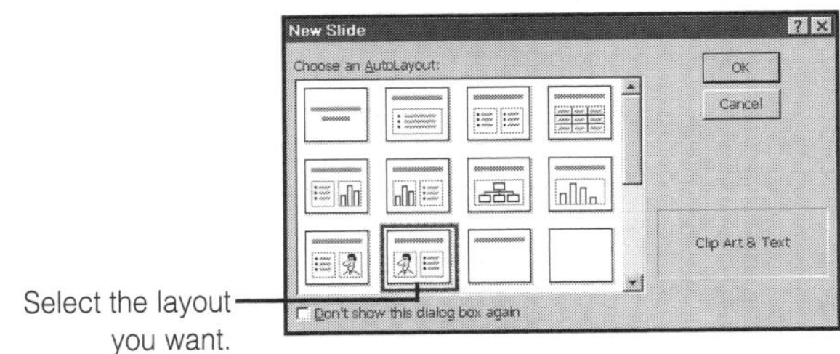

Select the layout you want.

3. Select the layout you want for the new slide, and click OK. The new slide is placed behind the slide on which you were originally working.

Placeholders that represent where text, graphics, and other elements should go appear on the slide. To add text, click on a text placeholder and type. To add other elements, double-click instead. See Chapter 39 for more help using a placeholder.

You can insert a duplicate of an existing slide if you want (including text, graphics, charts, and so); just select the slide you want to duplicate, and then open the Insert menu and select Duplicate Slide. The new slide appears behind the original slide. For help in moving your new slide within the presentation, see the "Beyond Survival" section.

Selecting Slides

Before you can delete, rearrange, or perform other tasks on an existing slide, you must select it first.

- If you're using Slide view or Normal view, the slide currently being displayed is considered the selected slide.
- To select a slide using Outline view, click its number. To select several contiguous (neighboring) slides, click the first slide in the group, then press and hold the Shift key as you click the last slide in the group. The slides between the first and last ones you clicked are also selected.
- If you're using Slide Sorter view, click on a slide to select it. To select several slides, press and hold the Ctrl key as you click the slides you want. To select contiguous slides, press Shift as you click the first and last slide in the set.

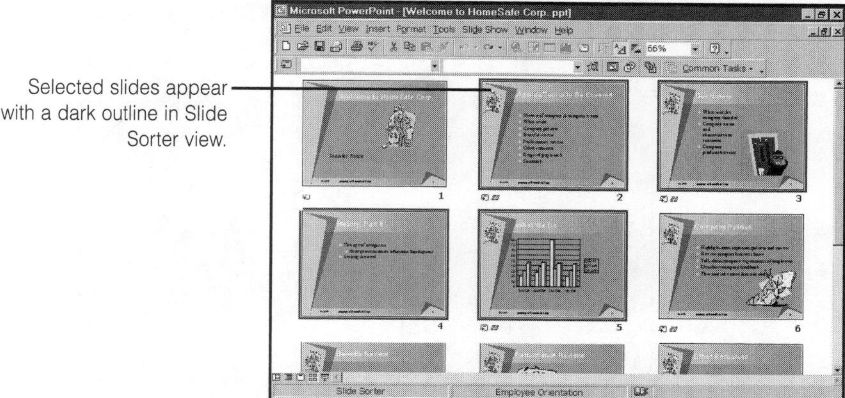

Selected slides appear with a dark outline in Slide Sorter view.

Deleting Selected Slides

Deleting slides couldn't be any easier:

1. While in Slide Sorter view or Outline view, select the slide you want to delete.
2. Press Delete. The remaining slides are automatically renumbered.

If you accidentally delete a slide, click the Undo button to restore it.

Beyond Survival

Rearranging Slides Using Slide Sorter View

As you begin to fine-tune your presentation, you'll probably find it necessary to rearrange your slides a little. Follow these steps:

1. Switch to Slide Sorter view. (It's the easiest view in which to rearrange slides.)
2. Click the slide you want to move.
3. Drag the slide where you want it to go. As you do, a vertical line marks your place in the presentation. When the vertical line appears in the spot where you want the slide moved, release the mouse button.

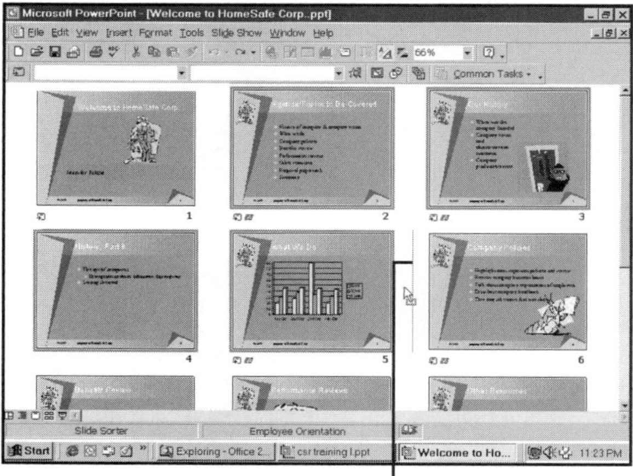

This line marks the spot to which the slide will be moved.

Cheat Sheet

Creating a Text Box

1. Switch to Normal view or Slide view and click the Text Box button on the Drawing toolbar.
2. Click on the slide to establish the upper-left corner of the text box.
3. Drag downward and to the right, until the text box is the size you want.
4. Release the mouse button, and the text box appears.
5. Begin typing your text. Use the tools on the Formatting toolbar to change the text as needed. When you're finished, click outside the text box.
6. To resize the box, click in the box and drag a sizing handle to a new position.

Adding a Bulleted List

1. Create a text box as described in steps 1-4 above.
2. Click the Bullets button on the Formatting toolbar. A bullet appears.
3. Type your first list item and press Enter.
4. Another bullet appears. Type your next list item and press Enter. Repeat this step to add additional items to the list.
5. To turn off the bullets for a line, click the Bullets button.

Adding a Numbered List

1. Create a text box as described in steps 1-4 above.
2. Click the Numbering button on the Formatting toolbar.
3. Type your first item and press Enter.
4. The number 2 appears. Type your next item and press Enter. Repeat this step to add additional items to the list.
5. To turn off the numbering for a line, click the Numbering button.

Changing Text Alignment

1. Select the text you want to change.
2. Click the appropriate button on the Formatting toolbar:

   Left Alignment

   Center Alignment

   Right Alignment

41

Adding New Text to a Slide

When you insert a new slide into your presentation, you select an AutoFormat for it. Each format contains several placeholders for text, clip art, or charts. If you want to add more text to a slide than its original format offers, you have to create an additional placeholder for text (a text box). You'll learn how to do just that in this chapter. In addition, you'll learn how to change the alignment of text, how to change plain text into a bulleted list, and how to change the bullet character.

Basic Survival

Creating a Text Box

If you want to add text to a slide, you must type your text into a text placeholder, otherwise known as a text box. Most slides already contain a text box, but if you want more than one, you'll probably have to add the text box yourself. After you create the text box, you can move it around and resize it to fit within the existing elements on the slide. Follow these steps:

1. While in the Normal view or Slide view, click the Text Box button on the Drawing toolbar.
2. Click on the slide to establish the upper-left corner of the text box.
3. Drag downward and to the right, until the text box is the size you want.
4. Release the mouse button, and the text box appears.
5. Begin typing your text. Use the tools on the Formatting toolbar to change the appearance of your text as needed. (See Chapter 42 for help.) When you're finished, click outside the text box.

Text placeholder = text box.

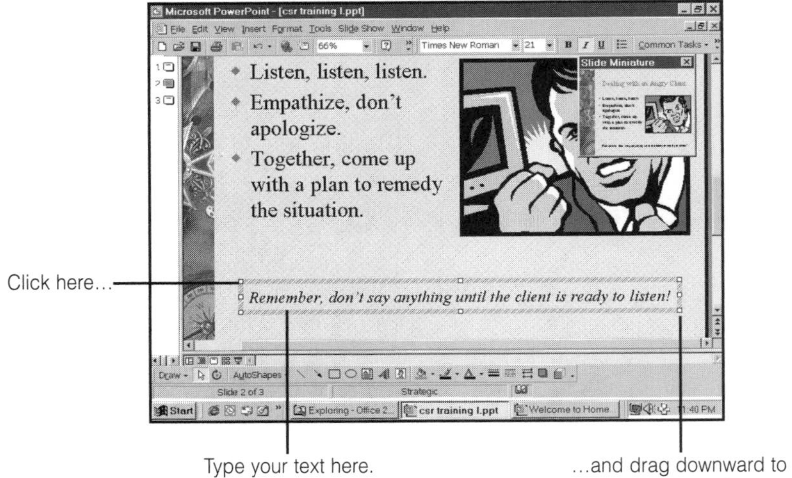

After the text box is created, you can move it if you need to by clicking on the box, moving the mouse pointer to an edge, and then dragging the box wherever you want.

To resize the box, click on it, and small handles appear (they look like small white boxes). Drag one of these boxes outward to make the text box bigger, or inward to make it smaller.

Can move and resize box.

Normally, the text box's outline is invisible and no shading fills the box. Click on the text box, then select a line style for the Line Style button on the Drawing toolbar. Use the Line Color button to change the color of the outline. To change the color of your text, select it and use the Font Color button; use the Fill Color button to fill the text box with color.

Adding a Bulleted List

When you create a text box, the text you type into it is plain. If you need to create a bulleted list, follow these steps:

1. Click the Bullets button. A bullet appears.
2. Type your first list item and press Enter.
3. Another bullet appears. Type your next list item and press Enter. Repeat this step to add additional items to the list.

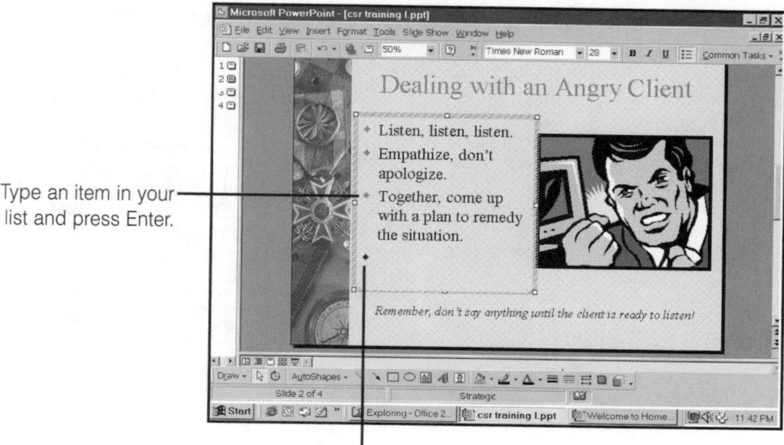

Type an item in your list and press Enter.

Another bullet appears.

Change text into a bulleted list.

If you've already typed the text you want to make into a bulleted list, just select the text first, then click the Bullets button. If you want to remove the bullets from an existing list, that's no problem either: just select the list and click the Bullets button.

Adding a Numbered List

Instead of creating a bulleted list, you can create a numbered list when needed. Follow these steps:

1. Click the Numbering button. A bullet appears.
2. Type your first item and press Enter.
3. The number 2 appears. Type your next item and press Enter. Repeat this step to add additional items to the list.

Use num list for steps.

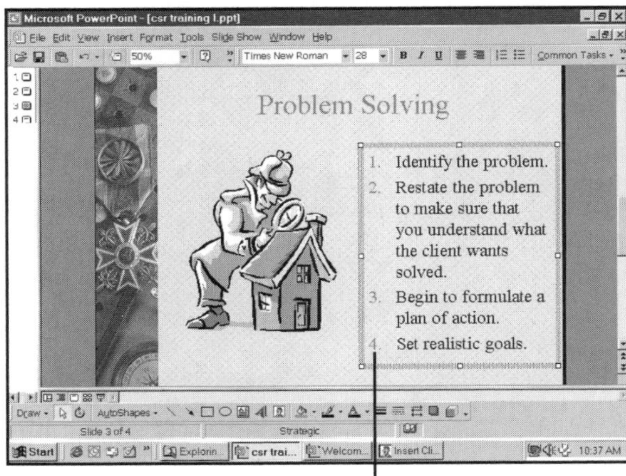

Typing an item in your list and pressing Enter inserts another number.

If you've already typed the text you want to make into a numbered list, just select the text first, then click the Numbering button. If you want to remove the bullets from an existing list, simply select the list and click the Numbering button.

In a process that's similar to changing a bullet symbol, you can change the numbering style of your list: select the list, choose Format, Bullets and Numbering, then select the numbering style you want. You can also change the size and color of the numbers, and reset the starting number, if needed.

Beyond Survival

Changing Text Alignment

Normally, text you type is left-aligned (placed against the left margin). You can change the alignment of text to right-align or center. You can even justify text, a process that adds spaces between words as needed, so that the text touches both the left and right margins.

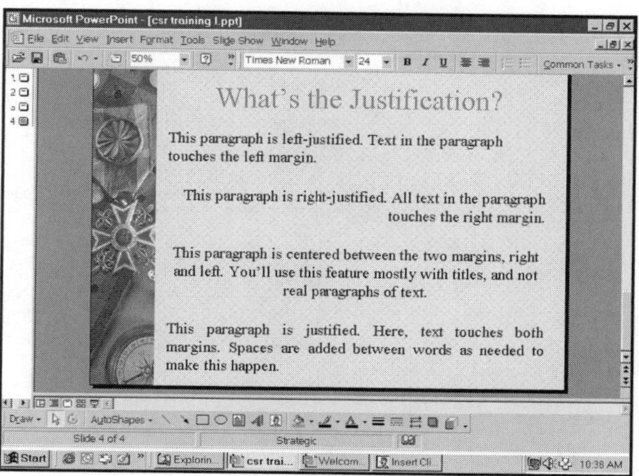

Here's how to center text!

Follow these steps to change the alignment of text:

1. Select the text you want to change.
2. Click the appropriate button on the Formatting toolbar:

   Left Alignment

   Center Alignment

   Right Alignment

If you want to justify text, select it. Then open the Format menu, select Alignment, and select Justify.

Changing the Bullet Character

Try this!

A simple thing you can do to make your presentation really stand out is to change the bullet symbol used in your bulleted lists. Normally, the bullet is a simple black dot. But you can easily change it to something else:

1. Select the bulleted list with bullets you want to change. (You select just the text—you can't select the bullets themselves.)
2. Open the Format menu and select Bullets and Numbering. The Bullets and Numbering dialog box appears.
3. Select a bullet from those showing, or click the Character button to choose from hundreds of symbols.

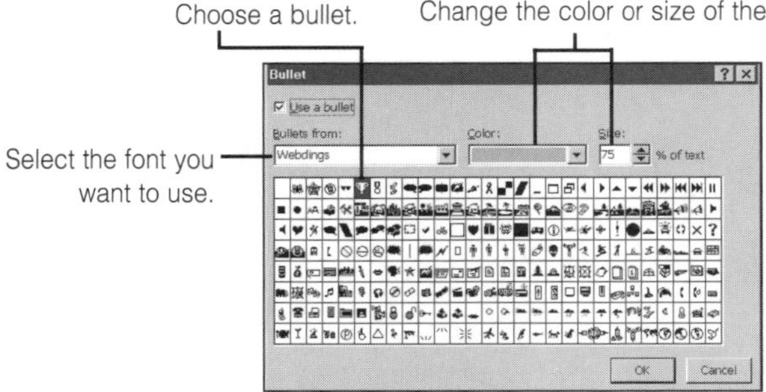
Choose a bullet.
Change the color or size of the bullet, if you want.
Select the font you want to use.
Bullet
Use a bullet
Bullets from:
Webdings
Color:
Size:
75
% of text
OK
Cancel

4. Select the bullet you want.
5. If you like, you can also change the Color or the Size of the bullet, then click OK.

You can select a different bullet from those listed by following these steps:

1. In the Bullets and Numbering dialog box, click Character.
2. If needed, select the font that contains the bullet you want to use from the Bullets from list.
3. Select the bullet you want. You can change its size and color as well.
4. Click OK.

Can use animated GIFs and pictures as bullets.

To use a graphic image as a bullet (something you've pulled off the Internet perhaps—including animated GIFs), follow these steps:

1. In the Bullets and Numbering dialog box, click Picture.
2. Choose one of the graphic bullets supplied with PowerPoint, or change to the Motion Clips tab to select an animated GIF.
3. Click OK.

If you have your own clip that you want to use, click Import Clips and select it from those listed. You can also click Clips Online to visit the Microsoft Web site for additional clips.

Cheat Sheet

Using the Formatting Toolbar

1. Select the text you want to change by dragging over it.
2. Click the appropriate button on the Formatting toolbar.

   Some buttons on the Formatting toolbar:

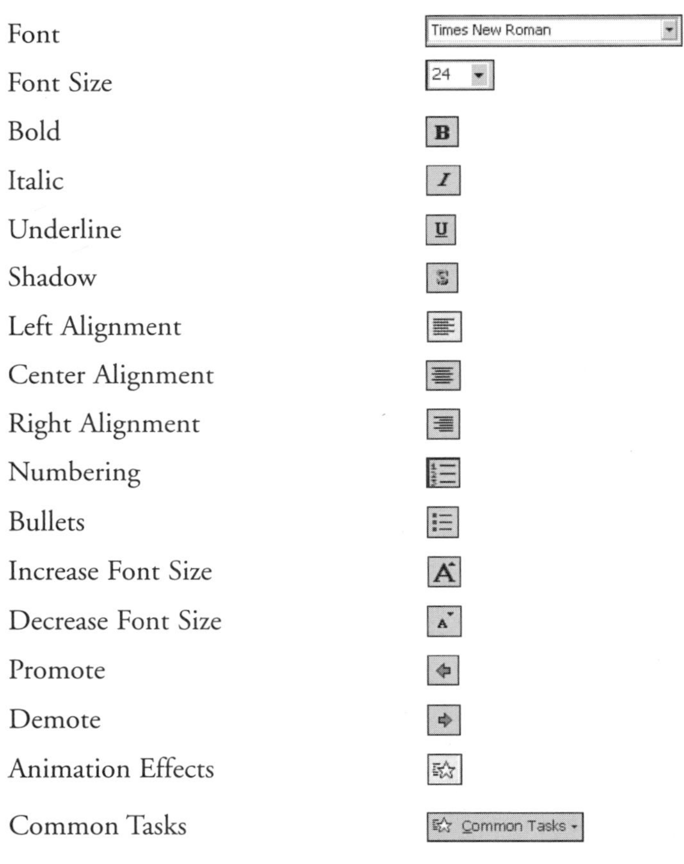

Font
Times New Roman
Font Size
24
Bold
B
Italic
I
Underline
U
Shadow
S
Left Alignment
Center Alignment
Right Alignment
Numbering
Bullets
Increase Font Size
A
Decrease Font Size
A
Promote
Demote
Animation Effects
Common Tasks
Common Tasks

42

Changing the Look of Text

Each presentation should have its own look, its own style. One way to distinguish your presentation from somebody else's is with the style of your text. For example, the *font* or typeface you select presents your words with a particular emphasis: funny, professional, light-hearted, or determined. In addition, you can use other formats as well, including bold, italic, or underline. You can even add color, as you'll learn in this chapter.

Basic Survival

Using the Formatting Toolbar

The simplest way to change the way your text looks is with the Formatting toolbar. Just select the text you want to change, and click the appropriate button:

Name	Button	Function
Font	Times New Roman ▾	Changes the typeface of text.
Font Size	24 ▾	Changes the size of text.
Bold	B	Makes text bold.
Italic	I	Makes text italic.
Underline	U	Underlines text.
Shadow	S	Adds a shadow behind text.
Left Alignment		Aligns text to left margin. (See Chapter 41 for help.)
Center Alignment		Centers text. (See Chapter 41 for help.)

continues

continued

Name	Button	Function
Right Alignment		Aligns text to right margin. (See Chapter 41 for help.)
Bullets		Adds a bullet in front of text.
Numbering		Adds a number in front of text.
Increase Font Size		Increases the size of text to the next point size.
Decrease Font Size		Decreases the size of text to the previous point size.
Promote		Promotes text one level up in outline. (See Chapter 39 for help.)
Demote		Demotes text one level down in outline. (See Chapter 39 for help.)
Animation Effects		Adds animation to text. (See Chapter 43 for help.)
Common Tasks	Common Tasks	Provides a list of commands for commons tasks such as inserting a new slide.

Beyond Survival

Changing Font Color

Changing the color of your text is simple to do, and it is sometimes even necessary, especially when the background of your slide is also a dark color. To change the color of your text, follow these steps:

Make text lighter on a dark background.

1. Select the text you want to change by dragging over it or clicking the text frame to change all the text within the text box.
2. Click the arrow on the Font Color button, located on the Drawing toolbar.
3. Select a color you like. If you want to see more colors, click More Font Colors, then select a color from the dialog box that appears.

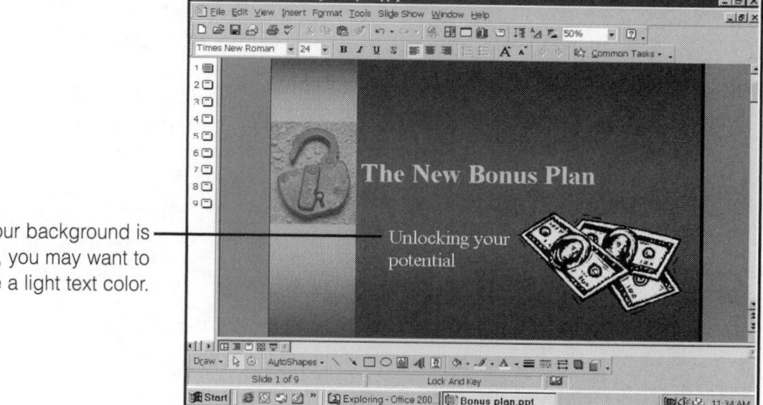

If your background is dark, you may want to use a light text color.

You can quickly apply the color displayed on the Font Color button by just clicking the button rather than the arrow.

Cheat Sheet

Animation Effects Toolbar

Button	Name	Function
	Animate Title	Title flies in from top of slide.
	Animate Slide Text	Each item in a bulleted list appears independently.
	Drive-In Effect	With car sound, selected object flies in from right.
	Flying Effect	With whooshing sound, selected object flies in from left.
	Camera Effect	With the click of a shutter, object appears from center outward.
	Flash Once	Object is flashed onscreen, then appears permanently.
	Laser Text Effect	With laser sound, each letter appears, one at a time.
	Typewriter Text Effect	With sound of a typewriter, each letter appears, one at a time.
	Reverse Text Order Effect	Items in bulleted list appear in reverse order, reading left to right.
	Drop-In	Words appear one at a time, as if dropped from top of slide.
	Custom Animation	Displays the Custom Animation dialog box.
	Animation Preview	Allows you to preview the animation on the slide.

43

Changing the Look of Your Presentation

The one thing that sets your presentation above any other is its overall look. A presentation that uses a pleasing background, an interesting and easy-to-read font, and effective clip art tells a dynamic story, helps sell your ideas, and makes your point. In this chapter, you'll learn how to change the background of your slides and add clip art and animation.

Basic Survival

Using a Presentation Design Template

Changing templates changes all slides!

When you created your presentation, you may have selected a design template. This template included a background design and color scheme. If, after playing around a while, you've decided that you don't like the look of your presentation, don't worry—it's easy to change to a different design template. Keep in mind that selecting a different template affects all the slides in your presentation—if you want to change the background of just one or two slides, use the Format/Background command instead.

To select a new design template for your presentation:

1. Choose Format, Apply Design Template.
2. Select the presentation design you want. A preview of the design appears in the preview panel on the right.
3. Click Apply, and the design is applied to all the slides in your presentation.

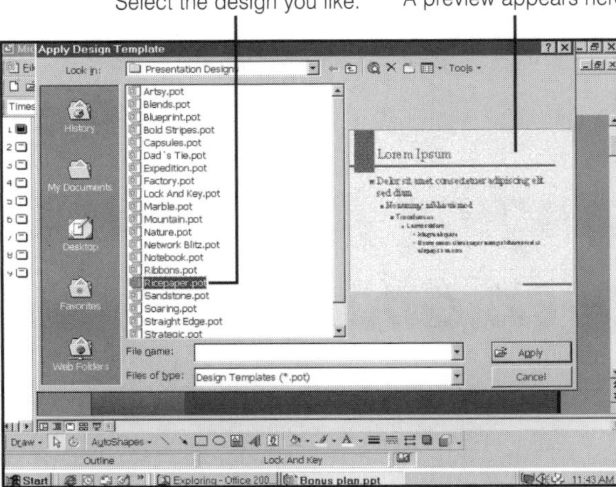

Once you've chosen a design for your overall presentation. You can change the background of just one or two slides using the Format menu.

1. Display the slide that is to have a different background and select Format, Background.
2. Click Omit background graphics from master to remove designs from this slide.
3. Click the drop-down arrow next to the background fill area and select a different color for the background or fill effects.
4. After selecting a new background color, click on Apply to change this slide only.

Adding Clip Art

One of the easiest ways to add some punch to your presentation is with clip art. PowerPoint comes with a generous supply of clip art, but you can supply your own if you like. Here's what to do:

You can import clip art!

1. Change to the slide to which you want to add the clip art or insert a new slide with a clip art Auto layout.
2. Double-click the clip art placeholder on the slide. If you're adding clip art to a slide that does not already have a placeholder, then just click the Insert Clip Art button on the Drawing toolbar instead.

3. You may see a dialog box telling you to insert the Office 2000 CD; if so, then insert the CD-ROM and click OK.

4. Click the category that best fits the type of image for which you're looking. Clip art images in that category appear in the large window. You can also type a few keywords in the Search for Clips box and press Enter.

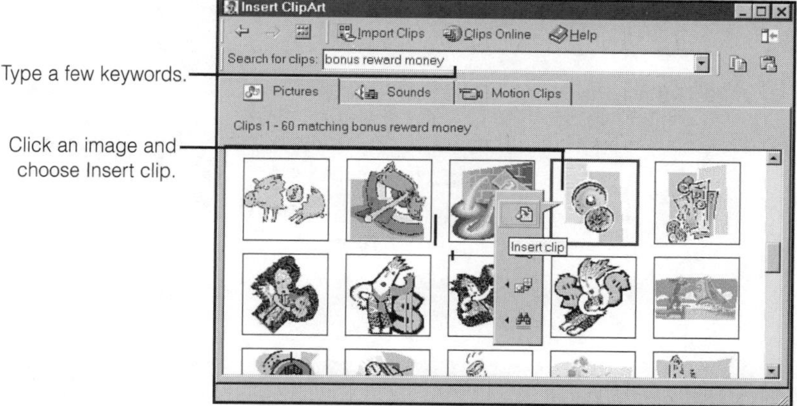

5. Click the image you want to add, then click Insert Clip from the drop-down menu of icons. The image you selected is placed on the slide and the Picture toolbar appears.

You can get on the Internet and search for an image by clicking the Clips Online button inside the Clip Art Gallery (Insert, Pictures, Clip Art). Of course, make sure you get the proper permissions before you try to use the image in any way.

PowerPoint can select images for you.

Tired of selecting images yourself? Well, just let PowerPoint do the hard work for you. When entering text in a slide, watch for a lightbulb. When it appears, click it. If the Office Assistant is offering to look for a related image, select that option to let it find clips for you.

To resize your clip art image, drag one of its corners inward to make the image smaller, or outward to make it bigger. To move the image, click in the center of the clip art and drag it wherever you want. To delete an image, click the image and press Delete.

Beyond Survival

Adding Animation

You can add animation to your presentation in many ways. For example, you can animate an object such as the title and make it appear from the left in one swift motion. Animations (in this case) control the manner in which objects appear.

Animating means controlling how objects appear.

If you don't want to animate individual objects (such as the title, clip art, text, or a chart), then you can add animation effects to provide transitions between slides.

To animate an object on a slide:

1. While in the Normal Viewer Slide view, click the Animation Effects button on the Formatting toolbar. (You might need to click the More Buttons button to see the button.) The Animation Effects toolbar appears.
2. Click the first object you want to animate, such as the title.
3. Select the effect you want from the Animation Effects toolbar, such as Drive-In Effect. (See the Cheat Sheet at the beginning of this chapter for help in making your selection.)
4. Repeat steps 2 and 3 for additional objects.

Transitions control how the next slide appears.

If you want to preview your animations, click the Animation Preview button on the Animation toolbar. A small window appears, displaying the slide as it will look during the actual slide show.

To add transitions between slides:

1. In Slide view, select the slide or slides that you would like to add a transition.
2. Open the Slide Show menu and select Slide Transition. The Slide Transition dialog box appears.

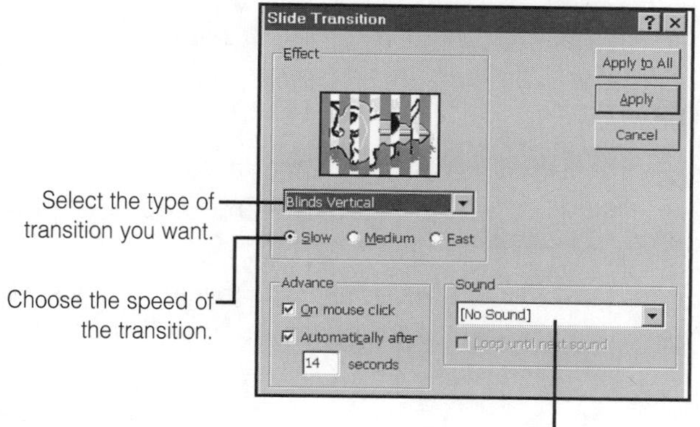

3. Select the type of transition you want from the drop-down list box. As you make a selection, it's previewed in the window above the drop-down list box.

4. Select the speed you want the transition to use: Slow, Medium, or Fast.

5. Select a Sound effect if you like.

6. Adjust the point at which the transition occurs during the slide show: on your mouse click, or automatically, after so many seconds.

7. Click Apply to apply your selections to the selected slides, or Apply to All, to apply this transition style to each slide in your presentation.

A transition icon appears below each slide.

8. To preview a slide's transition, click the tiny transition icon beneath the slide.

Cheat Sheet

Starting the Show

1. Move to the first slide in your presentation.
2. Click the Slide Show button, located on the left side of the vertical scrollbar.
3. The first slide appears automatically. To move to the next slide, click the mouse button. (If you are using animation, then clicking the mouse causes the first object to appear.)
4. During the presentation, you can perform any of the following:
   - To advance to the next slide, press N.
   - To return to a previous slide, press P.
   - To display the mouse pointer, press A.
   - To draw on a slide, press Ctrl+P. Drag the mouse pointer on the slide to draw. To turn the pen off, press Esc, or click to proceed to the next slide. (What you draw is not permanent.)
   - To pause an automated slide show, press S. To resume, press S again.
   - To end the slide show prematurely, press Esc.
   - To toggle between the current slide and a black screen, press B.
   - To toggle between the current slide and a white screen, press W.

44

Viewing Your Slide Show

Now that you've put your presentation together, the next step is to give it a run-through and work out any last-minute kinks. PowerPoint provides a way to display each slide in your presentation, one at a time, as you deliver your talk. You can control when each slide appears, or you can automate the process. You can even stop the slide show when needed to accommodate listeners who are taking notes.

If you don't have a computer handy for your presentation, you can print your slides and copy them onto transparencies. Even so, you should still run through the presentation to find a comfortable pace and smooth out any awkward spots.

Basic Survival

Starting the Show

Add animations and transitions!

Before you run through your presentation, you might want to jump back to Chapter 43 and add some animation and slide transitions to make your presentation more interesting. When you're ready to start the slide show, follow these steps:

1. Move to the first slide in your presentation.
2. Click the Slide Show button, located on the left-hand side of the vertical scrollbar.
3. The first slide appears automatically. To move to the next slide, click the mouse button or press N.
4. During the presentation, you can perform any of the following:
   - To return to a previous slide, press P.
   - To display the mouse pointer, press A.

- To draw on a slide, press Ctrl+P. Drag the mouse pointer on the slide to draw. To turn the pen off, press Esc, or click to proceed to the next slide. (What you draw is not permanent.)
- To pause an automated slide show, press S. To resume, press S again.
- To end the slide show prematurely, press Esc.
- To toggle between the current slide and a black screen, type B. To toggle between the current slide and a white screen, type W.

You may want to automate the slide show by adding timings, so PowerPoint will know how much time you want to display each slide. See the "Beyond Survival" section for help.

Use two monitors!

If you've attached two monitors (or a monitor and a TV) to your computer, you can have PowerPoint display your presentation on both your monitor (for you) and the TV (for your audience). (Just open the Slide Show menu and select Set Up Show. Then choose the monitor you want the slide show to appear on from the Show On list.) That way, if you want to display your notes on your monitor as well, you can, and no one will be able to see them. To display your notes, while the slide show is running, right-click on the first slide, and select Speaker Notes from the shortcut menu.

Beyond Survival

Automating a Slide Show

If you'd like the presentation to run without your help, you can insert timings that tell PowerPoint when to switch to the next slide. Here's how:

1. Open the Slide Show menu and select Rehearse Timings.
2. The slide show begins as usual. Rehearse the points you want to make about the slide. PowerPoint keeps track of the amount of time you spend on each slide. When you're ready to move to the next slide, click the mouse button or press N.
3. During the rehearsal, you can do any of the following:

- To pause the timing, click the Pause button in the the Rehearsal dialog box. (It has two vertical lines on it.)
- To resume the timing, click the Pause button again.
- To repeat the timing process for a slide, click the Repeat button. (It looks like a loop with an arrow on it.)

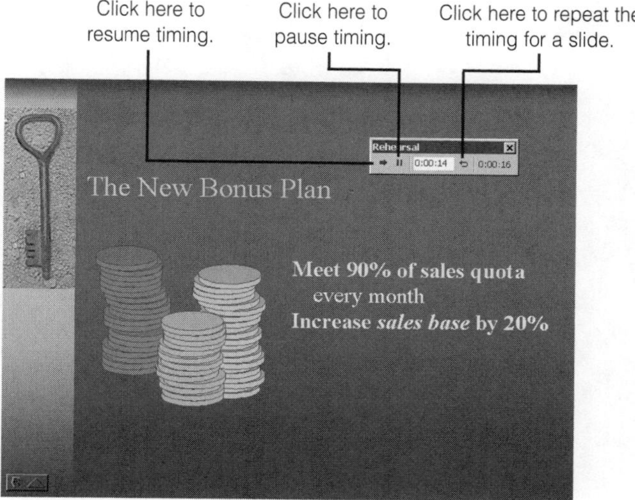

4. When you're finished, PowerPoint displays the total time for the presentation. If you want to save your timings, click Yes. If you think you've messed up on the timings, click No, and then repeat these steps to record accurate timings.

To preview your presentation using the timings you recorded, click the Slide Show button .

You can loop your presentation.

You can also have the presentation loop continuously whenever you run it (which is helpful if you're presenting it at a trade show) by opening the Slide Show menu, selecting Set Up Show, and choosing the Loop continuously until Esc option. Your presentation loops continuously until you press Esc.

PART 5

Outlook 2000

If you're like most of us, juggling email, meetings, appointments and tasks can become almost unbearable. With Outlook on your side, you can handle your mail, schedule your meetings and keep track of your contacts—it's just the type of companion you need.

In this part, you'll learn about the following topics:

- Taking a Look Around
- Creating and Sending a Message
- Checking for Messages
- Answering Your Messages
- Scheduling an Appointment, Meeting, or Event
- Managing Your Contacts
- Keeping Track of Things to Do

Cheat Sheet

Understanding the Outlook Screen

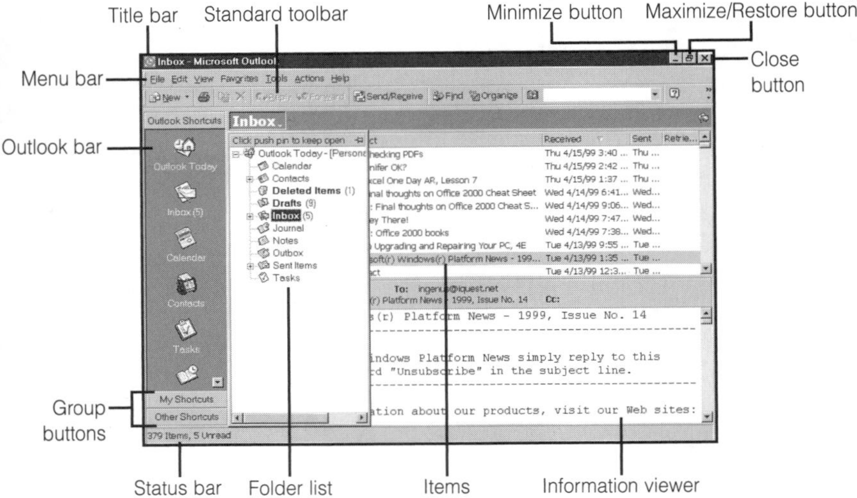

45

Taking a Look Around

Outlook is a personal information organizer that enables you to manage the wide variety of information you receive every day. With Outlook, you can:

- Send and receive electronic mail (email).
- Keep track of names, addresses, phone numbers, fax numbers, email and Web addresses, and more (contacts).
- Manage your appointments, meetings, and other special events such as birthdays and anniversaries (calendars).
- Organize the things you need to get done (tasks).

Before you can use Outlook to perform all these wonderful tasks, you must learn a bit more about it. In this chapter, you'll learn the parts of the Outlook screen, how to move around the program, and how to control the manner in which information is displayed.

Basic Survival

Understanding the Outlook Screen

The following list includes a brief description of the elements of the Outlook screen (see the Cheat Sheet at the beginning of the chapter for pointers to where each of these items is located):

- **Title bar** Displays the name of the current folder.
- **Window controls** With the Minimize and the Maximize/Restore buttons, you can control the size of the window in which you work. To exit Outlook, you use the Close button, which closes (removes) the Outlook window.
- **Menu bar** This bar contains the Outlook menus. To open a menu, click on it. For example, to open the File

menu, click on the word, File. A list of commands appears; to select one, click it. In Outlook, as in all the other Office programs, only the most commonly used commands appear on a menu when you first open it. To display all the commands on a menu, point to the expansion arrow at the bottom of the menu.

- **Toolbars** Use the Standard toolbar to accomplish common tasks quickly. Display the Advanced toolbar (View, Toolbars, Advanced) for more buttons used regularly. At the right end of each toolbar is the More Buttons button. Click this button and select Add or Remove Buttons to display a list of additional icons you can add or remove from the toolbar.
- **Outlook bar** Information in Outlook is organized into folders—the same way in which your files are organized in Windows. Icons for each of the Outlook folders are displayed on the Outlook bar. To change to a particular folder, such as Contacts, click its icon. At the bottom of the Outlook bar are the group buttons; if you click one of these buttons, a different group of icons is displayed. The main group is called Outlook Shortcuts; the My Shortcuts group contains icons for all the email folders: Draft, Outbox, Sent Items, and Personal. The Other Shortcuts group provides access to your files, with icons for My Computer, My Documents, and Favorites (enabling you to use Outlook much as you use the Windows Explorer in Windows 95 or 98). You can add or delete icons from a group to customize Outlook to the way you want to work.
- **Folder list** Provides an alternative to the Outlook bar for switching from folder to folder. To use the Folder list, click the Folder list button on the Advanced toolbar. Then click the folder you wish to view.
- **Information viewer** When you select a folder from the Outlook bar, its contents are displayed in the Information viewer. You can change the way in which this information is displayed by selecting a different view (see the "Beyond Survival" section for help).

Outlook items include messages, appointments, tasks, and so forth.

- **Items** Outlook enables you to create, copy, move, and delete many types of items, including email messages, contacts, tasks, appointments, and so on. Items are organized by folders. For example, you'll find all your incoming email messages in the Inbox folder. Appointments, on the other hand, are kept in the Calendar folder. To create a new item, click the New button on the Standard toolbar, then select the type of item you want to create. You'll learn more about creating items in the chapters that follow.
- **Status bar** This bar displays information about the contents of the current folder. For example, in the Inbox, the Status bar displays the number of unread messages and the number of total messages.

Switching Between Outlook Folders

Outlook items, such as email messages, appointments, and tasks, are organized in folders. To display a particular type of item, such as a contact, you must change to the appropriate folder. Follow these steps:

1. If needed, click the group button (Outlook Shortcuts, My Shortcuts, or Other Shortcuts) that contains the icon for the folder you wish to view.

Use Outlook bar to change folders.

2. Click the icon for the folder that includes contents you wish to display. If you can't see the icon you want, use the up or down arrows on the Outlook bar to display it. For example, click Contacts. The items in the Contacts folder are displayed.

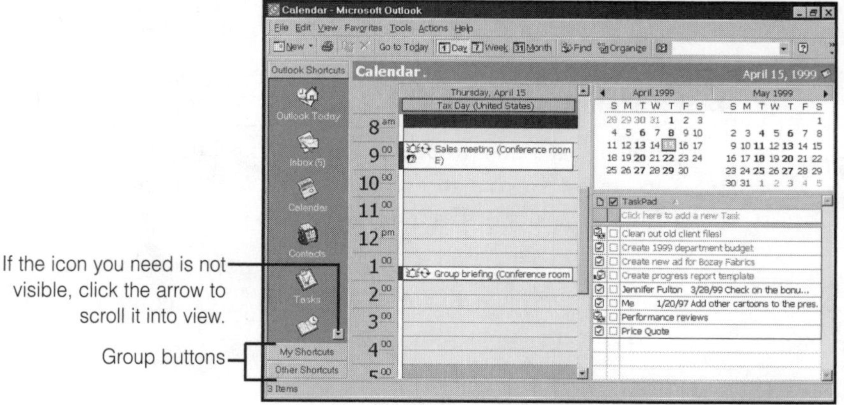

You can also use the Folder list to change from folder to folder. Just click the Folder list button on the Advanced toolbar (View, Toolbars, Advanced), and then click the folder you want to see from the list that appears.

Check this out!

One special folder you might want to look at is the Outlook Today folder. It presents a quick overview of the next few days' appointments, tasks, and the number of unread messages in your Inbox. If you want, you can tell Outlook to open this folder, rather than the Inbox, every time it's started. Just switch to Outlook Today by clicking its icon on the Outlook bar. Then click Customize Outlook Today at the top of the screen. On the Customize page, select When Starting and Go directly to Outlook Today. Click Save Changes to return to the Outlook Today page.

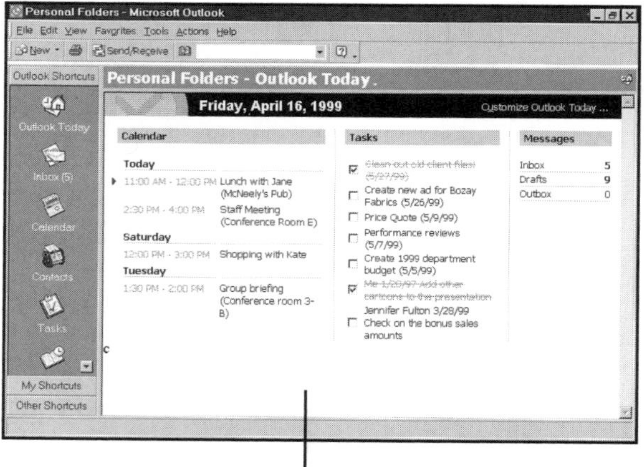

Outlook Today presents an overview of today's appointments, tasks, and incoming messages.

Beyond Survival

Changing Views

Each folder has a default or standard method in which it displays its items. To change the method in which items are displayed, change to a different view:

1. Open the View menu and select Current view. A list of views is displayed. The view currently being used appears with a check mark in front of it.

2. Select a view from the list. Items are displayed using that view.

3. To display a preview of an item in a separate pane while still showing the item's list, select View, Preview Pane. This adds an additional pane to the bottom of any view that is displayed.

While viewing the Inbox or Tasks folders, you can also select View, AutoPreview to display only a few lines of an item's contents.

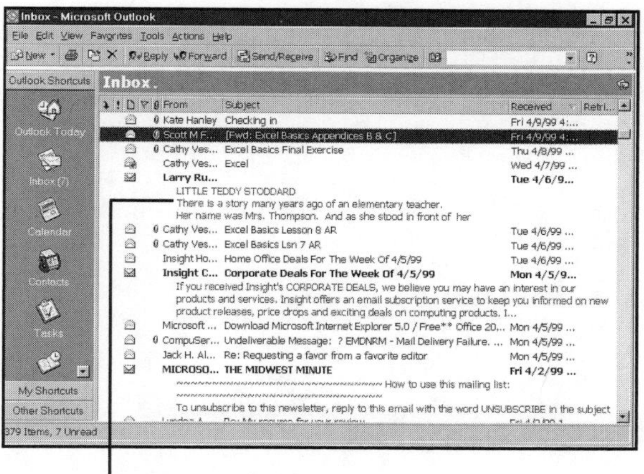

This view displays unread email messages with an AutoPreview of each item.

Cheat Sheet

Creating a Message and Sending It

1. From the Inbox, click the New Mail Message button on the Standard toolbar .
2. In the To box, type the address of the person to whom you wish to send the email message. To type a second name, first type a semi-colon (;) then type the additional address.

   If you're not certain of the email address, click the To button to display the Select Names dialog box. Select a name and click To. Repeat to add more names.
3. To send a copy of the message to someone, enter an address in the Cc box.
4. Type the subject of the message in the Subject text box.
5. Type your message in the large text area at the bottom of the window. You can use any of the tools on the Formatting toolbar to enhance your text.
6. To spell check your message, open the Tools menu and select Spelling, or press F7.
7. Attach an importance to the message by clicking either the Importance: High or the Importance: Low button on the Standard toolbar to indicate your intent.
8. To attach a file to the message, click the Insert File button, select the file you want to attach, and then click OK.
9. To send the message, click Send.

46

Creating and Sending a Message

As long as you have the email address, you can send a message to anyone. An Internet email address is made up of two parts: the person's name or nickname, followed by the @ sign, and the location of the person's email server. (The *server* is the computer that handles the recipient's email; it is often called a *domain*.) For example:

```
jfulton@speedy.net
```

If you're on a company network, you can also send email to your colleagues—as long as you have their proper addresses. (See your network system administrator if you need help.)

You can type any address manually, or you can enter addresses in the Contacts list to keep a permanent record. While you're adding someone to the Contact list, you can record other information, such as mailing addresses, phone numbers, birth dates, and other personal and business information. (See Chapter 50 for help.)

Enter addresses in Contacts for a permanent record.

Along with the text of your message, you can attach files that you want to share. You'll learn how to send messages and attach files later in this chapter.

Basic Survival

Creating a Message and Sending It

If you've used Word or some other word processor, you'll find that creating an email message is easy:

1. From the Inbox on the Standard toolbar click the New Mail Message button .

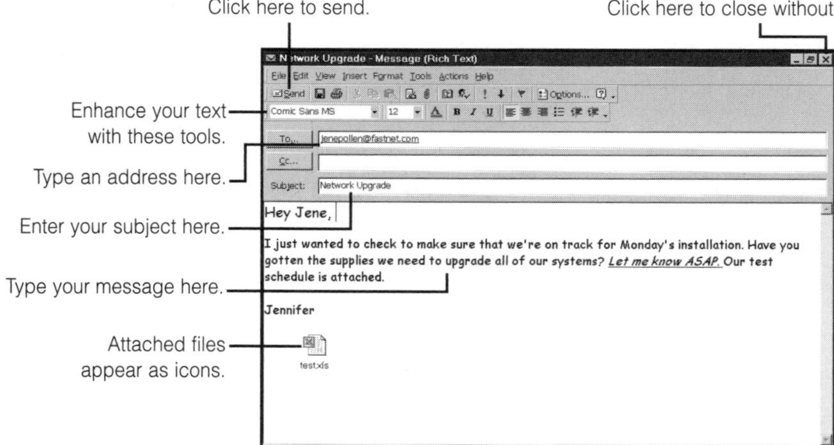

2. In the To box, type the address of the person to whom you wish to send the email message. To type a second name, first type a semicolon (;) then type the additional address.

   If you're not certain of the email address, click the To button to display the Select Names dialog box. Select a name and click To. Repeat to add more names.

3. To send a copy of the message to someone, enter an address in the Cc box.
4. Type the subject of the message in the Subject text box.
5. Type your message in the large text area at the bottom of the window. You can use any of the tools on the Formatting toolbar to enhance your text, however, the recipient of the message may or may not be able to see them (depending on which email program the recipient is using).
6. To spell check your message, open the Tools menu and select Spelling, or press F7.

   Check spelling first!

7. Attach an importance to the message by clicking either the Importance: High or the Importance: Low button to indicate your intent. (Remember, if you can't see a button on a toolbar, click on More Buttons.)

8. To send the message, click Send. To send the message later, click Save [icon]. The message is placed in the Drafts folder. To send it later, go to the Drafts folder on the My Shortcuts group and double-click the message to open it. Make any additional changes as needed, then click Send.
9. To close the message without sending it, click the Close box (the message is deleted).

If you want to attach a file to the email message for review, see the "Beyond Survival" section in this chapter for help.

You can use stationery to jazz up your email messages (this assumes that the recipient has an email program that supports HTML formatting, such as Internet Mail with Internet Explorer, Windows Messaging, Netscape Communicator, Outlook, or Outlook Express). To select a stationery for your new message, do not click the New Mail Message button. Instead, open the Actions menu and select New Mail Message Using. Select a stationery from the cascading menu that appears, or click More Stationery to view additional selections that Outlook provides.

Beyond Survival

Attaching a File to a Message

The most common reason for sending email messages is to communicate and share ideas. And what better way to do that then with sharing a Word report, Excel worksheet, or PowerPoint presentation? It's easy to attach any file to a message that you send. Here's what to do:

1. Compose the message as usual.
2. Click the Insert File button (it looks like a small paper-clip). The Insert File dialog box appears.

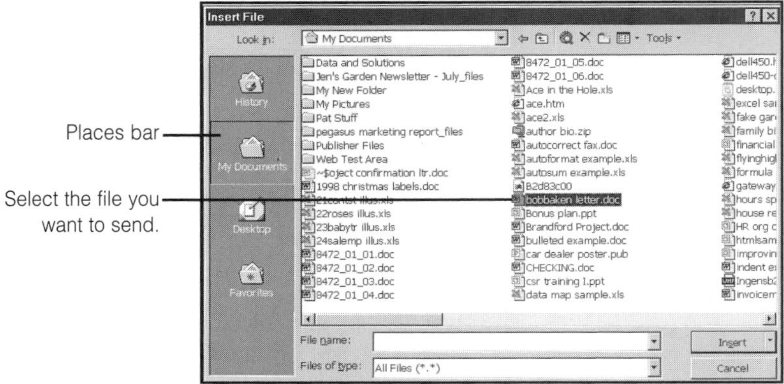

3. Change to the drive and directory that contains the file you want to send. You can change to common directories such as My Documents by clicking that icon in the Places bar.

4. Select the file and click OK. The file appears as an icon within the message (see the first figure in this chapter).

Check to see whether the recipient can read the file format before sending.

Although you can send any file you wish, the recipient may not be able to view the contents of that file if he or she does not have a compatible program with which to open it.

If you've received an email message with a file attached, double-click the icon to open it. See Chapter 47 for more help in displaying, saving, and printing its contents.

Cheat Sheet

Checking for New Messages and Viewing Them

- To check for mail, click the Send and Receive button.
- New messages appear in bold text, with a closed envelope icon. To view an unread message, click it, and the content of the message appears in the Preview Pane, located in the lower half of the window. (If the Preview Pane did not appear, select View, Preview Pane.)
- The content of a new message can also be displayed in its own window—just double-click the message header. To view the next message (read or unread), click the Next Item button.

Opening an Attached File

1. Double-click the message that contains the attached file.
2. Double-click the attachment icon you want to open. The file opens in its application, such as Word or PowerPoint.

Viewing an Attached File

1. Double-click the message that contains the attached file.
2. Right-click the attachment icon and click on Quick View.

Saving an Attached File

1. Double-click the message that contains the attached file.
2. Right-click the attachment icon and select Save As.
3. Change to the folder in which you want to save the file (and type a different filename in the File name box if you want to change the file's name), then click Save.

Printing an Attached File

1. Double-click the message that contains the attached file.
2. Right-click the attachment icon and click Print.

47

Checking for Messages

Incoming messages appear in the Inbox. New messages are typically displayed at the top of the window, where they are easy to spot. After you receive a message, you can view its contents, reply to it, and even forward it to someone else, as you'll learn in Chapter 48. In this chapter, you'll learn how to check for new messages, view them, and display or save file attachments.

Basic Survival

Checking for New Messages and Viewing Them

If you're attached to your company's network, you don't have to do anything to receive new mail. Outlook is set up to automatically receive new mail through the network about every 10 minutes. However, you can still check for new mail yourself, if you like.

If you dial into the Internet to receive mail, you can configure Outlook to receive mail periodically, or you can check for mail yourself when needed.

- To check for mail, click the Send and Receive buttons. Outlook connects to your mail server and downloads new mail. Incoming messages appear in the Inbox.
- New messages appear in bold text with a closed envelope icon. To view an unread message, click it, and the content of the message appears in the Preview Pane, located in the lower half of the window. If the Preview Pane did not appear, select View, Preview Pane.
- The content of a new message can also be displayed in its own window—just double-click the message header. To view the next message (read or unread), click the Next Item button.

- After viewing a new message, you may wish to reply to it or forward it to someone else. See Chapter 48 for help with replying and forwarding.
- If you want to filter out junk mail or adult content, click the Organize button, and click the Junk E-Mail tab. Click the drop-down arrows to make choices as to how Outlook should handle junk mail and adult content messages. You can assign a color to any mail that Outlook flags as junk or adult content, or ask Outlook to automatically move those messages to a folder such as Deleted Items. Be sure to click the Turn On button in the Organize box so unwanted messages don't appear in your inbox.
- If you do get a piece of junk mail that Outlook didn't catch, add the sender's name to the master list by right-clicking on the message in the inbox, selecting Junk E-Mail, and selecting a category from the list.
- After viewing a message, you can easily delete it by clicking the Delete button. Deleted messages are moved to the Deleted Items folder, where you can retrieve them should you discover that you deleted a message accidentally. To empty the Deleted Items folder (and permanently delete the items in it), open the Tools menu and select Empty Deleted Items folder.

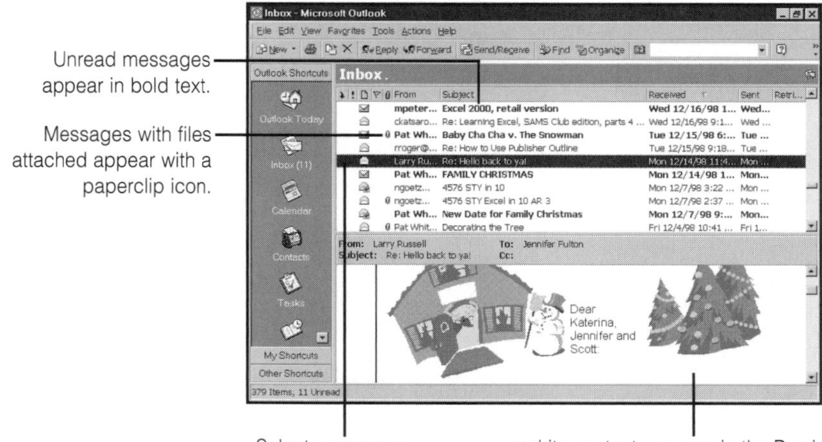
Unread messages appear in bold text.
Messages with files attached appear with a paperclip icon.
Inbox - Microsoft Outlook
Inbox
Select a message...
...and its content appears in the Preview Pane.

To set up Outlook so that it checks for new mail automatically, use your dial-up connection to:

1. Open the Tools menu and select Options.
2. Click the Internet E-mail tab.

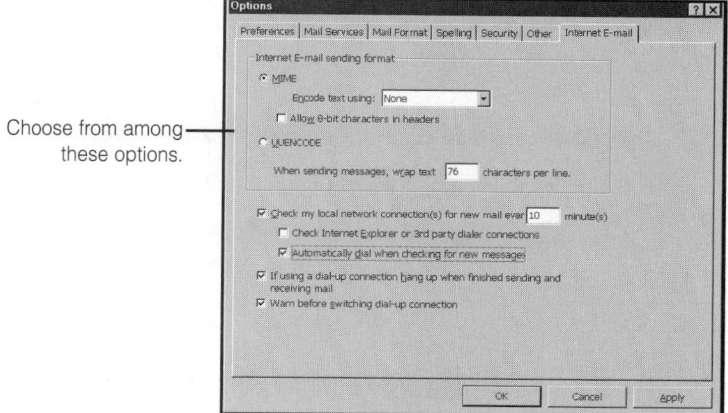

3. Select the Check Internet Explorer or third-party dialer connection option.
4. If you want Outlook to dial the connection for you and you're not already connected to the Internet, select the Automatically dial when checking for new messages option. You might want to select the option, If using a dial-up connection hang up when finished sending and receiving mail, as well.
5. Click OK.

If you would like to see whether you have any new mail when you start Outlook, jump to the Outlook Today folder. Better yet, set up Outlook so that it displays the Outlook Today page every time you start the program. See Chapter 46 for details.

Beyond Survival

Viewing, Opening, Saving, and Printing an Attached File

If a message you receive has a file attached to it, it appears with a small paperclip icon (see the first figure in this chapter). Provided you have a compatible program, you can open the file. You can also view the file in read-only format (which means you can't make changes) as well as print the attachment. You can also save the file to your hard disk for later editing and viewing.

You can view, open, save, or print attached files.

To view (not change) the contents of an attached file:

1. Double-click the message that contains the attached file.
2. Right-click the attachment icon and select Quick View. The file opens in a separate window where you can view the content.

   If you want to view the attachment without opening the message, right-click the message in the inbox and select View Attachments. Select the attachment from the list to view it. You cannot make changes to this file; you can only view it. To edit the file, you must open it as described in the following section.

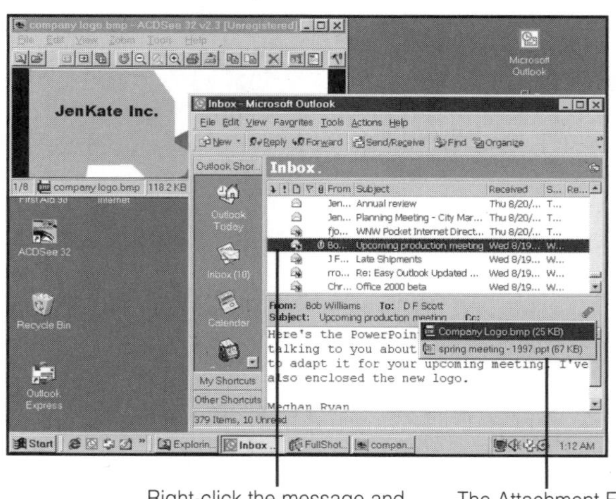

Right-click the message and select View Attachments.

The Attachment File list appears.

To open an attached file (so that it can be changed):

1. Double-click the message that contains the attached file.
2. Right-click the attachment icon and select Open. The file opens in its associated program. You can edit and revise this file and save it to your hard drive (File, Save As).

To save an attached file to the hard drive (without opening it first):

1. Click the message that contains the attached file.
2. Open the File menu and select Save Attachments. Then select the file you wish to save from the menu that appears. If you choose All Attachments, you can save all file attachments to the same folder in one step.
3. Change to the folder in which you want to save the file, then click Save. You can quickly change to a common folder such as My Documents by clicking its icon on the Places bar.

Use All Attachments to save all files to the same folder.

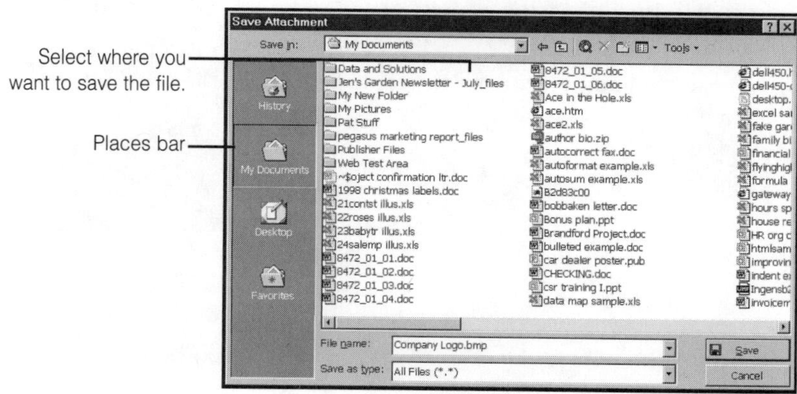

If you've opened the file within its associated program, such as Word or Excel, you can save it to your hard disk with the File/Save As command.

To print an attached file:

1. Double-click the message that contains the attached file.
2. Right-click the attachment icon and select Print.
3. Make your printing choices and click OK.

Cheat Sheet

Replying to a Message

1. Select the message to which you want to reply.
2. Click either the Reply button (to reply to the originator only) or the Reply to All button (to reply to the originator and all recipients of the original message). If the Reply buttons are not showing, click the More Buttons icon on the Standard toolbar.
3. Delete the original text, if needed, by selecting it and pressing Delete.
4. Type your reply above the copied text.
5. Click Send.

Forwarding a Message

1. Select the message you want to forward.
2. Click the Forward button.
3. Delete the original text, if needed, by selecting it and pressing Delete.
4. In the To box, enter the address of the person to whom you are forwarding the message.
5. Type an explanation for the forwarded message (if any) above the copied text.
6. Click Send.

48

Answering Your Messages

After reading a message, you may want to reply to it, or you may decide to forward the message to someone else. You can perform both tasks easily within Outlook.

Reply to sender OR sender plus other recipients.

When you reply to a message, you can send your reply to the sender only, or to the sender and anyone else who might have also received a copy of the message. You can, of course, forward the message to anyone you like.

When you forward a message, files attached to the original message are included as well as the text of the original message. To remove a file from the message you are forwarding, click on it and press the Delete key. If you reply to a message, only the original text is included in the reply.

Basic Survival

Replying to a Message

When you reply to a message, the text of the original message is copied to your reply. This makes it easier for the reader to recall the message to which you are referring. This also enables you to add your responses to a particular statement or question. However, you can remove this copied text from your reply by simply deleting it. The original text is easy to distinguish from any text you add to the message, because each line of the original text is preceded by a > symbol.

Again, keep in mind that when you reply to a message, attached files are not sent along with the reply—this is because you would not, under most circumstances, want to send them back. However, this also means that if you include in the recipient list any people who did not get the original message, they won't get the attached file. In such a case, you should send a forwarded message, rather than a copy of the reply, to those people.

To reply to a message, follow these steps:

1. Select the message to which you want to reply.
2. Click either the Reply button (to reply to the originator only) or the Reply to All button (to reply to the originator and all recipients of the original message). To access the Reply to All button, you may have to click the More Buttons button at the end of the Standard toolbar, and select it from the list that appears.
3. A new message window appears. The address of the originator (and recipients, if you selected Reply to All) appears in the To box. The text of the original message is copied to your reply—sometimes it is preceded by > symbols and other times it is simply separated from your reply with "---Original Message---." You can delete this text if needed by selecting it and pressing Delete.
4. Type your reply above the copied text. You can also press Enter to insert a blank line, and add comments within the copied text.
5. Click Send.

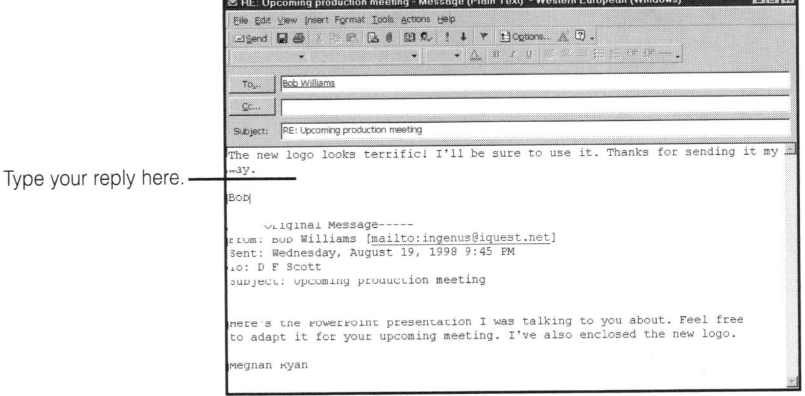

Icon with face and left-pointing arrow = reply.

Messages to which you've replied appear with an open envelope icon containing a small purple arrow that points to the left. If you're unsure later on when you might have sent a reply, just open the message by double-clicking it. At the top of the message window, you'll see a reminder telling you not only whether you replied, but when.

Beyond Survival

Forwarding a Message

Rather than reply to a message, you may decide to forward it to a colleague. When a message is forwarded, the original text and attached files are sent to whomever you specify. In addition, you can add your own text as well, to explain to the recipient why you're forwarding the message to him.

Text and files are included with forwarded messages.

The process of forwarding a message is similar to replying to one:

1. Select the message you want to forward.
2. Click the Forward button.
3. A new message window appears. The text of the original message is copied to this new message. You can delete this text if needed by selecting it and pressing Delete.
4. In the To box, type the address of the person to whom you are forwarding the message. You can also click the To button and select the address you need from the Contacts list.
5. Type an explanation for the forwarded message (if any) above the copied text.
6. Click Send.

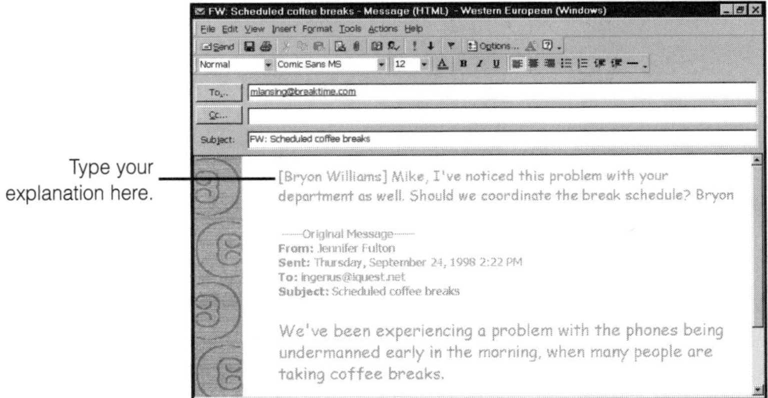

Later, if you're unsure whether or not you've forwarded a message, just look at the message icon. Forwarded messages appear with an open envelope icon that contains a blue right-pointing arrow. If you want to know when you forwarded the message, double-click it. At the top of the message window, you'll see a reminder telling you whether you forwarded this particular message and when.

Cheat Sheet

Setting Up an Appointment or Meeting

1. Drag over the beginning and ending time in which the appointment/meeting is to occur.
2. Right-click in the highlighted area, and select New Appointment or New Meeting Request from the shortcut menu.
3. Type a description in the Subject box and enter a Location for the appointment/meeting.
4. Select the Reminder check box and select the amount of lead time you want.
5. Select how you want the time scheduled for this appointment/meeting to appear in your calendar from the Show Time As drop-down list box.
6. In the large text box, add any notes you need for the appointment/meeting.
7. Assign a Category to this appointment/meeting if you like. You can also link this appointment/meeting to anyone in the Contacts list by clicking Contacts and selecting the names you need.
8. If this is a meeting, change to the Attendee Availability tab and choose Invite Others to select the people you want to invite. Select the contacts to invite to your meeting and click Required for each contact. Click on OK.
9. If you invited attendees, click the Send button to send meeting invitations and to schedule the meeting on your calendar. Otherwise, click Save and Close to add the appointment to your calendar.

49

Scheduling an Appointment, Meeting, or Event

Using the Calendar, you can keep track of appointments, meetings, and all-day events. You can even keep track of the things you need to do (tasks) from within the Calendar. You'll learn how to create tasks in Chapter 51. In this chapter, you'll learn how to add appointments, meetings, and events to your calendar.

Basic Survival

Displaying a Particular Date

When you switch to the Calendar, it displays today's appointments, meetings, and events. In the Date Navigator, today's date is marked with a square outline. The date currently being displayed appears in a small gray box. Dates that contain appointments, meetings, or events (in which your time is marked as busy and not free) appear in bold.

Dates in bold = scheduled items.

You can easily change to another date, scroll to view other times, and display more than one day at a time:

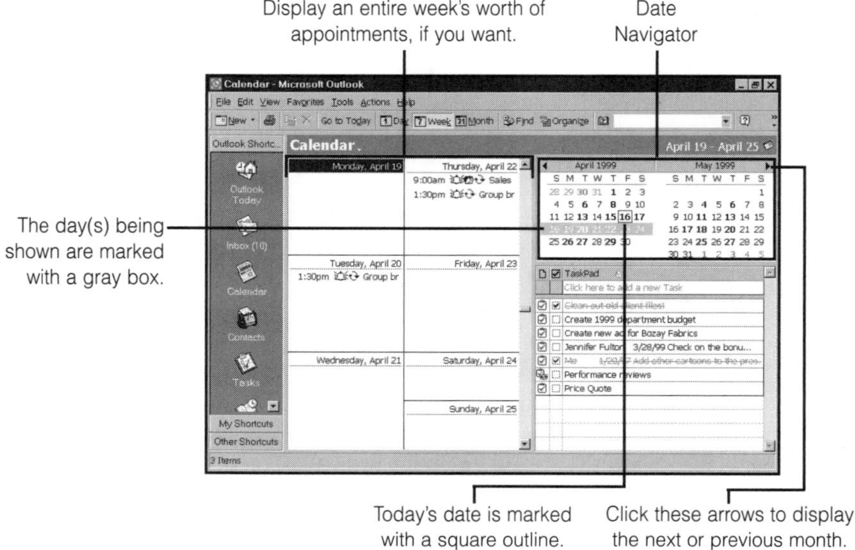
Display an entire week's worth of appointments, if you want.
Date Navigator
The day(s) being shown are marked with a gray box.
Today's date is marked with a square outline.
Click these arrows to display the next or previous month.
Calendar - Microsoft Outlook
Calendar
April 19 - April 25
TaskPad

- Scroll through the times displayed in the Appointment area by clicking the up or down arrows on the vertical scrollbar. If your Preview Pane is showing at the bottom, you might want to turn this off (View, Preview Pane) so you can see more of your calendar.
- Display another date by clicking it within the Date Navigator.
- To jump to today's date, click the Go to Today button.
- Change to another month in the Date Navigator by clicking the left or right arrows.
- Display a day [1], a week [7], or a month [31], by clicking the appropriate buttons on the Standard toolbar.
- Display any series of days by selecting them in the Date Navigator. To select consecutive days, drag over them. To select non-consecutive days, press and hold the Ctrl key as you click each day.

Setting Up an Appointment

To add an appointment to the Calendar, follow these steps:

1. Change to the day on which the appointment will occur.
2. If you're displaying only a single day, go to the Appointment area, and drag over the time in which the appointment is to occur. For example, drag over the 11:30 to 1:00 time segment.
3. Right-click in the highlighted area and select New Appointment from the shortcut menu. The Appointment dialog box appears.

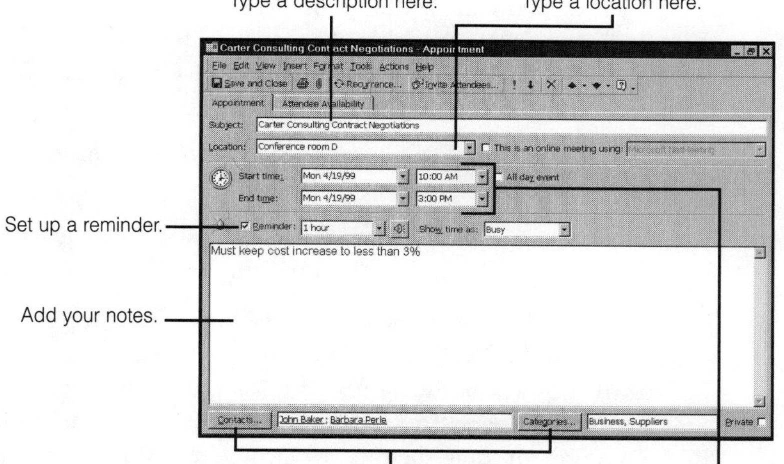

4. Type a description for the appointment in the Subject text box.
5. Type a location for the appointment in the Location text box. If you've used this location before, you can select it from the drop-down list.
6. Adjust the start time and end time, if needed. If this is a recurring appointment, see the "Beyond Survival" section for help.
7. Outlook can remind you of the appointment prior to its occurrence, if you want. Select the Reminder check box and select the amount of lead time you want.

Outlook will personally remind you of an appointment!

8. If you're connected to a network, your colleagues can look at your appointments and select the best time to schedule a meeting with you. To help them out, select how you want the time scheduled for this appointment to appear in your calendar from the Show Time As drop-down list box.
9. In the large text box, add any notes you need for the appointment.
10. Assign a Category to this appointment, if you like. Categories help you identify and organize your appointments. In addition, you can associate this appointment with anyone in your Contacts list. This places the appointment within the activities file of that contact. You can review this information on the Contact's Activities tab.
11. Click Save and Close. The appointment appears in the Calendar.

You can create an appointment without selecting the date or the time by clicking the New Appointment button.

If you need to move the time of the appointment, place the cursor on the blue bar at the left of the appointment (cursor turns to a four-headed arrow) and drag it within the Appointment area to a new time. To change the duration of the appointment, drag the top or bottom edge of the appointment (cursor turns to a two-headed arrow).

To move the appointment to another day, drag and drop it on a date within the Date Navigator. To delete the appointment, click it and then click the Delete button [X]. To make other changes to the appointment, double-click it, and the Appointment window reappears. Make your changes and click Save and Close.

Scheduling a Meeting

A meeting is similar to an appointment, but when you schedule a meeting, you're given the opportunity to send meeting requests to other people. In addition, provided your network administrator has set up the feature, you can schedule resources for the meeting, such as the meeting room, an overhead projector, and so forth.

You can invite others via email.

To schedule a meeting, follow these steps:

1. Change to the day on which the meeting is to occur.
2. In the Appointment area, drag over the time in which the meeting is to occur. For example, drag over the 2:00 to 3:00 time segment. (If this is a recurring meeting, see the "Beyond Survival" section for additional help.)
3. Right-click in the highlighted area, and select New Meeting Request from the shortcut menu. The Meeting dialog box appears.
4. Complete the usual appointment information: Type a description in the Subject text box, enter a Location if needed, set up a reminder, select how you want the time scheduled for the meeting to appear, add any notes, and then select a category and contact associations, if you want.
5. Change to the Attendee Availability tab and choose Invite Others. The Select Attendees and Resources dialog box appears.

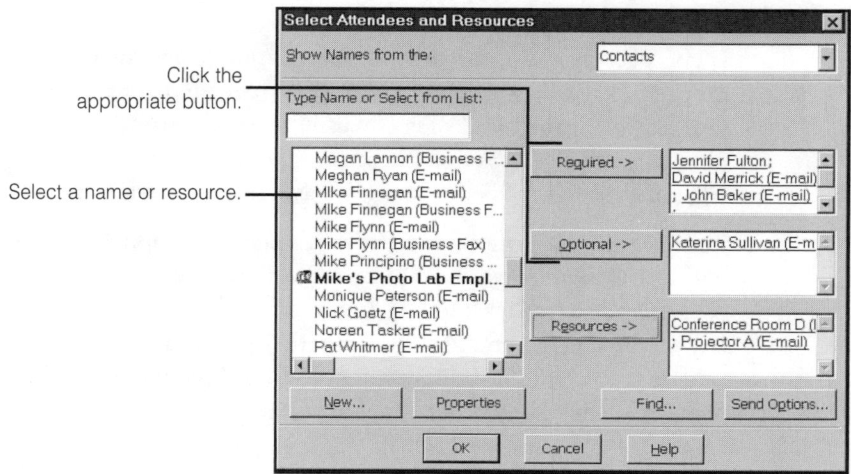

6. Select a name from the list on the left, then click the appropriate button: Required or Optional.

7. Select a resource such as a meeting room from the list on the left and click Resources.
8. When you're finished, click OK. You're returned to the Meeting dialog box.
9. If the people you select are connected to you through your company's network, you should be able to see their schedules on the Attendee Availability tab. If you see a lot of conflicts, click AutoPick to have Outlook check schedules and find the first available time when everyone can attend.
10. Click Send. The meeting appears in the Calendar, and email messages are created for each attendee.

Check the status of a meeting on the Attendee Availability tab.

After receiving the email request, each attendee should respond. You can check the status of responses from attendees connected to you through the network by double-clicking the meeting to open it and clicking the Attendee Availability tab. Select the show attendee status option if needed, and the response for each invited coworker is displayed. If you need to respond to a meeting request you've received, see the "Beyond Survival" section for help.

If you need to move the time of the meeting, place the cursor on the blue bar at the left of the appointment (cursor turns to a four-headed arrow) and drag it within the Appointment area. To change the duration of the meeting, drag the top or bottom edge of the appointment (cursor turns to a two-headed arrow).

To move the meeting to another day, drag and drop it on a date within the Date Navigator. To delete the meeting (cancel it), click it and then click the Delete button [X]. If you perform any of these tasks, you are asked whether you want to send an update to each attendee. Click Yes, and the Meeting dialog box reappears. Make any other changes as needed, and click Send Update.

Scheduling an Event

An event is an all-day affair, at least as far as Calendar is concerned. Events therefore appear at the top of the calendar, in a gray banner. Events typically do not block time from your cal-

Event = all day or several days.

endar as appointments do. An event can last several days, such as a week-long conference. Scheduling an event is fairly simple:

1. Change to the day on which the event is to occur.
2. Right-click, and select New All Day Event from the shortcut menu. The Event dialog box appears.
3. Completing this dialog box is similar to setting up an appointment: Type a description for the event in the Subject text box, enter a Location if needed, set up a reminder, add any notes, and select category and contact associations, if you want. To set up a recurring event, see the "Beyond Survival" section for help.
4. Normally, an event appears to others as time that is still free. The logic here is that the event might be a holiday, birthday, or anniversary, and that it would not interfere with your ability to schedule appointments and meetings that same day. If your time will be taken up by the event, then from the Show time as drop-down list, select how you want the time scheduled for the event to appear.
5. Click Save and Close. The name of the event appears at the top of the Calendar; it does not appear within the appointment area.

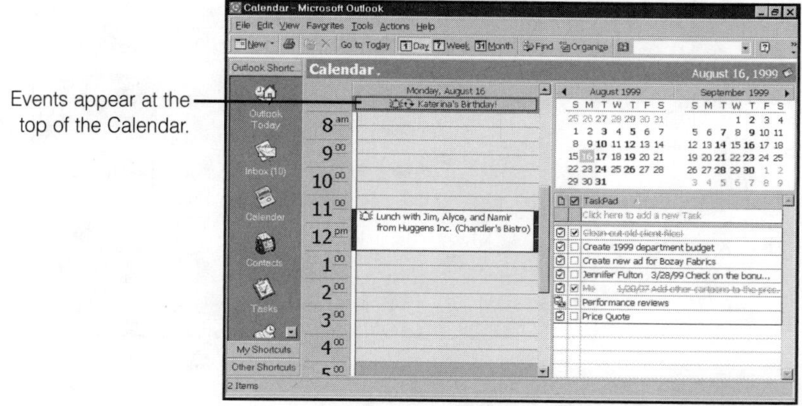

To move the event to another day, drag and drop it on a date within the Date Navigator. To delete the event, click it and then click the Delete button [X]. To make other changes to the event, double-click it to open the Event dialog box.

Beyond Survival

Setting Up a Recurring Appointment, Meeting, or Event

You can repeat appointments, meetings and events.

If an appointment, meeting, or event recurs in some kind of discernible pattern, Outlook can use that pattern to copy it throughout your calendar. Follow these steps:

1. Double-click the existing appointment, meeting, or event to open it.

   If you're creating a new appointment, meeting, or event, select the day and time as usual, then right-click and select New Recurring Appointment, New Recurring Meeting, or New Recurring Event from the shortcut menu that appears (skip to step 3).

2. In the Appointment, Meeting, or Event dialog box, click Recurrence.

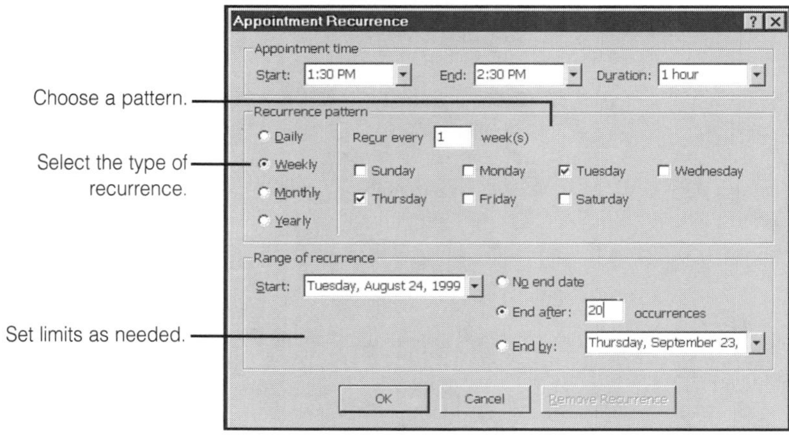

3. Select the type of recurrence: daily, weekly, monthly, or yearly.

4. Select a pattern for the recurrence, such as every Tuesday and Thursday.

5. In the Range of recurrence area, set any limits you desire, such as End after 20 occurrences.
6. Click OK. You're returned to the Recurring Appointment, Meeting, or Event dialog box.
7. Click Save and Close. When a recurring appointment, meeting, or event appears in the Calendar, it is preceded by a circular double-arrow icon.

If you need to make changes to a recurring item, double-click it to open it. You'll see a dialog box asking whether you wish to change just this one occurrence, or the recurring series. You can do either; make your selection and click OK. Make your changes as needed and then save them as usual.

Responding to a Request for a Meeting

If someone invites you to a meeting, the request is likely to come in the form of an email message. Follow these steps to respond to that request:

1. If needed, change to the Inbox folder, and open the message for viewing by double-clicking it.
2. Scan the details of the meeting, and then click the appropriate response button: Accept, Tentative, or Decline. (If you want to check your calendar first, click the Calendar button.)

You can check your calendar by clicking here.

Click the appropriate response.

Department Review - Meeting
File Edit View Insert Format Tools Actions Help
Accept ? Tentative X Decline Calendar...
From: on behalf of Jennifer Fulton [ingenus@iquest.net] Sent: Wed 9/30/98 1:53 PM
Required: Katerina Sullivan (E-mail); Mike Finnegan (E-mail)
Optional: Meghan Ryan (E-mail)
Subject: Department Review
Location: Conference Room E
When: Monday, October 05, 1998 10:00 AM-12:00 PM.
Bring revised budget

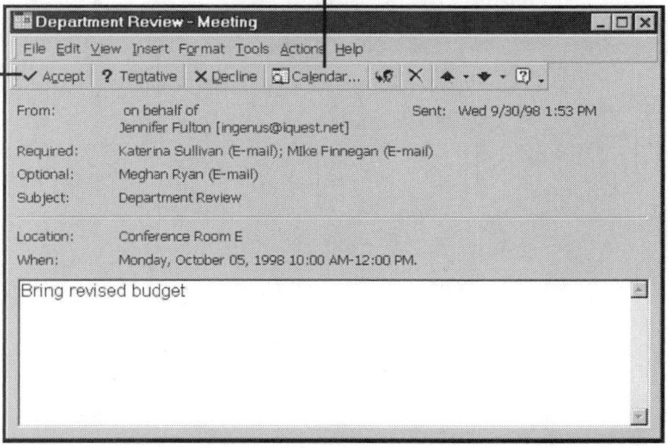

You can send a message with response.

3. You'll see a dialog box listing some options. Select the one you desire and click OK.

   - Edit the response before sending This option enables you to send a message back with the response.
   - Send the response now This option sends only your response: accepted, tentative, or declined.
   - Don't send a response You might choose this option if you've changed your mind about the way in which you responded and wish to backtrack and change your response before sending.

4. If you're adding a message with the response, you'll see the message window. Type your comments and click Send. If you accepted or tentatively accepted the invitation, then the meeting is added to your calendar automatically.

If you accept a meeting for a time that is already scheduled on your calendar, Outlook schedules both appointments side by side. If you open the meeting, a warning notice appears at the top of the appointment letting you know that it conflicts with another appointment.

You can have Calendar automatically respond to meeting requests by opening the Tools menu, selecting Options, and clicking Calendar Options on the Preferences tab. Click Resource Scheduling. Select the options you want, such as Automatically accept meeting requests and process cancellations, and click OK three times to return to Calendar.

Cheat Sheet

Adding a Contact

1. Click the New Contact button.
2. Type the contact's full name into the Full Name text box. Select the field by which you want this contact filed (such as last name, first name) from the File as drop-down list, or typing one in, such as Company.
3. Enter any additional information you like on the General tab.
4. Click the Details tab and enter additional details about the contact.
5. Click Save and Close.

50

Managing Your Contacts

You can keep information about your business and personal contacts in the Contacts list. After you enter a contact, you can send email messages, plan meetings and appointments, assign tasks, and even place phone calls to that contact.

The Contacts list can maintain just about any information you might have on a contact, including his or her email address, business and personal address and phone number, fax, pager and cell phone numbers, nickname, secretary's name, spouse and children's names, Web site address, and so on. In this chapter, you'll learn how to enter and change your contact information.

Basic Survival

Adding a Contact

The Contact list contains several fields for storing a lot of information about a contact; however, this does not mean you have to enter data into every field. Feel free to leave certain fields blank as you enter only the information you need:

1. Click the New Contact button. The Contact dialog box appears.

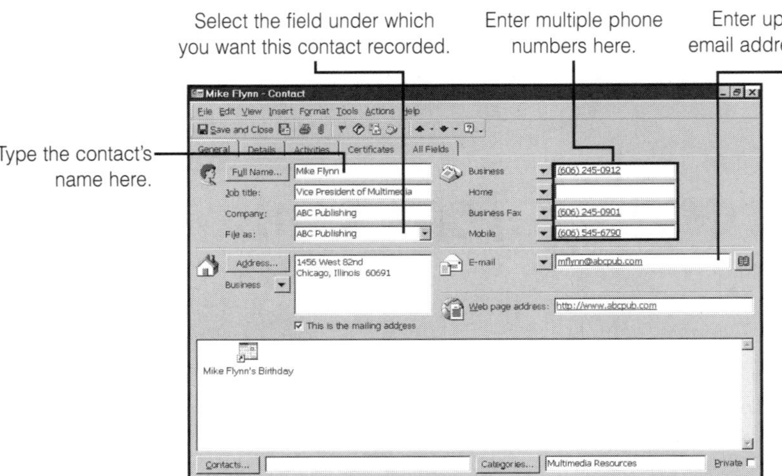

2. Type the contact's full name into the Full Name text box. Select the field by which you want this contact filed (such as last name, first name) by selecting an option from the File As drop-down list, or typing one in, such as Company.

3. Enter any additional information you like on the General tab. Some fields enable you to use them for something else, if you like. For example, you can click the down arrow next to the Mobile phone number field and select Pager. You can even use the fields with the down arrows to store multiple bits of information. For example, you could enter a Mobile phone number, select Pager, and enter that as well. You can even store up to three email addresses!

Entering a birthday or anniversary date automatically enters a recurring event on your calendar.

4. Click the Details tab and enter additional details about the contact, such as his or her department name, manager's name, spouse's name, birthday, anniversary, and so on.

5. Click Save and Close.

If you have only a minimum of information to enter, you can add a contact quickly by typing your data in the text boxes at the top of the Contacts list.

To change the information on a contact, you can click in any field that's displayed and simply make your change. If the field you need to change is not displayed, then double-click the contact to redisplay the Contact dialog box, make the change, and click Save and Close. To delete a contact, select the item and click the Delete button [X].

Change to the Detailed Address Card view to see the most information.

Contacts are usually displayed in a simple phone list. To change how contacts are viewed, open the View menu, select Current View, and select a view from the menu that appears.

If you want to quickly create a new message to a contact, drag the contact and drop it on top of the Inbox in the Outlook bar. This automatically opens a new message window addressed to the contact. Try dragging a contact and dropping it on the Calendar icon to create a new meeting notice.

If your modem is connected to the phone line through your telephone, you can use Outlook to quickly dial a contact's phone number. Open the contact you want to dial, then click the down arrow on the AutoDialer button and select the phone number you want to dial. In the dialog box that appears, click Start Call. (If you want a record of the call, select Create New Journal Entry When Starting New Call.) After you connect, click Talk, then pick up the receiver and begin talking. When you're finished, click Hang Up.

Beyond Survival

Creating a Distribution List

If you often send the same information to several people, you can group them together in a distribution list. You can then use this list to invite the group to meetings, or to send group email messages. To create a distribution group, first enter each person into the Contacts list. Then follow these steps:

Make some distribution lists!

1. Open the Actions menu and select New Distribution List.
2. Type a Name for the distribution list. Select a category to associate with this list, if you want.

3. Click Select Members. The Select Members dialog box appears.

4. Select a name from the list on the left, then click Add. Repeat to add more names. When you're finished, click OK. You're returned to the Distribution List dialog box.

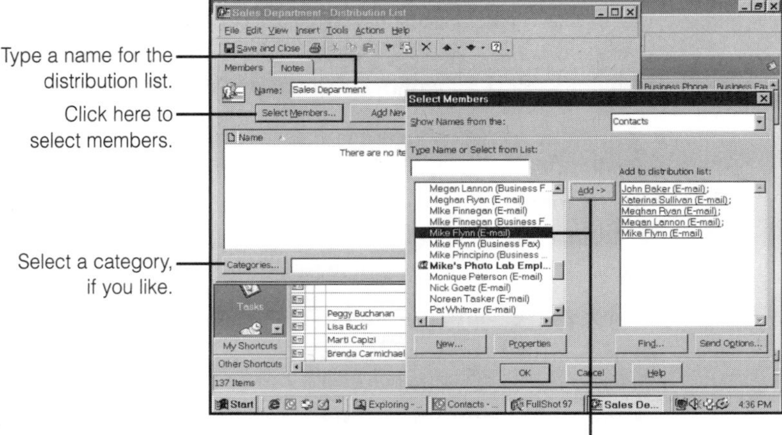
Type a name for the distribution list.
Click here to select members.
Select a category, if you like.
Choose a name and click Add.

5. If you need to add any notes about this list, click the Notes tab and type your note into the large text box.

6. When you're finished, click Save and Close. Distribution lists appear in the Contact list in bold type with an icon that includes two faces on top of an address card.

To use the distribution list to send an email message, select the list then click the New Meeting Request to Contact button. You can also click To within a message window and select the distribution list just as you might any other name. Remember that distribution lists appear in bold type to help you distinguish them from regular contacts. You can follow this same procedure to invite the members of the distribution list to a meeting.

To add or remove members from the list, double-click the list to open it, then either click Select Members to add a member, or choose a member and click Remove to delete a contact. Click Save and Close when all changes are made.

Cheat Sheet

Adding a Task Through the Calendar

1. Click at the top of the TaskPad in the Calendar, where it says, "Click here to add a new Task."
2. Type a description for the task and press Enter. The task is added to the Task list, but it is not assigned a due date.

Adding a Task Through the Task List

1. Change to the Task list and click the New Task button.
2. Type a description of the task in the Subject text box.
3. Select a Due date for the task. If you've already started working on the task, select a Start date as well.
4. If you like, you can change the Status of the task, select a Priority, and enter the percentage complete.
5. To be reminded of the task before it's due, click the Reminder check box and select a date and time.
6. Select a contact and/or category to associate with this task.
7. Add any notes about the task in the large text box at the bottom of the window.
8. If this is a recurring task, click the Recurrence button. Then select the recurrence pattern and click OK.
9. Click Save and Close.

51

Keeping Track of Things to Do

We all have a lot to do, and there are only so many hours in a day in which to do them. Why not let Outlook help you manage your tasks? It's easy to do, as you'll learn in this chapter.

Basic Survival

Adding a Task

Tasks appear in both the Calendar (on the TaskPad) and in the Tasks folder. In addition, tasks also appear on the Outlook Today page. To enter a task while you are viewing the Calendar:

1. Click at the top of the TaskPad, where it says, "Click here to add a new Task."
2. Type a description for the task and press Enter. The task is added to the Task list, but it is not assigned a due date.

Use TaskPad to add a task, but remember it has no date due.

Tasks listed on the TaskPad appear only when they are due (and not before). If a task has no due date, it appears every day in the Calendar. If a task is overdue, it appears in red.

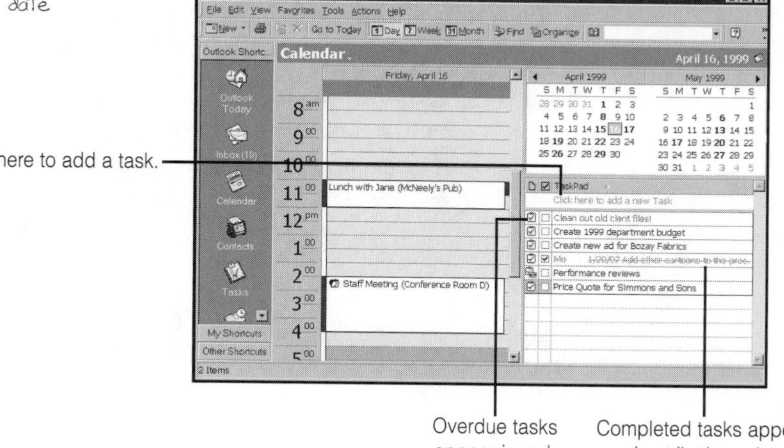

If you need to record more details about a task, such as the date on which you started working on it, or the date when the task is due, follow these steps:

1. Change to the Task list and click the New Task button. The Task dialog box appears.

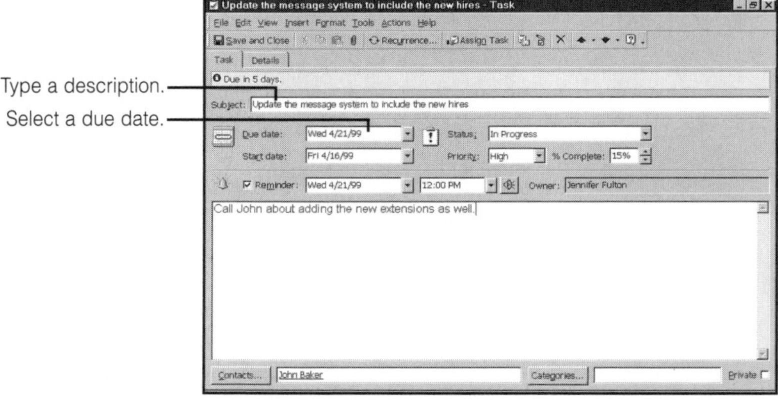

2. Type a description of the task in the Subject text box.
3. Select a Due date for the task. If you're planning a task to be started in the future, select a Start date. Or if you've already started working on the task, select a Start date as well.
4. If you like, you can change the Status of the task, select a Priority, and enter the percentage complete.
5. If you want to be reminded of the task before it's due, click the Reminder check box and select a day and time.
6. Select a category for this task, if you want. Categories help you organize your tasks into logical groups. You can choose a Contact name as well; this information will then appear on the Activities tab for that contact.
7. Add any notes about the task in the large text box at the bottom of the window.
8. If this is a recurring task, click the Recurrence button. Then select the recurrence pattern and click OK.

9. To assign the task to someone else, click the Assign Task button and complete the task information. Click the Send button to send the contact a notice about the assigned task.

Overdue tasks appear in red.

10. Click Save and Close. The task is added to the Task list.

As you work on a task (or if you complete it) you can update its status. See the "Beyond Survival" section for help. To remove a task, select it and then click the Delete button [X].

Beyond Survival

Updating the Status of a Task

If you've just completed a project, it's easy to check it off your list: just click the check box in front of the item, either in the Calendar, Outlook Today, or in the Task list itself. One catch, however: completed tasks are never removed from the Task list, so they keep appearing everywhere. To remove tasks, select them and click the Delete button [X]. Deleted items, by the way, are placed in the Deleted Items folder, where they remain until you empty the folder with the Tools, Empty "Deleted Items" folder command. This enables you to retrieve items that are accidentally deleted.

Check off completed tasks!

If you're managing a big project, on the other hand, you may wish to update its status from time to time—even before the project is actually completed. Here's how:

1. Double-click the task to open it.
2. On the Task tab, select the current status from the Status drop-down list box. Update the percentage completed.
3. Click the Details tab.
4. If you've completed the task, you can make a note of that fact by selecting the date on which the task was completed from the Date Completed drop-down list.
5. If you know about how many hours it will take to complete the project, enter that number in the Total Work text box.

6. If you've kept track of the total number of hours on which you've worked on the project, enter that number in the Actual Work text box.
7. Enter the names of any companies associated with this project in the Companies text box.
8. If this project has been assigned a billing number, enter it in the Billing information text field. You can enter other billing-related data here as well, such as the cost per hour/day, billable resources used, and so on. In addition, if you've accumulated any mileage costs associated with the task, enter that in the Mileage box.
9. When you finish updating the task, click Save and Close.

If you need to send someone an update on the status of this task, click the Send Status Report button in the Task window and select a contact to which you want to send the email. Type any additional comments you wish to add in the text box and click Send.

Index

A

B

C

D

E

F

G - H

I

J - L

M

N

P

Q - R

S

T

U - V

W - Z